CONSPIRACY

THE PLOT TO STOP THE KENNEDYS

CONSPIRACY

THE PLOT TO STOP THE KENNEDYS

MATTHEW SMITH

× × ×

CITADEL PRESS
Kensington Publishing Corp.
www.kensingtonbooks.com

CITADEL PRESS BOOKS are published by

Kensington Publishing Corp.
850 Third Avenue
New York, NY 10022

All Kensington titles, imprints, and distributed lines are available at special quantity discounts for bulk purchases for sales promotions, premiums, fund-raising, educational, or institutional use. Special book excerpts or customized printings can also be created to fit specific needs. For details, write or phone the office of the Kensington special sales manager: Kensington Publishing Corp., 850 Third Avenue, New York, NY 10022, attn: Special Sales Department; phone 1-800-221-2647.

CITADEL PRESS and the Citadel logo are Reg. U.S. Pat. & TM Off.

First printing: July 2005

10 9 8 7 6 5 4 3 2 1

Printed in the United States of America

Library of Congress Control Number: 2005922702

ISBN 0-8065-2701-3

This book is dedicated to the memory of my parents,
Matthew and Georgina.
I love you both.

Contents

Strike 3. *Senator Robert F. Kennedy*

Strike 4. *Senator Edward M. Kennedy*

Acknowledgments

As each stage of my story unfolds, there is layer upon layer of people who have helped me in a whole variety of ways. Those whose help I record with gratitude extend from the people who contributed to the very first book I wrote, all the way through to my most recent work.

I think first of the late Wayne January, who patiently led me into the nether world of deep conspiracy that he abhorred, but in the midst of which he found himself to his intense surprise, sorrow, and embarrassment. He waited thirty years to confide what he knew to someone, anxious for his life in view of all those of whom he knew who possessed some kind of evidence and died unexpectedly, unaccountably, or violently. I am greatly indebted to January that he felt he could trust me and chose me as the one to whom he could unburden himself.

Debra Conway and Larry Hancock of JFK Lancer have kept me updated with important new data, for which I am grateful, and my thanks also go to Dulaney Howland, Vicki Howland, and Brookie Vangerbig for fascinating new input. Joachim Markus, in Germany, knows how greatly I value the friendship we formed during the four years we worked on an advanced and very revealing computer study, which changed vital perspectives and confirmed others.

Mary Ferrell, a senior researcher and accomplished archivist, sadly passed away in 2004. She was an enormous help to me through years of my research and was another who became a good friend. The late, great Harold Weisberg was another to whom I owe a debt of gratitude, and my thanks are also due to the late Madeleine Brown. It has been sad these last few years to part with so many of those who knew so much about the events of the 1960s, but I am glad to say their legacies of knowledge and wisdom have been handed down to us.

John Miner, who was serving as the deputy to the district attorney in the days when Marilyn Monroe met her death; Natalie Jacobs and the late Robert Mitchum gave me unswerving help; and I am grateful also to Cyril Wecht for his comments and advice. Tom Reddin, who became the chief of police in Los Angeles, was kind enough to assist me in research, as was Jeanne Carmen and the late Jack Clemmons. Ted Landreth, Patte Barham, and Dr. Thomas Noguchi all contributed time and energy to answering my questions, for which I am grateful. I am indebted also to Robert Slatzer and Debbie Slatzer for both information and printed data, and I do not overlook the help received from the National Archives in Washington, D.C., and Maryland, the John F. Kennedy Library in Boston, and the British Library in London.

More recently, I have obtained help from William Law, whose concentration on the detail of events and procedures during the autopsy on President John F. Kennedy has produced incredible insight into what occurred and created a unique perspective with which to guide our researches. William Baillie, Scott Enyart, and Rose Lynne Mangan have also contributed to my understanding of the investigation into the death of Robert F. Kennedy and the trial of Sirhan Bishara Sirhan. I am grateful to each one of them.

I am greatly indebted to Gary Goldstein, my editor at Citadel. His transatlantic operation has made things incredibly smooth and I much appreciate his efforts on my behalf.

If I leave the debt of thanks I owe to my wife, Margaret, and to those other members of my family whose continuous support I enjoy until the end, it is only to add emphasis to my appreciation for all their encouragement and practical help.

Introduction

To the vast number of books written on the assassination of President John F. Kennedy, I have contributed two. Effectively, while paying tribute to the work of those distinguished researchers who have served the cause of truth since the time Kennedy died, my work—involving more than thirty years of research—involved approaching the mysteries surrounding Kennedy's death with a clean slate, starting from scratch, and seeking where a fresh approach would lead.

It was fruitful, in that it did not follow the pattern set by earlier writers, and I did not assume data correct merely because others before assumed such. The path I chose, I am happy to state, did not lead me to wild surmise or totally different results from my fellows, though some valuable new results emerged from a different approach and new thinking. I also met a lot of people, some of whom I talked to in person, and others I corresponded with by phone, fax, and letter, resulting in a flow of data that has not yet stopped.

In the course of time, I ventured to investigate the death of Senator Robert F. Kennedy and later still, the tragedy at Chappaquiddick, Massachusetts. I saw a thread connecting all these events, and later received compelling evidence that I was right. The distressing story told in this book is not, therefore, simply based on an inspired idea. I know I am not alone in the belief that a connection between all these events exists, but, uniquely, what I write has the support of testimony deriving directly from one of those involved in the serial conspiracy, coming to me firsthand by way of a man of enormous integrity. It is a sad story I tell. It is a story of the determination of a handful of people to control the U.S. government. It is sadder because it succeeded, and sadder still because those in a position to investigate and expose the work of the handful who carried out the extended coup d'état did not act with the required dedication to bring the conspirators to justice. I do not believe that all these people are disinterested and unwilling to help, however, and what you are about to read may assist in obtaining the result of one of them taking steps to expose the hijack of the United States in the 1960s.

As you read, do not think of the contents of this book as several stories. If you do, I have failed, for it is one continuous story. It is a story of intense hatred, greed, ambition, and gain. At best, there may be an element of totally erroneous and misplaced loyalty, but make no mistake: in no sense was what these conspirators achieved laudable, honest, or American. It is foreign to everything Americans believe in and stand for. It is the result of two extremely different strands of power fusing into a covert force able to control the lives—and deaths—of people in high places to achieve its own ends. Those making up this covert force then think nothing of the many ordinary people it "disposes of" to keep their identities secret. This speaks of an evil pact.

When a poison invades a system of any kind it must be expelled at all costs, by one means or another. The worrying factor in this story is that this poison has not been expelled. It is something still remaining to be done.

CONSPIRACY

THE PLOT TO STOP THE KENNEDYS

CHAPTER 1

Statistics and Curses

The fault, dear Brutus, lies not in our stars, but in
ourselves, that we are underlings.

—Shakespeare, *Julius Caesar*

THERE ARE THOSE who insist the tragedies that befell the family of
Joseph P. Kennedy were all the consequence of a curse. Interesting
though the idea may be, it can only be justified by a belief in astrol-
ogy or, perhaps, even the occult. There is no rational foundation for
a belief of this kind.

The first of Joseph's family to die was his eldest son, Joe. In the
early days of America's involvement in World War II, Joe Kennedy
Jr. volunteered to become an aviation cadet, giving this preference
over completing his final year at Harvard Law School. In 1943, he
went with the U.S. Fairwing Seven Squadron to serve with the Royal
Air Force, and regularly flew patrols from England. At the time he
was due to return home, Joe volunteered for a highly dangerous
mission. It was "Project Anvil," a mission that would require dedication, nerves of steel, and resolution of the highest degree. He and
his copilot were to fly a Liberator bomber packed with over 20,000
pounds of explosives to a point approaching the French coast
where they would bail out, leaving accompanying aircraft to guide
the enormous bomb, which the Liberator effectively was, by remote
control to explode on a V-2 rocket site. The Liberator unaccountably exploded in midair, before either pilot was able to bail out.

Joe's mother, Rose, and his father, Joseph, were devastated by

1

the loss of their eldest son. This tragic event is pointed to as the first of a whole series of deaths and misfortunes attributed to the "Kennedy curse."

Rosemary, born in 1918, Joseph and Rose's first daughter was, as she grew up, recognized as retarded. To most families, this would distinctly have been a misfortune. The statistics relating to the number of retarded children—who live loving and loved lives—born to American parents, or for that matter European parents and parents across the other continents, do not need reciting. To the Kennedy family, however, this was regarded as an enormous tragedy, which is sad. But, like her brother's unfortunate death in action, it was certainly not the result of a curse.

During the war, Rosemary's younger sister, Kathleen, went to London to become a Red Cross worker. She met—again—Billy Hartington, son of the tenth Duke of Devonshire, who had accompanied her around London in the days when her father was Ambassador to the United Kingdom. They fell in love, and despite problems relating to religion and not to mention both families being unenthusiastic, were married in May 1944 in a civil ceremony at Chelsea, Massachusetts. Unhappily, Billy was killed in action during the 1944 invasion of France. Kathleen, known to her friends as "Kick," who had by now been accepted by the Duchess of Devonshire, Billy's mother, still suffered the coolness of her own family. But in May 1948, when the war was ended, she flew to spend a holiday with her father in the French Riviera. Caught in fog and bad weather in France, the plane crashed, killing all onboard, including Kathleen, Earl Fitzwilliam, her host, two crew members, and another passenger. She was buried in England at Chatsworth, Devonshire, the ducal home of her husband.

The assassination of President John F. Kennedy in 1963 cannot be the consequence of a curse any more than Caesar's death was the consequence of the Ides of March. Caesar was the victim of a conspiracy, viciously stabbed to death by those around him, which included so-called friends. Similarly, Kennedy's death was the result of a deep-seated conspiracy on the part of enemies and some who should have been his friends. As to the perpetrators, the "lone nut" theory that branded Lee Harvey Oswald the killer and that is supported and promoted by the U.S. government, has long since been discredited. Besides which, Oswald, had he been guilty, was neither the agent of a curse nor a Brutus.

The murder of Robert F. Kennedy in 1968 should have alerted the U.S. government to something sinister going on. It would seem it chose to close a blind eye, while the authorities in Los Angeles, where he was shot down, became preoccupied with an anxiety that the city did not become another Dallas. The night he was murdered, Senator Kennedy had won a huge electoral victory that clearly set him on the road to the White House. By now extremely popular with the electorate in his own right, his supporters were confident he would be swept to victory in the forthcoming presidential election. Those who made sure this did not happen were certainly not enacting a curse. They were dedicated to keeping him out of the presidency: They were murderers dictating the future of U.S. politics and government.

So, the following year when another Kennedy death would have totally exposed what was going on, even to those covering their eyes and holding their ears, the events at Chappaquiddick, Massachusetts, made absolutely sure the third Kennedy brother did not get near to occupying the White House. This did not mean that blood was not shed: it was the sad death of Mary Jo Kopechne that made sure her killers succeeded in what they had set about. She died so that this diabolical plan, hatched as long ago as 1961 to keep the Kennedys out of power, extended to Edward M. Kennedy. Was she the victim of a Kennedy curse? Patently, she was not.

In 1964, Edward Kennedy had broken his back when a small private aircraft in which he was traveling crashed in fog approaching a landing strip. The pilot was killed and others in the party injured. Kennedy was lucky to escape with his life. He was not paralyzed, as was at first suspected, and survived well, in spite of terrible injuries. It was Edward who engendered the "curse" notion when he spoke of "whether some awful curse did actually hang over all the Kennedys."

In fact, his escape from the plane crash belied any idea there was a curse about, and the fact that fog played a critical part in the crash is a much more likely indicator of the source of many of the Kennedy problems. Kathleen Kennedy's plane was also in the grip of fog and bad weather when it crashed, as was the plane John Kennedy Jr. and his wife were in when it crashed off the Massachusetts coast in July 1999. Statistics will show that fog is a frequent factor in the cause of the crashes of light aircraft. There is nothing supernatural about that.

Those determined to press the idea of a curse will, no doubt, also quote the misfortune that befell Ethel Kennedy when both of her parents were killed in a light aircraft crash in 1955. Ethel was to suffer again in 1966 when her brother, George, died in another light airplane crash and two years afterward, when George's widow choked to death at a celebration of Robert F. Kennedy's electoral victory in California.

Once in the way of translating all misfortunes as the result of a curse, it is not difficult to extend the pattern to include such events as John F. Kennedy's heroic wartime escapade when his PT boat was broken in two in Far Eastern waters and he nearly lost his life, and the physical problems that dogged him for years. Then there was the stroke his father suffered. . . . To be totally realistic, Joseph had been warned he might have a stroke and was prescribed anti-coagulants by his doctor. He refused to take them, and the consequence was a blood clot in a brain artery.

One wonders what those who speak of curses would make of a little publicized event in London that involved the young Caroline Kennedy. It was while she was taking a year-long course in fine arts at Sotheby's in the early 1970s, and was staying with Sir Hugh and Lady Frazer in Camden Hill Square. Sir Hugh was a member of Parliament, and before he drove to the House of Commons each day, he made a detour to take Caroline to Sotheby's.

On the day in question, his Jaguar was parked in the square, waiting for him, when, before they could leave, the telephone rang. Frazer returned to answer the phone while Caroline waited for her ride. Meanwhile, Sir Hamilton Fairley, an eminent children's cancer specialist who lived next door to the Frazers, was walking his dog past the car. The dog sniffed at one of the curbside wheels and the car blew up. Fairley was killed instantly and the car was blown some distance away, landing on its roof. Caroline had a narrow escape that day, but the curse theory does not fit the circumstances at all. It was extremely unlikely that Caroline was the bombers' target. The bomb was planted by the Irish Republican Army, who, it seems, had Sir Hugh Frazer on its death list, though it is not impossible the blast was intended for Lady Frazer's father, Lord Longford, a renowned campaigner for the welfare of prisoners.

The idea of a family curse provides a fascinating, dark, and overall answer for those prepared to subscribe to it and hide the truth, but the reality of the individual "evidences" of such a curse do not really stand up to scrutiny. I have little doubt there are those who are delighted that such a theory has reared its head, notably those who put into motion the events that led to the deaths of a high-profile film star, a president, a senator, and an innocent woman who provided the means by which they could achieve their political ends. With a curse involved, nobody looks for other causes, and certainly not conspiracy.

But, putting aside such fanciful notions, let us face up to considering the "kernel" of the "curse," the first three deaths just mentioned that gave rise to such speculation. It is time to face reality and begin to unravel the sequence of events that led to these deaths, beginning with the death of a world-renowned film star, which is necessary to complete the hard and fast pattern that accounts for all these occurrences.

CHAPTER 2

Origins

*There is nothing makes a man suspect much, more than
to know little.*

—Francis Bacon

THE STORY BEHIND the tragedies that befell the Kennedy brothers
began some time before John F. Kennedy became president. It was
when Dwight D. Eisenhower occupied the Oval Office that the
National Security Council put forward proposals for a secret committee, which became known as the 5412 Committee, empowering
the Central Intelligence Agency (CIA) to formulate plans to bring
about a reversal of the political coup in Cuba. National Security
Council Directive No. 5412/2 set out four essential points: they
were to (1) create a Cuban government in exile; (2) start a powerful
propaganda offensive; (3) create a covert intelligence and action organization inside Cuba; and (4) create a paramilitary force outside
of Cuba for future guerrilla action.

The action officer for the 5412 Committee was Vice President
Richard Nixon, who was confidently expected by many to become
the next president. Suffering from failing health, Eisenhower was
not enlightened as to the details of what the CIA, liasing with
Nixon, had in mind, thus Nixon was very much running the show.

The CIA brought to Nixon a plan to strike back at Fidel Castro
and the communist regime he had brought to Cuba. Through the
5412/2 directive, they had the president's permission to recruit a
band of Cuban dissidents from those who had fled to American

shores following the Castro revolution. The plan involved training and arming them so that they could be sent back to Cuba as guerrillas. Once landed on Cuban shores the guerrillas would attract the support of the Cuban people, who would rally to their side and overthrow Castro. The plan had the support of those who had been approached in the Pentagon, though it appears those who approved it were more concerned with being seen not to disapprove it than expressing enthusiasm for it. Allen Dulles, the CIA director, saw that the Democratic candidate John F. Kennedy was "briefed" about the Cuban situation. That is, he told him about National Security Council Directive 5412/2. This did not fill him in on what was really happening in respect of invasion plans, but then Dulles did not expect Kennedy to be successful in the election. Before the mini-invasion could be executed, however, Eisenhower had left office, and, against all predictions, Nixon failed to get a majority in the presidential elections. Meanwhile, Kennedy had capitalized on what he had been told by Dulles, which resulted in the vote-winning *New York Times* headline: KENNEDY ASKS AID FOR CUBAN REBELS TO DEFEAT CASTRO.

However, not mentioned by Dulles was the plan for invasion, which was left on the Oval Office desk for the perusal of, and the final approval of, the new incumbent, who, to the surprise of many, would be Kennedy.

It is my belief that Kennedy would be quite suspicious of any plan emanating from the CIA, but there were pressing reasons for him to look carefully at it. Having just arrived in the White House, he did not want to turn down the plan out of hand if such indifference would mark him out as being happy to have Castro as his neighbor. As it was for those in the Pentagon, they felt compelled to approve the plan, because opposition attracted criticism and brought problems. On the face of it, it was only permitting Cubans to go back to Cuba to overthrow Castro, which was a popular idea.

Kennedy, however, made a speech that set out his position clearly, one that echoed Eisenhower's position. In it he said:

There will not be, under any conditions, any intervention in Cuba by United States armed forces, and this government will do everything it possibly can—and I think it can meet its responsibilities—to make sure that there are no Americans involved in any actions inside Cuba. . . . The basic issue is in Cuba and is not one between the United States and Cuba; it is between the Cubans themselves. And I intend to see that we adhere to that principle. . . . This administration's attitude is so understood and shared by the anti-Castro exiles from Cuba in this country.

In the meantime, the CIA took advantage of the political situation by increasing the number of Cuban exiles put into training. This was not what Eisenhower had authorized. There was a 300-strong guerrilla band already operating in the Cuban hills, and it had now recruited a force far in excess of a second guerrilla band. It was a small army of 1,200 to 1,400 that was trained and armed and that waited for the word to overthrow Castro.

Kennedy was put on the spot. He was told the plan would not wait, that it was a now or never scenario. Therefore, he was unable to scrutinize the details of the plan and obtain advice from elsewhere; nor was he helped by the fact that Langley kept him in the dark. He was rushed into a decision, and not the kind of decision a new president likes to face on arrival at the White House. Kennedy had little choice. He was warned that Castro's army was about to be equipped by the Soviets, and MiG fighters were soon to be delivered, followed by pilots trained in the Soviet Union.

It did not help when Dulles stepped in to publicly argue that here were "a group of fine young men who asked nothing other than the opportunity to try and restore a free government to their country. [They were] ready to risk their lives. . . . Were they to receive 'no sympathy, no support, no aid from the United States?' "

Besides other considerations, the existence of the CIA-backed guerrilla camps in Guatemala was well known. The CIA told Kennedy he must act now or it would be too late. As an interesting side issue, whether the 12,000-plus insurgents realized they were on their own in this enterprise is a question to which we do not have an answer.

CHAPTER 3

The Bay of Pigs

It is the disease of not listening, the malady of not marking, that I am troubled withal.
—Shakespeare, *Henry IV*

WHEN PRESIDENT JOHN F. Kennedy finally obtained more information about the planning for the invasion of Cuba by the rebel army, he was dumbfounded to learn that Mafia money was being used to finance the guerrillas already operating in the Cuban hills. Robert F. Kennedy's jaw must have dropped even further, for, as the newly appointed U.S. attorney general, he had planning in progress for a full-scale attack on the Mafia. The brothers were incensed, and President Kennedy began to assemble what he could of the fine detail of what the CIA intended. Regardless of how much he needed to know what was happening, the CIA did not take him into its confidence, and it has been claimed the agency secretly told the rebels the invasion would happen whatever the president decided.

It appears the plan involved the insurgents linking up with the small band already in Cuba, and the strategic planning, if it could be called that, was quite advanced. At this stage, the Cuban rebel leader Mario Garcia Kholy, with whom the CIA was in close contact, was already established with the guerrillas, and he had plans to head a new government when Fidel Castro was overthrown. How much the president ever found out about such things we are not sure, but it was later discovered that Castro was well informed via carefully placed agents. Kholy, also, was kept in the dark and

9

was not allowed to know that the CIA was to be completely in charge of the invasion. To add to a heady mix of secrecy and the left hand not being told what the right was doing or even thinking, infighting was taking place between factions within the agency, adding complication to complications.

Agent E. Howard Hunt was appointed coordinator of the plan to invade Cuba, and he appeared to know a great deal more than the president. He rendered certain advice in a memo, the echoes to which were exposed some time later. He wrote, "Assassinate Castro before or coincident with the invasion (a task for Cuban patriots). Discard any thought of a popular uprising against Castro until the issue has already been militarily decided."

President Kennedy, who found himself in a classic no-win situation, finally authorized the confused invasion plans, as much as he knew of them. It was probably the decision he regretted most in his presidency. The landing of the Cuban rebels' army began on Monday, April 17, 1961. Unfortunately, it all came as no surprise to Castro since the CIA had carried out initial air strikes two days before the landings. Castro was ready for this miniarmy in no uncertain terms. The logic for the air strike was unbelievable: The CIA thought that the world would believe the strikes were the work of Castro's pilots revolting against the regime. It was no surprise that the world simply did not believe this and was shocked at what the United States had done. The astute Kennedy ordered the cancellation of a second air strike scheduled for the day of the invasion.

Incredibly enough, the real problem with the Bay of Pigs (Bahia de Cochinos) invasion was either poor intelligence or unwillingness to accept what had been learned. Regardless, it amounted to the same thing: The CIA believed that once the insurgents had landed, the Cuban people would rally to their side and rout Castro and his communist regime. Furthermore, they acted on the assumption that, prior to the delivery of promised aircraft and newly trained pilots, Castro did not have the fire power to cope with the insurgents. On both counts, the CIA was singularly wrong. The people did not rally to the side of the invading army; it appears that by and large they were happy enough for Castro to head the nation, communist or not. And the strength of Castro's army and air force was totally miscalculated by the CIA. With a 20,000-strong force, he was amply able to deal with 1,200-plus rebels. They were decimated.

The insurgents' air support consisted of sixteen outdated B-26 aircraft that were easily outmaneuvered by Castro's jets. In any case, the B-26s had to come from such a distance that they could only conduct a one-hour engagement before having to return home. Adding fatally to the insurgents' problems, two of the four ships carrying the much needed ammunition were sunk and the remaining two were driven away. The insurgent troops on the ground were cut adrift. Everything had gone wrong. It is truly remarkable that the basic cause for the tragedy that followed was the poor and inaccurate intelligence supplied by the intelligence arm of the world's most powerful nation.

The invaders were mowed down on the beaches, and with them their CIA masters, who had been strictly forbidden by the president to take an active part in the landings. The 1,200 troops were simply insufficient to mount a realistic threat to Castro. The original plan for a guerrilla force might, arguably, in its own way, have achieved more. The CIA agents soon found themselves in a position where withdrawal was the only alternative available to them. Then followed the desperate arguments over air cover for retreat.

The CIA claimed it beseeched the president for air cover for their withdrawal and were refused, abandoning them and those left of the insurgents to their fate. The president, it said, had promised such aid and then had reneged. Theodore C. Sorensen, a close aide to the president, told a very different story. One of the two supply ships that had been driven away from Cuban waters returned with the rebels' essential ammunition and other supplies, but the crew threatened to mutiny unless the United States provided destroyer escort and jet aircraft cover. The beleaguered convoy commander radioed the CIA in Washington asking for the help of the navy, but Langley was not abreast of the developments at the Bay of Pigs at that time and as a consequence did not approach the president.

Instead, the CIA canceled the convoy. Sorensen claimed this was the only request made for air cover and that it never reached the president.

On the night of the supply ship crisis, Kennedy was pressed by the Pentagon to get behind the rebels and turn the lowly insurgent invasion into a regular war against Cuba. It appears the CIA planners had, in fact, banked on those back in Washington being able to persuade the president to change his mind and send military assistance: it was part of the planning for the operation. Kennedy said that if it was ever wise for the United States to enter into a war with Cuba, it would not be on the coattails of a small exile force. Under great pressure from those around him, however, the president agreed to send unmarked navy jets to provide cover for the elderly B-26s, which in turn would provide cover for the insurgents the following morning. Perhaps by a time-zone error, the allocated planes took off an hour too late and the result was devastating. The B-26s were either shot down or forced to scuttle to their base. It was over. The consequence of this to the surviving insurgents and CIA agents was incalculable.

The Bay of Pigs invasion was an out and out debacle. Those who survived, particularly the CIA agents, blamed the president for forsaking them in their hour of need. About a thousand rebels were rounded up and sent to a Cuban jail. The bungled CIA intelligence, it seemed, did not enter into the reckoning for the disaster. The project was not so much ill fated as ill founded. But in an interview with the researcher Anthony Summers, E. Howard Hunt blamed it all on Kennedy "losing his nerve."

Notwithstanding, the president gallantly accepted the blame for the fiasco. But there were immediate consequences to the events in Cuba. The president had learned a great deal about the CIA he did not know before, and his deep suspicion of what went on at Langley would affect the rest of his brief presidency. The agency planners did not take Kennedy into their confidence, and, not surprisingly, the relationship between the CIA and the president had sunk to an all-time low. Outrageous situations arose in which, regardless of the wishes of the president or the U.S. government—and sometimes in defiance of them—the agency went its own way.

As far as the CIA personnel who survived the Bay of Pigs were concerned, the president and his brother became objects of their intense hatred. U.S. Attorney General Robert F. Kennedy was known to have played a big part in the monitoring of the invasion and was accused by the survivors of having been the overriding influence in the president's decision to withhold support. The agency's plans for Cuba, however, were by no means finished. The attorney general would learn a few months later that, quite apart from the financial arrangements with the Mafia over the Bay of Pigs invasion, the CIA had "engaged" Mafiosi to kill Castro. This was not the first time "arrangements" had been made between U.S. intelligence and Mafia figures. It had started during World War II when the Office of Naval Intelligence negotiated the help of the notorious Lucky Luciano, and the liaison with the gangsters was developed by the Office of Strategic Services, which later became the CIA. Incredibly, the CIA would continue a relationship with the Mafia at least until the time of the Vietnam War.

The Mafia was greatly displeased that it had lost its gambling interests in Havana when Castro came to power, and the idea of reversing the situation with the blessing of the U.S. government, in the shape of the CIA, was no doubt hugely attractive to the Chicago hoodlum Sam Giancana and his henchman, the Las Vegas boss Johnny Roselli. They were approached by an agency representative some months before Kennedy was elected president, and, with the sanction of planners at the very top of the CIA hierarchy, they met at a hotel in Miami with one item on the agenda: the assassination of Castro.

It would appear the plan was hatched by Richard Bissell, the CIA deputy director of planning, with Sheffield Edwards, the agency's director of security, but Director Dulles was put in the picture, as was Deputy Director Pierre Charles Cabell, the brother of Earle Cabell, who would be the mayor of Dallas in 1963 when President Kennedy visited that city. As a safety net against any leaks, the decision was taken to use a former Federal Bureau of Investigation (FBI) man, rather than a current CIA employee, as their agent in the negotiations. That man was Robert Maheu. And thereby hangs a tale.

It was Giancana's love problems that were the cause of the very secret link between the Mafia and the CIA being exposed. Giancana was romancing a well-known singer, believed to have been Phyllis McGuire. Suspecting her to be two-timing him and sleeping with comedian Dan Rowan, he asked Maheu to obtain from the CIA a listening device that would be planted in Rowan's hotel bedroom. The CIA obliged and went further; it even engaged a private detective to plant the bug in Rowan's bedroom for him. It transpired, however, that he was caught red handed by a maid. She told the manager, who informed the sheriff, and the detective, whose name was Balletti, was arrested.

Not willing to carry the blame alone in these circumstances, Balletti volunteered he was carrying out orders from the CIA. The sheriff took the matter to the FBI; this led to Maheu, then to Giancana, and the whole nasty mess returned home to roost in the high places from which it had come. Finally, a memorandum was sent to Robert Kennedy, and his brother, the president, was told what had been going on. Director Dulles managed to resign before he was fired, Bissell was fired, and Cabell did not survive in his job long.

Unbelievably, at a later stage it was discovered the CIA was preparing another invasion of Cuba. This was after President Kennedy had given his word that there would be no further attempts to invade Cuba or on Castro's life. The president sent in the police and the FBI to dismantle the camps set up by the agency and to destroy the armaments they found.

Meanwhile, the president and his brother rushed along a plan to obtain release of the Bay of Pigs captives. With an agreed ransom offered, the last of the captives was released and returned to the United States, but this was not until January, 1963. The tailpiece to the story came much later when the scandal of the Nixon tapes was revealed. Nixon, then president, was recorded recounting his misgivings about what—even at that stage—could still come out of the Cuban mess, "You open that scab, there's a hell of a lot of things and we just felt it would be very detrimental to have this thing go any further. . . . If it gets out that this is all involved . . . it would be a fiasco."

Early in his presidency, Kennedy, daily juggling all kinds of problems at home and in various parts of the world, found himself fencing with an agency of government that should have been his prime ally. But then, the CIA was never his friend, and the agent-survivors of the Bay of Pigs nursed their hardening, intense hatred of Kennedy.

CHAPTER 4

Total Autonomy

Commit the oldest sins the newest kind of ways.
—Shakespeare, *Henry IV*

IF JOHN F. KENNEDY did not know what was going on at Langley, he became well aware the CIA was a loose canon, a rampant rogue elephant that neither the White House nor anyone on Capitol Hill could contain. The agency was a law unto itself. It had its own program; it served neither the president nor the U.S. government, unless their wishes coincided with those of the agency. The nature of the animal was such that it sheltered under its own secrecy, becoming totally secure and untouchable. It might well have been described as a form of government in its own assumed right.

By 1956, President Dwight D. Eisenhower was being pressed to look to the future in his decisions, but he did not really want to make decisions. He "really didn't want to do or decide anything," wrote Harry S. Truman. "He passed the buck, down." Meanwhile, the CIA was making decisions and spending most of its budget on activities that would not have met with the approval of the president, the government, or the people: activities that entered the annals of government as "clandestine." Eisenhower must have had some idea of what was going on, however. Before leaving office, he warned against the military-industrial complex being allowed to acquire more power.

In the early days of U.S. involvement in Vietnam, the question of how to deal with Ngo Dinh Diem arose. Kennedy positively ruled

16

out murder. Notwithstanding, Diem was ruthlessly overthrown and killed. The president was livid, but he soon realized this was an example of the CIA having its own agenda. Another example of the agency's duplicity, directly in defiance of the president, surfaced when a Yale professor of history was arrested in the Soviet Union for spying. Kennedy, assured by the CIA of the professor's innocence, made a personal plea on his behalf to the Russian president Nikita Khrushchev. Khrushchev, in response to Kennedy's intervention, released his prisoner. When the professor had been invited to meet Kennedy at the White House, the president only then learned that the CIA had lied and that the professor *had* been an agent of the CIA all along. Clearly, the president could not rely on the word of the CIA at any level. It was embarrassing, and Khrushchev probably realized he was better informed about what was happening in the CIA than Kennedy.

When President Kennedy accepted the resignation of Allen Dulles and fired Pierre Charles Cabell and Richard Bissell, he put Robert F. Kennedy temporarily in charge of the CIA, which was probably not a wise thing to do. Robert had a bull-in-a-china-shop manner that did not endear him to those he might have made his allies. But how many of the staff at Langley were potential allies? John McCone became the new director in Dulles's place, and Richard Helms—later to become director himself—took Bissell's place as the CIA deputy director of planning. That said, the relationship between the agency and the president was set to continue much as before.

William Harvey was the chief of the CIA's "Executive Action" operation. Harvey's brief was the removal—even by assassination—of troublesome foreign leaders, monitoring and progressing ZR/RIFLE—murder—activities, and the covert, anti-Castro "Project Mongoose" program; he also provided another example of the CIA's independence of the president and the government. It happened during the Cuban missile crisis in the fall of 1962. Delicate negotiations were in progress to defuse the desperately dangerous situation brought about by the installation of Soviet missiles in Cuba, while the world held its breath minute by minute, terrified this situation might lead to a devastating nuclear world war. Meanwhile, Harvey was crassly running commando operations into Cuba, thus directly undermining the president's delicate negotiations and the security of the entire nation. When this came to light, Harvey was shipped off to a post in Rome, and Tracy Barnes became the head of the Domestic Operation Division—the "Department of Dirty Tricks"—though Harvey still turned up periodically in the United States in connection with the Cuban projects. E. Howard Hunt was brought in to run covert activities. Hunt would later be convicted and jailed in connection with the Watergate scandal.

Following the disclosures about the CIA-Mafia alliance and having rid the CIA of its top men, Kennedy declared his intention to dismantle the agency. This was a private comment made by the president that soon assumed the proportions of a very public pronouncement. He said he planned to "tear the CIA into a thousand pieces and scatter it to the winds." Such comments were not calculated to make friends or influence people in the CIA, but then, had that ever been possible?

And while the president saw to the affairs of state, those agents who had survived the Bay of Pigs disaster continued to hold their grievances, their acrimony fermenting and festering, acrimony that would lead to unbelievable consequences.

Marilyn Monroe

CHAPTER 5

Action and Reaction

*Seek not to know who said this or that, but take note of
what has been said.*

—Thomas à Kempis

IT WAS 1962, just a few months after the Bay of Pigs tragedy.
Marilyn Monroe was having trouble with Twentieth Century–Fox
over her current movie *Something's Got to Give*, or, to be more precise, she was having trouble with the director of the movie, George
Cukor. There had been an earlier version of the story, titled *My
Favorite Wife*, that in the early 1940s had featured Cary Grant and
Irene Dunne. *Something's Got to Give* was the final movie Cukor
had to make with Fox under his present contract, and he would
much rather have been elsewhere, directing a movie he would have
enjoyed doing and that would have brought him much more credit.

To say that Cukor and Monroe did not see eye to eye was putting
it mildly. Monroe had held Cukor in the highest esteem as far as his
directing abilities went, but he was now demolishing this new movie
with endless rewrites to the script, which she had the greatest difficulty keeping up with. It was not so much the rewrites as the rewrites
of the rewrites that upset her, not to mention the rewrites of the
rewrites of the rewrites. Cukor was not getting that sparkle from
Monroe, and it was not surprising. Monroe was suffering from hypoglycemia, a sugar-related problem, that required strict monitoring and rigid dietary control, neither of which had been prescribed
for her. This, in addition to an inability to sleep, rendered her diffi-

cult to rouse in the mornings, tired and twitchy, and tiresome to cope with on the set. Though it was the studio doctor who had diagnosed her with hypoglycemia, no one was treating her for the problem, neither him nor her personal physician, Dr. Hyman Engelberg. Dr. Engelberg appeared to be oblivious of the complaint, and his answer to what ailed her was drugs. To complicate matters further, her psychiatrist, Dr. Ralph Greenson, was at this point, and for good reasons, weaning her off the drugs she was using.

The script was typed up on white paper, while revisions were typed on yellow paper and revisions to the revisions were typed on blue paper. Monroe found that the words she had memorized from a revised script delivered to her late at night were changed again by the time she reached the studio the following morning. There were some changes she insisted on having made herself, which only poured fuel on the fire, but no one knew better than Monroe that the movie was bogged down. The presence of her acting coach, Paula Strasberg, on the set—called "Black Bart" by studio hands because she always dressed in black—and Dr. Greenson, who had become directly involved with her work schedules, like a shadow in the background, did nothing to help. Matters came to a head when Monroe, supposedly at home sick, was found to have flown to New York to sing at the celebration of President John F. Kennedy's birthday at Madison Square Garden. She had had permission to go, but progress—or lack of it—now made her absence unacceptable. She was fired.

Her smoochy, sexy performance at Madison Square Garden set tongues wagging. The president's wife, Jacqueline, had refused to attend the function, and this added to the speculation among those who wondered what was going on between Kennedy and Monroe. Indeed, they had reason to be suspicious, as we shall later see. In the meantime, Monroe went back to her home in Los Angeles and planned her reinstatement to Twentieth Century–Fox. Fox was in deep financial trouble, and by the time Monroe had been fired, *Something's Got to Give* was running $1 million over budget, a huge amount in those days, with only six minutes of film in the can.

Her plan for reinstatement involved the release of photographs by three illustrious photographers: Bert Stern, George Barris, and Douglas Kirkland. The result was immediate, and she did not wait long for a Fox executive to make contact. Her reinstatement to the production was something of a triumph for her. She negotiated a contract worth three times the one she had before she was fired, and, not surprisingly, she was elated. It was the best deal she had ever had from the studio.

There had been a number of provisos to which she had agreed. Strasberg had to go, and this did not devastate Monroe. Dr. Greenson had to butt out of any interference in the production of the movie, and this did not faze her, either. Things were looking up, and it was time for her to examine the relationships she had with others around her. Eunice Murray, her housekeeper, was another who definitely had to go. Monroe had discovered she was little more than a spy for Dr. Greenson, and that would not do.

It was rumored Monroe had been involved in an affair with Kennedy since before he became president. Already indicated by several writers including myself, Kennedy rendezvoused with Monroe at the Santa Monica beach house of his brother-in-law, the actor Peter Lawford, among other places (Lawford was married to Patricia, the second youngest of the Kennedy girls). By the time she was sorting out her relationships with those around her, Monroe had accepted that her relationship with Jack—now the president—was over. Attorney General Robert F. Kennedy, Jack's younger brother, was suddenly to come on the scene, however, sent, many believed, to put a final stop to the liaison between Monroe and the president.

The scenario, as those in the know saw it, was that a "love at first sight" situation arose. It bore the appearance of being such. Robert Kennedy, it was believed, became besotted and wanted to take up where his brother had left off. Monroe, deprived, as she thought, of any chance of becoming America's first lady, now saw her chance renewed, since it was commonly believed that Kennedy would follow his brother into the presidency. On the face of it, it was a hot, passionate romance, but some suspect Kennedy had another agenda in making advances on Monroe.

It is my belief the president had an urgent need to recover documents, letters, and photographs in Monroe's possession, and it was Robert Kennedy's mission to obtain them. He saw a romance with Monroe as the way to achieve this. He had no intention of leaving his wife, Ethel, and his children to marry Monroe. This would have been disastrous to his career, apart from anything else, but he led her on, and starry-eyed Monroe believed him. Matters came to a swift and abrupt head for two reasons. One, it appears, was that there was strong evidence that Monroe had become pregnant, and the scandal of a child from a liaison with either of the Kennedy brothers would have been devastating. It would have brought the political ambitions of the Kennedy dynasty to a dramatic end. This was 1962, and that kind of thing was not tolerated by the electorate. The other was that Ethel, perhaps the only member of the family who did not know about her husband's mission to Hollywood, found out about it.

This was the making of a disaster of the first order. The indications are Monroe was reluctantly persuaded to have an abortion. Her close friends spoke of her telling them about it at the time she appeared to have had a head-on clash with Robert Kennedy. Things were never the same again. She received phone calls telling her to "keep away from Bobbie, you tramp," which, if not from Ethel herself, Monroe believed were sent at Ethel's instruction. This may have given Monroe a bad time, but it probably did not hold a candle to what Kennedy suffered. It was later popularly believed that it was at this point her world began to simply melt away, bringing with it despair. This was far from the truth. By this time she had finally seen a clear perspective in which she had been used—indeed abused—by the Kennedy brothers, and she wanted nothing more to do with them.

She was visited on Saturday, August 4, 1962, by Robert Kennedy. He tried bullying her, probably to retrieve the file of documents the president wanted, but she was not having any. She unceremoniously threw the attorney general out of her house. Those who knew about the situation may well have believed that matters had reached the point of no return for her on that Saturday. They were mistaken. By then she had everything in hand. But it was that night Monroe, inexplicably, fell into a coma, and she died early the following morning.

CHAPTER 6

Friday Night and Saturday

There are no Second Acts in American Lives.
—F. Scott Fitzgerald, *The Last Tycoon*

MARILYN MONROE HAD declined a Saturday night dinner engagement at Peter Lawford's beach-side mansion, where Robert F. Kennedy was expected to be a guest. She had intended to accept the offer, and said so to Sidney Skolsky, a journalist friend, in a telephone conversation on Saturday morning, but things changed dramatically as the day progressed.

Monroe received a package that day, probably in the late morning, that contained a soft toy tiger. There was likely a note with it, but we can only speculate as to what it said. Agnes Flanagan, her hairdresser, was present at the time it arrived and saw that Monroe became quite upset. Flanagan said she quietly left afterward. If it was not the contents of a note that upset Monroe, it may have been the tiger itself that was the message. Looking at the events of the day, however, it is reasonable to speculate it was some message from Robert Kennedy, perhaps telling her Ethel knew what was going on and it had to stop. We now know that by this time Monroe had made up her mind to abandon any relationship she had had with the attorney general. Therefore, it would seem it was not the termination of the relationship that bothered her; it was the circumstances in which *he* thought he was dumping *her* that caused her grief.

We know she felt that she had been "passed around like a piece of meat" (as she herself said) by the Kennedys, and here was a second example of her being dropped like a hot potato. John F. Kennedy had dropped her thus, but by all accounts, she had expected to see Robert Kennedy to tell him a fond farewell the previous evening. She ordered an expensive meal to be delivered to her house and he failed to appear. That was on Friday, and it was later that night she was virtually lured into having supper with Lawford at a noted restaurant. When she got there, she found Kennedy waiting to see her.

This is likely the time Kennedy spelled it out to her that it was not safe for him to be paying social visits and sharing a meal at her house anymore. Perhaps Ethel was now hyposensitive. Perhaps she had someone watching him. But he was not to know that Monroe had decided to stop seeing him, that it was all over. And up to this point he had led Monroe to believe—as she clearly understood him—that he would divorce Ethel and marry her, and now he was revealing that had never been a possibility. He was in fear that *Ethel* would divorce *him*. Had Monroe not already made up her mind to end her relationship with him, this would have devastated her. As it was, she was extremely disillusioned and suddenly saw Kennedy in an altogether different light. He had been leading her on to get his way with her. But far from being depressed or even furious, Monroe no doubt felt just a bit pleased with herself that *she* had made the decision to dump *him*.

Since her abortion, she had repeatedly tried to reach Kennedy, but he had behaved as though she had the plague. He would not take her calls, and he would not contact her. But Monroe knew how to get his attention. She passed the word around in certain quarters that she intended holding a press conference in which she would "tell all." He came scurrying. He need not have worried. By all accounts, all she wanted was his attention while she said goodbye. It was over as far as she was concerned. But the discovery that Friday night that he had been insincere all along shattered any illusions she still retained about him.

The restaurant meeting was not a pleasant one. It became quite acrimonious, and after she left Kennedy she went elsewhere with

Pat Newcomb, her press agent friend, and got drunk before returning home. I believe Kennedy was not in the mood for polite good-byes: he had not yet collected the file for his brother, and that may be an indication he had "wooed" Monroe just to get his hands on the file his brother wanted. As far as Monroe was concerned, it is likely that if he had allowed her to say her polite good-bye instead of revealing he had not been honest with her over his promise to marry her, he would have gone home with the items he had come to collect. But then Kennedy was an aggressive man: he was capable of being his own worst enemy.

Unabashed, Kennedy turned up uninvited on Saturday afternoon, bringing with him someone who was suspected of having administered an injection to calm Monroe down. Kennedy and Monroe argued. He was incensed she was not handing over what he wanted, but she was very much in command in her own home. After kicking them out, she was quite unruffled and turned her attention to the absence of confirmation from Ralph Roberts, her masseur, about an evening meal they had tentatively arranged. She did not know that Roberts had telephoned while Dr. Ralph Greenson was at her house and that he had taken the call. The psychiatrist, who did not like Roberts, told him she was not at home, and, no doubt baffled, the masseur went off for the evening with other friends, leaving Monroe alone when she would have appreciated the company of a friend.

Lawford telephoned her during the late afternoon, after Kennedy's visit. The attorney general was most anxious for her to come to dinner that night. But she told Lawford she would not be going and that, no doubt, would come as no surprise to him in view of what had happened on Friday night and Saturday afternoon. It was during this conversation that Monroe told Lawford about her disillusionment with Kennedy and used the expression she felt that she had been "passed around like a piece of meat." She had tried to telephone John Kennedy earlier, most likely simply to tell him to call his brother off, but she could not to reach him. The president was at his family home at Hyannis Port, Massachusetts, at the time.

Although we know she retained enormous admiration for John

Kennedy, she was making it abundantly clear she was cutting herself off from both of the Kennedy brothers. She left a message for Lawford to pass on, in which she said "good-bye" to the president, having failed to reach him in Washington. In spite of her surviving affection for him, she would not be bothering him again.

Having still not obtained from her the items his brother wanted him to recover, Robert Kennedy really needed to see Monroe at the Lawfords' dinner party, and he was frustrated that she had cried off. Again uninvited, he paid another visit to her home that evening, probably shortly before seven o'clock. He turned up with Lawford this time and tried to browbeat her into handing over the file he wanted. Nobody browbeat Monroe, and Kennedy had not yet learned that. Tapes made from taps and bugs by Bernard Spindel for Jimmy Hoffa and Giancana of what transpired at her house that night left no doubt he was given short shrift. And when she decided enough was enough, she ignominiously threw both Kennedy and Lawford out.

Afterward, she suffered from no depression or any ill effects at all from her evening encounter with Kennedy. At about 7:30 P.M., Joe DiMaggio Jr. telephoned to tell her he had broken up with his girlfriend, and Monroe was delighted. She believed the girl was unsuitable for him and was quite elated by the news. Eunice Murray, the housekeeper, heard her on the phone and said she was happy and light hearted. This offers evidence that Monroe was suffering from no ill effects from her meetings with Kennedy. That was behind her.

She was home alone that Saturday night, thanks to Dr. Greenson's interference. She had had food sent in for a barbecue supper for herself and Roberts, but having no company, she went to bed early, soon after DiMaggio Jr's call. Newcomb, who had slept over on the previous night, had been included in the invitation to dinner at the Lawfords', and she had accepted. Other friends, Arthur Jacobs and Natalie Trundy, were enjoying a Henry Mancini concert at the Hollywood Bowl that night. Jacobs was Newcomb's boss and the head of the publicity company that represented Monroe, and he and Trundy, his fiancé, were good friends to Monroe; she thought of Jacobs as something of an "anchor." "He'll always be there for me," she confided to Trundy. And a bewildered Roberts linked up with other friends since his supper date with Monroe had inexplicably fizzled out. Murray decided to sleep over on that last Saturday night. Dr. Greenson later said he had not asked her to and that would have been the usual procedure for the odd night she stayed. Certainly, Monroe would not have asked her to stay. Therefore, the presence of Murray that night remains a mystery, though, in view of the circumstances, her being there might have been a boon. She might have been able to enlighten us about what actually did happen on the night Monroe died. Instead, she made matters worse by telling one story then another until no one could believe what she said. However, this did underline clearly that a cover-up was being put in place. A blanket of secrecy shrouded the truth from being known for forty years afterward about how Marilyn Monroe died.

CHAPTER 7

Death of an Icon

*It hath been often said, that it is not death, but dying,
which is terrible.*

— Henry Fielding, *Amelia*

ARTHUR P. JACOBS was summoned to Marilyn Monroe's house by a
telephone call to the Hollywood Bowl. He left Natalie Trundy to
hear the rest of the concert and drove directly to Monroe's home at
Fifth Helena Drive, where he found her in a coma and without anyone present able to tell him what had happened. Who was actually
present is still a mystery. Eunice Murray was there, but at that time
she had been unable to make contact either with Dr. Hyman Engelberg, Monroe's physician, or her psychiatrist, Dr. Ralph Greenson.
Trundy said she thought Pat Newcomb made the telephone call to
Jacobs at the Hollywood Bowl, but Newcomb strongly denies this.
The call was made at about 10:30 P.M., and it took Jacobs roughly
half an hour to reach Monroe's bedside.

The problem was that those present, whoever they were, did not
know what Monroe was suffering from. For any star in this kind of
situation, it was always best if she could be treated at home to
avoid publicity. But they made no progress with her, so they eventually called an ambulance to take her to the hospital. By then, after
midnight, Peter Lawford was at her house, and it was he who accompanied her to Santa Monica Hospital. But it was too late: when
she arrived, Monroe was pronounced dead.

The ambulance driver was not keen to turn his vehicle around and take Monroe home, but it seems he was persuaded. Ambulances were not used as hearses. It was bad for business. A great deal of what we now know about this was confirmed by Walt Schaefer, the owner of the ambulance company in the early 1980s. She was driven back to her home where she was laid on a bed and prepared for a police investigation. It is believed she had been found in her guesthouse, but she was laid in her own bed before the police were called.

The people there had various priorities before they wanted the police on the scene. Having said that, it is quite likely a senior officer, perhaps Chief of Police William Parker himself, had been at the house immediately after Monroe died. Police cars were seen outside the house by neighbors at about the same time the ambulance was noticed when it returned from the hospital, probably nearing 1:00 A.M. But by the time all had been arranged to the satisfaction of those present, the official call to the police was not made until 4:25 A.M., when Duty Sergeant Jack Clemmons, at the local police station, took the call. Wondering if he had taken a hoax call from, perhaps, a mischievous student, he decided to go to the house himself to confirm that the story of Marilyn Monroe being dead was true.

Though *officially* the first officer on the scene, he told me he had the feeling all was not what it was purported to be, as he looked at Monroe's body and interviewed Murray and Dr. Engelberg. Their interviews were peripheral, however; it was Dr. Greenson who appeared to be the elected spokesman. Sergeant Clemmons felt the presence of others in the house, others who never showed themselves. We know he was right, for Newcomb admitted she was there before the call was made to the police. Whoever else was there we do not know, but it was quite likely Milton Rudin, Monroe's lawyer, Jacobs, and perhaps Lawford, who had certainly been there earlier: it was Lawford who accompanied Monroe in the ambulance to the hospital.

It has to be remembered that Sergeant Clemmons was not there as an investigating officer: investigating officers would come later. He was there primarily to confirm that Monroe was dead, as reported to him on the telephone. He did a fair bit of poking around, however, and we are indebted to him for his observations, observations not made later on by the official police investigation team, who appeared to be there merely to go through the motions. For instance, he reported hearing the sound of a washing machine at near five o'clock in the morning, when Murray was washing what was probably vital evidence. The vacuum cleaner had also been busy, and he reported that the whole place appeared to have been cleaned up in preparation for his visit.

He looked in vain for documents, which he assumed would be in evidence, but found none. Amazingly, they were strewn about the floor in police photographs taken later. He also looked for a drinking glass, in view of the information that Monroe had swallowed several pills. He could not find one, and though he was assisted in his search by those present, Murray, Dr. Engelberg, and Dr. Greenson, they all drew a blank. Since there was no water to Monroe's bathroom, which was being renovated, it was wondered how she had managed to take so many pills without a drink. Remarkably, however, a glass of sorts appeared in a later police photograph. Sergeant Clemmons's attention was drawn by Dr. Greenson to her bedside table, where a number of pill bottles had been placed. The doctor indicated she must have taken all of them, because all the bottles, with caps removed, were empty. Sergeant Clemmons was later astounded to be told that partially filled bottles had been submitted to the coroner.

Murray regaled Sergeant Clemmons with the story of how she saw a light under Monroe's bedroom door at about midnight. The door was locked, she said, and it was when Dr. Greenson arrived that she was found dead, after he broke a window and climbed into her room. This was remarkable because the window, supposedly broken by Dr. Greenson, was found more likely to have been broken from the inside, and it was improbable Monroe was sleeping with her bedroom door locked, anyway. Add to this the likelihood she died in the guesthouse, and the whole story was nonsense. Murray later admitted she did not see a light under Monroe's bedroom door—

which would have been quite impossible, since Monroe had just had a thick white pile carpet laid throughout the house—and we knew that, for whatever reason, we were caught up in a cover-up of enormous proportions.

We did not have to search very far before finding the reason for the cover-up. Robert F. Kennedy having been in Monroe's house only hours before she died was bound to have far reaching consequences, if ever revealed. This is not to say Kennedy had anything to do with her death, but the proximity of him to Monroe at that time would have called for careful and close investigation. Such careful and close investigation of a U.S. attorney general, the country's top lawman, in relation to a sudden death, would certainly have resulted in his resignation being sought, and the likely consequence was that the president's resignation would also have been demanded. The press corps well knew about John F. Kennedy's dalliances with Monroe, details of which had been kept out of the newspapers, and the fact that Robert Kennedy was the president's brother holding the U.S. attorney general's post as a patronage appointment would have been more than sufficient to result in the fall of Camelot.

The fact that this did not happen was due to the Los Angeles police chief William Parker, who, to his credit, I believe, *knew* that Robert Kennedy had had nothing to do with Monroe's demise. Monroe had been murdered, and that fact had been thinly disguised as suicide. The patently obvious attempts to make the death appear a suicide were intended to be stripped away, indicating that Kennedy was the likely killer, since he had not long before left her house after an argument. And after all, if the autopsist did not find any drugs in her stomach, but her liver and blood were full of barbiturates, it is difficult to support a case for suicide.

One did not have far to look for those who would kill Monroe and rig everything to point at Kennedy. Both the CIA and the FBI had bugs in her house—on the grounds of national security since Kennedy was visiting—not to mention Jimmy Hoffa, who was listening in for the Mafia. They were all conversant with the affair that had gone on with John Kennedy, and doubly aware of the relationship between Robert Kennedy and Monroe. All were more than interested: Hoffa for blackmail possibilities, J. Edgar Hoover's FBI so that he could have more to hold over the Kennedys in his secret files, and the CIA, knowing its comrades, who had survived the Bay of Pigs debacle only a few months before, were anxious to nail both Kennedys, no matter how.

Monroe died and was declared a suicide. She was murdered, but not by the Kennedys.

CHAPTER 8

Conversations

Conversation is imperative if gaps are to be filled.
—Patrick White

IN THE COURSE of my research into the death of Marilyn Monroe, I met and talked with many people. With others, I had conversations on the telephone, and with some I communicated by letter and fax.

Jack Clemmons, a former sergeant of police and the policeman credited with being first at Monroe's house after a telephone call had broken the news of her death, was more than likely preceded by several other people long before he got there. Nontheless, his evidence and opinions are extremely valuable. Most outstanding is his certainty that Monroe was murdered. Reflecting on his lengthy visit to Fifth Helena Drive early that Sunday morning, he was convinced he had been at the scene of a homicide. I have recounted elsewhere what he told me he saw. He also told me that when he went to look at the body, he observed that Monroe was lying—as he put it—in the soldier position, arms by her sides, legs together. Her head was to top left of the bed and her feet to bottom right, the opposite way quoted by some. "Suicides don't die like that," he said to me.

As time progressed, Sergeant Clemmons realized how much evidence had been tampered with—the empty tablet bottles that were partially filled in time to be examined by the coroner, for instance—and how much was being concealed. He was criticized by some for not turning his visit into an investigation. Actually, he probably went as far as he could in that direction without putting himself directly at odds with his superiors. There were procedures, and he was there only to confirm that Monroe's death, as telephoned to the police, was genuine. His evidence that the place had been specially cleaned up before his visit—and continued to be cleaned up during his visit—was an extremely valuable pointer.

Retired Police Sergeant R. E. Byron, one of the first of the investigating officers to reach Monroe's house, said nothing. During a phone conversation, he gave me the impression he was having difficulty even remembering who Marilyn Monroe was. Much the same might be said of Beverley Chief of Police Marvin Iannone, who was another of the investigation team first at the scene. At the time of her death he was a sergeant, whose prime duty was to regulate the traffic coming and going outside Monroe's house, which was located at the end of a cul-de-sac. I went, personally, to meet him after arranging an appointment before leaving England. When he heard what I wanted to discuss with him, he barely spoke to me and was certainly not commenting on what he observed at Monroe's house.

Another to add to the list of those who are not talking is Pat Newcomb, Monroe's press secretary. Again, I made an appointment to meet her in advance and duly met up with her in a hotel lounge. She was charming, polite, and willing to talk, but she was very careful not to add anything to what she had already said during the years since Monroe's death. She stonewalled me. In this bracket also and possibly being my worst experience was Milton Rudin, Monroe's lawyer. He hung up on me when he heard what I wanted to talk about.

Tom Reddin, who was the assistant chief of police with the Los Angeles Police Department (LAPD), under Chief William Parker, when Monroe died, was extremely helpful. He confirmed some important assertions I had made, like the presence of Robert F. Kennedy in Los Angeles on the Saturday before Monroe's death. He also was the source of my information relating to the existence of a very big file on the investigation into Monroe's death, which disappeared and was replaced by a slender one containing, perhaps, fifty documents.

He told me he believed Chief Parker had taken the file to Washington, and that it never returned. Reddin and his wife are charming people with whom I still keep in touch.

Natalie Trundy, the wife of ace publicist Arthur Jacobs, and I never met, but we became great friends during the series of telephone calls I made to her. Our conversations covered some vital points that I have mentioned elsewhere. One unmentioned thing is that she told me that Newcomb was fired by Jacobs because of a verbal scrap she and Newcomb had after Monroe's death. One can only wonder about the subject of their argument. Trundy told me that she and Jacobs were quite close to Monroe and that they were good friends. She recounted spending hours with her on a "bad" night. For days on end after Monroe's death, Trundy did not hear at all from Jacobs. "He fudged the whole thing," she confessed to me.

I became friends with Robert Mitchum long before I met him; in numerous telephone calls that began, "I'm Matthew Smith," I always received the answer, "I do not doubt it." I remember with pleasure the time I spent with him at his home in Santa Barbara. We talked of a great many things, including the frustration he felt when Monroe died. She had tried to reach him shortly before her death and he grieved that he had never gotten back to her. To add to his discomfort, Newcomb told him that Monroe really did want to talk to him. Mitchum worked with Monroe on location for the film *River of No Return*. He told me he was in New York when John F. Kennedy was celebrating his forty-fifth birthday at a party at Madison Square Garden. This was the famous occasion when Monroe appeared in a gown that looked as if she had been poured into and sang a breathy "Happy Birthday" to the president. She might not have made it if Mitchum had not met her in his hotel beforehand and reassured her, telling her she should go ahead and keep her promise. She had thought of chickening out.

Mitchum told me how he had been working in the same plant as Monroe's first husband, Jim Dougherty, when they met up at a dance at which Tommy Dorsey was playing. Monroe was fascinated by the voice of a young singer whom Mitchum introduced to her. His name was Frank Sinatra. Mitchum had only kind words to say about Monroe, though he was not so kind to George Cukor, whom he called "a basket case."

I was pleased to speak to Antionette Giancana, the daughter of Sam Giancana, the infamous Mafioso. She was charming in her conversation with me. I asked her what she thought about the book written by "Sam and Chuck" Giancana, *Double Cross*, in which Monroe's murder is ascribed to the Mafia. She told me to ignore the book because it had no foundation.

The most constructive and helpful of all my conversations were with John Miner. Miner, who became a well-known lawyer in Los Angeles, had been the deputy district attorney at the time Monroe died. He was present throughout the autopsy carried out by Dr. Thomas Noguchi and even assisted at times. He later talked to the psychiatrist Dr. Ralph Greenson and listened to the tape recordings that were made just before she died. I recorded—with permission—the conversations I had with Miner, the following extract being of particular interest:

> *Smith:* I must say I believe unequivocally she did not commit suicide.
> *Miner:* Well, you've got good medical evidence to support that.
> *Smith:* Furthermore, considering all the facts in this case, I do not believe her death was an accident.
> *Miner:* I go with you there.

I had not expected such a positive reaction.

> *Smith:* And in that case there is only one alternative.

For the first time Miner said it to me:

> *Miner:* Homicide.

Smith: Is there any question of it? Can there be any question of it?

Miner: I would think the medical evidence strongly supports that.

Smith: Could anything contradict it?

There was a long pause while Miner considered his answer. I repeated the question, and when the answer came it was strong and clear:

Miner: No. I don't know of anything.

I also spoke to Dr. Noguchi in the course of my enquiries, accompanied by his lawyer, Godfrey Isaac. We talked about things in general until I suggested that there should be a disinterment and a new autopsy. Dr. Noguchi's eyes lit up and he said that he would like to be involved in any such move. He believed new techniques and equipment could provide answers not possible before. Since Miner has also expressed a wish to be present at any new autopsy carried out on Monroe, this has become one of my prime aims.

The work of the "Suicide Team" might be thought of as one of the nonstarters in respect to investigating the death of Marilyn Monroe. This was a team set up by the Los Angeles authorities to look into the background of suicides in the area. In Monroe's case, those involved had nothing to find that contradicted suicide, but then, their brief did not include investigating whether the death was due to suicide or not. It was a three-man team, known also as the "Suicide Investigation Team" and, somewhat curiously, as the "Suicide Prevention Team." Led by the psychologist Dr Norman Farberow, the team included the psychiatrist Dr. Robert E. Litman and Dr. Norman Tabachnik.

Dr. Farberow wrote to me stressing that he had attempted to learn "what the psychological status of Ms. Monroe was at the time of her death." The team's remit regarding its enquiries would have no limit, he asserted, though they were able to overlook, for instance, that she had just settled a deal with her studio for the highest salary she had ever had and had gone out and bought a whole new wardrobe. These and other indications did not seem to have registered with the team. I met Dr. Litman in his consultation suite in Los Angeles, to have it pointed out to me, quite rightly, that any investigation into the physical aspects of Monroe's death would have been for the LAPD to probe. Dr. Litman also told me—and I found this most interesting—that Monroe had been off drugs for some seven weeks before she died. For someone who had been a habitual taker of medicinal drugs, this was some accomplishment, fitting in with her assertion in the tapes she made for Dr. Greenson that she had flushed all her pills down the toilet.

Two other people I spent time in conversation with merit mention here. The first is Robert Slatzer, who had a friendship with Monroe for a number of years, and the second is Jean Carmen, a beautiful actress who was, at one time, a neighbor to Monroe. She maintained a friendship with her until the day Monroe died.

Conversations are never a waste of time. Sometimes they are most revealing. On others they often reveal just a small nugget of information, perhaps something that links with another small nugget, and that is how research builds up. I have to say that I met some very interesting people in and around Los Angeles, to whom I am greatly indebted for the contributions they made to my understanding of what happened—and of what did not happen—when Monroe died.

CHAPTER 9

New Insight

The voice of the dead was a living voice to me.
—Alfred, Lord Tennyson, *In the Valley of Cauteretz*

THE STORY OF Marilyn Monroe killing herself was started and circulated by Arthur Jacobs. As I understand it, it was not that he believed she had committed suicide; it represented the only way forward open to him—as he saw it—at that time. The indications are that Chief of Police William Parker had spoken to the principals involved in the tragedy that had overtaken Monroe. He had likely spoken to Robert F. Kennedy after hearing of the problem by phone before leaving his home. Satisfied that Kennedy was totally innocent of any involvement in the problem Monroe was suffering from—for it is my understanding that Parker heard of what was going on even before Monroe died—he decided the U.S. attorney general was to be protected. It was more than likely that he was astute enough to know exactly what was happening, that dark forces were out to involve Kennedy, and through him the president, in a mesh that would result in the fall of the House of Kennedy. That, he knew, would be a catastrophe.

It is one of the evidences to me that since the Kennedys did not have anything to do with Monroe's death Parker undertook to establish an incredible cover-up to protect them. He was a man of integrity, and though it is true he believed his future would come through the favors of the Kennedys, that by itself would certainly not have been enough for him to throw his professional standing behind a guilty Kennedy. He simply would not have done it. He must have been completely convinced the Kennedys were innocent before lending his help. And what help it was: it involved not only the LAPD but also the coroner's department and all other areas of concern in regard to Monroe's death, including the handling of the insatiable inquisitiveness of the press corps that was straining at the leash. The cover-up was complete: it was a blanketing of enormous proportions. It would not have succeeded, however, without the collaboration of all those nearest to Monroe, and it is this, perhaps, that is the most disturbing aspect of what happened.

There are three critical indications that Parker organized the cover-up of what happened to Monroe. One is that he was informed at his home of what was happening at about 11:30 P.M., well before Monroe died. If it was information important enough to be passed to the chief at such an hour at night, it was very important. It would also demand a response. The second is that there came to exist a bulky file consisting of all the documentation relating to the investigation of Monroe's murder. Tom Reddin, Parker's assistant and later chief of police himself, told me he had seen the file, but then it disappeared. He believed Parker took it to Washington on a visit and never brought it back. Later, a slim collection of documents became the "official" file, and still is. Third, the first police officer "officially" on the scene at Monroe's home that dreadful night was Sergeant Jack Clemmons, who assured me that such a cover-up could only have been carried out on Parker's orders. There was no one else who could have achieved such an incredible suppression of the truth.

Monroe's friends were left with two options: going along with Chief Parker and protecting the best interests of the innocent Kennedys, or telling the truth and throwing the Kennedys to the wolves. Neither was a great choice. But there is no reason for not telling the truth now, except that there are so few of those who knew what really happened left.

Not long before Monroe died, Dr. Ralph Greenson tried to get her into free-association analysis and failed. It was not his fault. She acknowledged it was her inability to let herself go while in her psychiatrist's office. She devised a means of overcoming this problem, however. She would record her innermost secrets on tape in the privacy of her bedroom and give Dr. Greenson the tape for analysis. She was so enthusiastic about this method that she encouraged Dr. Greenson to develop the idea professionally. She made her first tapes just before her death. Perhaps they were recorded—on her reel-to-reel tape machine—on the Friday before her death, but what she said precluded them from being recorded before Thursday or after Friday. It is likely she handed them over to Dr. Greenson on Saturday, her last full day of life, otherwise, seeing what happened to her other belongings, they would have never come to light.

We only learned that Dr. Greenson had them because he was the only one to quit the agreement made at Monroe's house in the hours after her death. He had, no doubt, decided his professional integrity was his highest priority, and when the coroner sent John Miner, the deputy district attorney, to interview him on the Wednesday following Monroe's death, he dropped his bombshell. "Marilyn did not commit suicide," he said to Miner. "I know that my defense of her will raise the accusation of vested interest, since it represents a dreadful failure for a psychiatrist to lose a patient by suicide, but listen to these tapes and make your own mind up." The deal, agreed by Miner, was that he could report his conclusions but not quote any part of the tapes. He listened to the two tapes and admitted that there was no way Monroe had committed suicide. This is what he reported, though his memo to the coroner and his copy to the district attorney have since disappeared. We assume this was not what they wanted to hear. Dr. Greenson had gone along with the suicide idea in the first place and it was expected by the coroner that his interview would support this.

In the tapes, Monroe outlined her plans for the future; they were positive plans. She did not use words like "perhaps" or "maybe"; instead, she presented carefully worked out intentions. Other aspects of the tapes showed that she was in a happy, buoyant, and forward-looking mood. There was nothing of committing suicide in them. She spoke about her marriages, her friends, and her future in positive terms. She also spoke, without vindictiveness, about her relationships with the Kennedy brothers.

So, Monroe was murdered; but how? Dr. Thomas Noguchi, the autopsist, found no evidence of the drugs that killed her in her stomach. Neither did he find any traces of the gelatine from the forty-seven Nembutal capsules she was said to have swallowed. The manufacturer of the drug, Abbot Laboratories, commented that the volume of Nembutal found in Monroe would have indicated an intake of over ninety capsules. What he did find was a large quantity of chloral hydrate in her blood. Given the amount of chloral hydrate, it was indicated that Monroe had been given a Mickey Finn.

Dr. Noguchi's next thought was injection. He, with the assistance of Miner, who attended the autopsy representing the district attorney, examined every inch of Monroe's skin with magnifying glasses. There was no sign of a "hot shot" having been administered. Besides, with an injection the drugs were not likely to reach the liver before death took place, and that, apart from the bloodstream, was the only place a huge volume of barbiturates was found.

The coroner said Monroe had quickly swallowed a large number of capsules that killed her, and this is patently not true, and if she was not killed by a hot shot, there remained only one means by which she could have been murdered. After a drink containing a strong Mickey Finn, which would knock her out quickly, the barbiturates must have been administered by enema. Suppositories, as some have suggested, could not have contained the volume of drugs found in her body. But she used enemas as part of her beauty treatment, as many other stars did, and all the gear was in her home.

Those who gathered at her home did not understand what was happening to her. Any ordinary person would have been rushed to the hospital as soon as her coma condition was discovered, when she likely would have been saved. But movie stars had to avoid the adverse publicity that went with that kind of action. Those around waited till the last minute by which time they, no doubt, believed they had tried everything. Then she was rushed to the hospital, but it was too late.

Having died on the way to the hospital, she was then taken back to her home, where the story line protective of the Kennedys was decided on and promulgated. Those who killed Monroe, no doubt, waited anxiously for news that the U.S. attorney general was hauled up for questioning, but it never happened. If he was questioned at all—and it is likely he was—it was in private and the interview was never placed on public record. Dr. Noguchi, puzzled by what he had found and not found, returned to extend the autopsy, but the means of doing so—the samples and smear slides—had all been disposed of.

The Kennedy family has not helped by pretending that nothing ever happened in regard to Monroe. It will not support even those such as myself who staunchly support the innocence of the Kennedy brothers in regard to Monroe's demise. The Kennedys were not responsible for her death, even though there are indications they "paid off" a number of people for silence relating to their proximity. The Kennedys would not have wished for her to die, neither would the act of killing her have fit their political or personal profiles. Far from it: From a realistic viewpoint, the enormous risk involved in killing anyone—or having anyone killed—would have placed the entire family in lasting jeopardy. And as far as the Kennedy family was concerned, murder was never a solution to infidelity.

It is not hard to speculate as to the likely murderers. The CIA was listening in to what was happening at Monroe's home, and a number of CIA agents, those who survived the Bay of Pigs debacle, were more than anxious to take advantage of such a situation as this. This was the political futures of John and Robert Kennedy falling into their laps. I cannot admit to unreasonable speculation when I accredit Monroe's murder to the CIA, for this is but a logical step to take in respect of the firsthand intelligence passed on to me by an extremely reliable source, which will be addressed in more detail in chapter 22.

The name of the individual who actually killed Monroe I do not know, but the indications are that she was knocked out by a Mickey Finn and killed by the injection of an enormous amount of Nembutal delivered by enema. More than likely the "lead" man was known to her. Perhaps, it was a member of the CIA-friendly Mafiosi. She knew one or two of them. When Monroe was knocked out by the Mickey Finn, the "lead" would only have to open the guesthouse outside door and admit those who would finish the job. Perhaps only one; probably no more than two. They worked fast, and when Monroe was next seen, she was in a coma and dying.

In their actions, Monroe's friends responded to the needs of the living. The fact that she would enter the annals of Hollywood history as a suicide came a poor second in their consideration, it appears. But, it is worth repeating, there is no need for the deception to continue now.

CHAPTER 10

Between the Lines of History

And even I can remember
A day when the historians left blanks in their writings,
I mean for things they didn't know.
　　　　　—Ezra Pound, *A Draft of XXX Cantos* (1930), no. 13

WHEN MARILYN MONROE was purported and universally accepted to have committed suicide, the CIA conspirators soon saw that ranks had been closed and their plans to remove the Kennedy brothers—and all other Kennedys—from American politics had failed abysmally.

There were others, however, who became very interested in the CIA Bay of Pigs survivors and what they had attempted. They were a privileged group that benefited from information fed to them by CIA personnel. These were people in high places in business—the American Establishment—and, generally, their benefits came from up-to-the-minute data relating to events and circumstances in countries in which they had investments. The CIA was their eyes and ears across the world. This conduit, no doubt, was linked to a "grapevine" via which all kinds of information was transmitted, for good measure.

It would be hard to believe that the gossip surrounding Monroe's death would not feature in word of mouth opinions of what had really happened. And it also would be hard to believe that those agents with direct contact with the Bay of Pigs survivors—or even some of them in person—would not reveal to trusted individuals what had really gone on, how Monroe died, and why. It would be of enormous interest to certain people who circulated in the highest places in industry and other parts of the American Establishment that there was already in existence a band of people sworn to bringing down the Kennedy dynasty, regardless of what it involved. That they actually killed Monroe would, no doubt, serve as a guarantee of their dedication. These were people who were as anxious as the Bay of Pigs survivors to get rid of the Kennedys, but for very different reasons.

There were, possibly, two reasons for the concern of Establishment members. One might well have been the genuine—though misguided—horror that, as they saw it, the president was taking a sharp turn to his political Left and showing determination to take the government with him. There were some who were highly suspicious of what might be termed his socialist traits. To these people this represented the road to communism, and they were opposed to it. It mattered not that the policies at issue carried great new benefits for disenfranchised Americans: the poor, the sick, the elderly, and the unemployed. At all costs, this socialist rot had to be cut out of the plans for development in the United States. It was a way forward they would not accept. Besides, it was big business that would be expected to produce the funding of benefits for the disenfranchised, one way or another.

Linked to this was more than uneasiness that John F. Kennedy was dedicated to finding, for America, a peaceful way through the jungle of international politics. This might be acceptable to the people, but to industrialists, oil men, and manufacturers of armaments, military aircraft, and other accoutrements of war, this was serious. For them, it was taking the path to ruin. Armaments had a distinctly limited shelf life when it came to new technologies and the relevant day-by-day expansions and developments of them. And if this were true in regard of those who manufactured armaments, it was even more true for the aircraft industry, which was expected to keep America ahead of international competition. It was said that designs were being developed so fast a new plane was obsolete before it left the drawing board. Therefore, the powerful military-industrial alliance, as it was known, was exceedingly frustrated.

As such, many members of the Establishment were feeling the effects of having Kennedy in the White House. Having shackled the Pentagon, Kennedy was showing he was not prepared to unleash U.S. military power to achieve political ends. Any lingering doubts on this were settled by the Cuban missile crisis. The Pentagon advised the president to blast the missile installations out of existence, but he chose eyeball-to-eyeball tactics instead. Therefore, the generals had a lot to be unhappy about. They headed the most powerful military force in the world, and yet they were prevented from as much as flexing their muscles by the new president. The success of the president's peaceful approach to the Cuban missile crisis was applauded the world over, but his means of obtaining it was seen as weakness by many nearer to home.

The "knock-on" effect of Kennedy's policies was that, quite apart from those industries directly affected by a reduced need for armaments, many "feeder" industries, such as steel and plastics, and many servant industries who depended on contracts from the "big boys" for survival, saw an uncertain future if Kennedy was allowed a second term and time to develop his fresh new way in politics. The oil millionaires were disturbed for other reasons, also. President Kennedy had been looking at the oil depletion allowances that had made them rich and were calculated to make them richer. This was a form of tax exemption established when oil was greatly needed and when the oil giants were being pressed to invest and reinvest in new drillings. It was a huge bonus that was long outdated and Kennedy was planning revisions to bring the oil producers into line with other industries.

By this time, the United States had a substantial presence in Vietnam, though it was not involved in war. The military there hid under the guise of "advisors," but this fooled no one. The political ideology of helping to fight communism in a distant country rather than risk the rise of communism at home had been inherited by

Kennedy, and by all indications he was preparing to withdraw U.S. presence from the volatile region. What could be done?

As if this were not enough, the balance of priorities in government had changed. Traditionally, the government had placed the needs of the Establishment first, no doubt in the belief that its success was necessary to providing for the working population. Even the military was regarded as being stationed overseas primarily to protect the interests of the Establishment. But now the people were being placed first. This was remarkable, and the consequences, which were only ripples at that point, were calculated to become waves. This young upstart who had crept into power by the smallest of margins was trouble, and there were more than murmurs that he had to be dealt with.

Kennedy, of course, had not been expected to become president. The very idea of a Kennedy occupying the White House was anathema to some. To them, in fact, it had come as a nasty shock. As some saw it, his father, Joseph P. Kennedy, was a scoundrel who had scandalously extended his wealth through bootlegging in the days of Prohibition and had abused his position as U.S. ambassador to Britain during World War II. Apparently, he had taken advantage of empty ships returning to the United States after discharging lend-lease goods to Britain by shipping home supplies of gin and other spirits, from which he made another fortune.

John Kennedy had won the presidency by only a hair's breadth. It was said that Sam Giancana and his henchmen had "elicited" votes from the Chicago area and that it was these votes that had made all the difference. If this had been true, there were certain ways of interpreting this: there were those who argued it was the Mafia who put Kennedy into the White House, and since Joseph Kennedy was believed to have links with the Mafia, the rumors took the edge off his son's victory for those who came across such stories. In fact, it was completely overlooked that Chicago's Mayor Richard Daley always produced the vote for the Democrats. It was unlikely he would have welcomed help from the Mafia.

Since his inauguration, Kennedy had worked hard to justify his election and was steadily gaining the confidence of the people. His popularity was increasing apace, and there was little doubt he was heading for a second term. That said, there was talk of Robert F. Kennedy following him into the White House for two terms, and their younger brother, Edward after that. To the disaffected this represented a crisis of the first order. To them it was unimaginable, but it was like the tide encroaching on the shore. It was happening. It was a nightmare turning into a reality.

I envisage that a meeting of minds took place. First, it was a meeting between like-minded friends in the Establishment, and they may have existed as a group long before the CIA came into the picture. More than likely this group expanded, though I do not see it as very large. Their meetings would become increasingly urgent and when the Monroe "termination" was identified by those in the know as a bold attempt to dislodge the Kennedys on the part of survivors of the Bay of Pigs, it would be an obvious step for them to make a tentative approach to someone belonging to that group. This would lead to other meetings, in which it would be eventually suggested any amount of money could be made available to finance a daring bid to kill Kennedy. As far as the Establishment members were concerned, the CIA renegades might lack funds, but they scored highly in respect to know how, contacts, and the illicit influence they could exert on the agency and its operatives. Their influence was of such a nature it would almost certainly lead to some agents contributing to their scheme without knowing it.

With terms having been agreed, we had here a combination of influential members of the Establishment with a group of men dedicated to avenge the treachery they believed to have been dealt them by the president and his brother. This was a volatile combination: a powder keg concentrated in one direction. On both sides there was resolution, a deadly intent to determine who would run the United States and how. Three plans to assassinate President Kennedy surfaced within a short time of each other, one in Miami, one in Chicago, and the other in Dallas. It is not unlikely they were all the work of this same group, giving the impression that plots to kill the president were springing up everywhere and confusing the issue of which one was the real one.

I cannot say the diabolical partnership plotting the death of the president did not have certain assistance from elsewhere. There are strong indications that a military brain was behind the planning, but this, of course, may have derived from the military-industrial input. Then the team to actually carry out the shooting may well have been supplied, at the request of the CIA renegades, by the Mafia, or on the "recommendation" of the Mafia. With the affluence of the Establishment members involved, there would now be no shortage of money to pay for whatever and whoever they wanted.

President John F. Kennedy

CHAPTER 11

The Texas Adventure

QED: *Quod erat demonstrandum. (Which was to be proved).*

—Euclid

IT MIGHT HAVE been called the Great Adventure, for there was a great deal to be proved by John F. Kennedy on his tour of Texas, and no one was more aware of it than Kennedy himself. Could he impose a peace on the warring factions that were tearing the Democrats to pieces in this, his period of consolidation, before the run up to the next election? Could he make popularity gains in a territory hostile to just about everything he stood for? Could he allay the fears of his well-intentioned advisers, those who feared for his safety on this visit? Everything had to be proved. Billy Graham, the respected American evangelist, had made known his forebodings about the trip to the president, and he was only one of several who tried to put the president off this visit. The Texas-based lawyer Byron Skelton was specifically worried about the proposal for the president to visit Dallas, and UN Representative Adlai Stevenson reminded Arthur M. Schlesinger Jr., Kennedy's aide, that he had been beaten and spat on during a visit to Dallas less than a month before Kennedy was due to go. Even the Texan Lyndon B. Johnson—one of their own— had had saliva poured over him.

At the heart of the divisions among the Democrats in Texas was the feud between Governor John Connally and Senator Ralph Yarborough, borne of the fact that the vice president had been awarded half the patronage of Texas by Kennedy—hitherto completely Yarborough's patronage—so he might reward those who supported him, and Connally was seen as Johnson's man by Yarborough. It befell Johnson to settle the personality disputes in Texas, but he appeared impotent. The president had taken matters in hand simply because it was necessary for someone to do so. Rancor spilled liberally on day-to-day events in Austin, and it even cast a cloud over Kennedy's visit when Yarborough refused to sit next to the vice president in the motorcade to the airport. Kennedy responded by sending word to Yarborough that he sit next to Johnson "or else he walked."

Connally had made the arrangements for the official Trade Mart reception and lunch at Dallas and had placed Yarborough at a lowly spot at the tables. He was to be shown as little respect or recognition as planning permitted, ignored as far as possible, and his wife was not even invited. When Kennedy found out, he pressured Connally to place the senator at the top table. Connally submitted, but had the lunch ever taken place, it is to be wondered whether the governor would have played his trump card: the top table had two tiers to it, and it had not been specified at which tier Yarborough would sit. Arrangements for the reception to be held at the governor's mansion later that day were completely in Connally's hands, and Senator Yarborough was not even invited. The Texas politicians were simply using the visit as an opportunity to get at each other's throats. In fact, things were getting worse, not better, and not unreasonably, the question springs to mind: With friends like these, who needs enemies?

The president had no complaints about the proceedings at San Antonio. At Houston, things also went well. By Thursday, November 21, Kennedy and his sizeable entourage had arrived at Fort Worth, where they would spend a night in the Hotel Texas. President Kennedy was to speak twice the following morning before moving on to Dallas. The first of these two speeches was delivered in spitting rain outside the hotel to workers who turned out to see him before they made their way to work. He mounted the rear of a truck and declined a raincoat, preferring to be identified with those in his audience who were getting wet. Despite the rain, the numbers were encouraging and his speech went well.

The second speech was after breakfast in the Grand Ballroom. "A few years ago in Paris," he said, "I introduced myself by saying that I was the man who accompanied Mrs. Kennedy to Paris." His audience was smiling and receptive. "I'm getting something of that same sensation as I travel around Texas." His listeners were falling under his spell. When the laughter and applause allowed him, he continued. "Nobody wonders what Lyndon and I wear." His audience was now captivated. His smile, his charm, his friendliness were winning hearts here in Fort Worth. He was offered and gracefully accepted a tall Stetson before he left the ballroom, and he could not have failed to be happy with his reception. Next, it was to Dallas.

Dallas is a relatively short car ride from Fort Worth. They are so close they share an international airport. The journey was deemed necessary to be taken by air, however, to obtain a full-scale reception and the best publicity, so Air Force One made its way to the relatively small Love Airfield, where that reception was to be held. The vice president, being a Texan, was obliged to take part in every reception, and the humor of this was not missed. Connally had approved the composition of the reception committee, which was made up largely of Republicans, but it was the impressive turnout of the minority-Kennedy supporters who supplied the warmth of welcome. However, this did not mean they were the only ones there, or that all the faces were smiling.

A watchful Larry O'Brien, a Kennedy aide, avoided an unpleasant moment when Yarborough went seeking a car with company more amenable to him. He was collared and gently guided to take his appointed seat next to Johnson's wife, Lady Bird. Then, the motorcade left the airfield and proceeded at a modest speed via Mockingbird Lane and Lemmon Street to downtown Dallas, which it was to thread on the route to the Trade Mart. The welcoming placards were interspersed by some hostile to the president, and the crowds were a mixture of smiling supporters and the straight-faced curious.

Turtle Creek Boulevard gave way to Cedar Spring Road, and Harwood brought the motorcade to Main Street, which eventually joined the Stemmons Freeway. Main Street ran into a tangle caused by a traffic island, however, so a diversion had been introduced to the route that, supposedly, allowed a smoother passage from Main to Stemmons. The motorcade would take a right at Houston Street and a sharp left on to Elm Street, where it would proceed under the railway overpass to Stemmons and then the short distance to the Trade Mart. The acute dog-leg left from Houston to Elm placed the motorcade into a classic ambush location, and this proved to be exactly what happened.

The president had hardly turned on to Elm Street, his Lincoln having slowed to accommodate the sharp dog-leg bend, when firing broke out. He was exposed to buildings behind him and to locations to his right and in front of him. It was all over in six seconds. He was caught in cross fire between snipers behind him and, as eye witnesses told, to his front right, and shot, it was said, three times. Within seconds, he was being rushed via the Stemmons Freeway to Parkland Hospital. Elm Street was part of a complex of roads running through the grassed Dealey Plaza, named after a local newspaper proprietor. Mayhem erupted during the shooting and for some time afterward. There was argument about the number of bullets fired: some said three, some said four, others said up to six. And those in the plaza were no surer about where the bullets had come from. Some said from behind the motorcade, some said from the front, and some said both. The Dealey Plaza was something of an echo chamber, which did not help to clarify things, and the arguments go on to this day.

The president arrived at Parkland Hospital, where a team of doctors unsuccessfully fought to save his life. His death was announced to a traumatized public at 1:00 P.M. The very heartbeat of the world was stopped for a moment when the news broke. Who had carried out this outrage? Was it the Soviets, in reply to Kennedy's victory over the Cuban missile crisis? Was it the Cubans? As time went by, a whole range of possible theories were tabled. Was it the Mafia? There were any number of scenarios put forward. Then a young man, Lee Harvey Oswald, an employee of the Texas School Book Depository, which the motorcade had just passed as the shooting started, was arrested in the Texas Theater, just a few miles away, and became the only suspect for the killing of the president. Oswald himself was cut down by a bullet two days later, when he was being led to a car for transfer from the police department to the county jail. The killer, small-time Mafiosi and strip club owner Jack Ruby, was arrested and later charged with Oswald's murder.

The Texas Adventure had ended in disaster.

CHAPTER 12

Investigation

I hate quotations. Tell me what you know.
—Ralph Waldo Emerson

LEE HARVEY OSWALD'S death and the manner of it immediately engendered suspicions of conspiracy, but an investigation, ordered immediately by the new president, Lyndon B. Johnson, reassured the people in a vast report published ten months later that Oswald had been the killer, that he had acted alone, and that no conspiracy had taken place. It was also asserted that one "lone nut" killer, Oswald, had been killed by another "lone nut" killer, Jack Ruby. The Warren Report, named after Chief Justice Earl Warren, who chaired the investigatory commission, consisted of twenty-six volumes and was 10 million words long. It told that only three bullets in total had been fired. One had missed and the other two had hit the president. To explain the fact that Governor John Connally had also suffered various wounds, the commission put forward the theory that one of the two bullets from Oswald's rifle hit the president in the upper back, then exited his throat and hit Governor Connally's back. But the bullet did not stop there. Amazingly, it traversed his body, exited again, and hit the governor in the wrist, passing through once more and coming to rest in his thigh. This became known as the single-bullet theory. The other bullet, also fired by Oswald, effectively blew the back of the president's head off. The commissioners had found themselves in a tight corner.

The problem they faced was that had more than three shots been fired, Oswald could not have fired them all in the time scale. Even one more bullet fired would have meant that there had been two snipers, and two snipers would have confirmed without a doubt that a conspiracy had taken place. To the consternation of the commissioners, the FBI put out a report asserting that four bullets had been fired, but this was soon "adjusted" to conform with Warren Commission requirements.

The time scale for the firing of the shots was established by a continuous sequence of film that had been taken by the tailor Abraham Zapruder. Zapruder had a point of vantage from which to shoot his film and his 8 mm amateur camera recorded the entire sequence in which the shots were fired. The speed of the camera he used was eighteen frames per second, and this translated to about six seconds of actual footage. The problem was that the rifle the commission said Oswald had used was a 6.5 Italian carbine, a Mannlicher-Carcano, which could not have been fired more than three times in the six seconds.

With the publication of the Warren Report, the government hoped it had consigned to history the events surrounding the murder of President Kennedy. This proved wishful thinking, since, even before the Warren Report was published, books had begun to appear challenging the "official" line. Since then, thousands of books have been written, and the status of the Warren Report has been so denigrated in the countless attacks made on it that it is now generally considered by increasing numbers as worthless. At worst, there are a significant number of people who would quote it as a shocking example of how far the government would go to avoid the truth being known. In general terms, it was found that there were numerous occasions on which the commission stifled those who might have contradicted the stance it had taken, ignoring them as witnesses, regardless of the information they had, while those who supported the commission's line, even though their testimony was doubtful, were accepted. Witnessess in the process of giving testimony were not infrequently cut off when what they were leading to was deemed "undesirable" to the commission's position, and on several occasions witness testimony was heard "off the record" and, therefore, not recorded. This practice might well be said to have been emulated by the FBI, which provided testimony to the commission. At one point, a witness anxious to tell FBI men what he had seen was stopped when they heard a description of a man he had witnessed. "If you didn't see Oswald, you didn't see," they said.

Oswald was drinking a coke from a bottle he had obtained from a machine in the second floor lunch room when Marion Baker, the first police officer to enter the Texas School Book Depository, appeared. The warehouse manager, Roy Truly, confirmed Oswald was a staff member and Baker was not interested in him. He was in the wrong place and this was but two minutes after the shooting had ceased. Amazingly, many have argued that Oswald hid his rifle and fled to the second floor lunch room after shooting the president. The shots fired, they said, came from the sixth floor where Oswald worked, but the elevator was not available to bring him down to the second floor. Officer Baker discovered this for himself when he tried to call it so that he might use it to continue his investigations higher up in the building. The elevator doors had been left open several floors above, and that made it impossible to be called. Officer Baker had to climb the stairs. If Oswald had carried out any shooting, he hid his rifle, dashed through the various piles of books on the sixth floor to the diagonally opposite corner of the long open-plan warehouse, rushed down several flights of stairs until he reached the second floor, when he produced coins, obtained a bottle of coke, and stood drinking it outside the lunch room without being at all breathless or agitated. Most reasonable people have declared this quite impossible.

Nonetheless, Oswald was not there to defend himself when the Warren Commission decided he was the guilty party. In a court of law, Oswald would have had little difficulty obtaining an acquittal, but this was not a court of law. It was a team of commissioners making decisions as they wished. There was no defending counsel or an impartial judge to assess the so-called evidence being "considered."

The Warren Commission arranged for a team of fine marksmen from various parts of the country to repeat the feat of marksmanship attributed to Oswald. Oswald was said to have fired at the president from the sixth-floor window, sixty feet high, at a moving target, discharging three bullets in the space of six seconds, two of them finding their target. The experts were located only forty feet high and were to fire at a stationary target. In spite of their advantages, not one of the marksmen achieved what had been attributed to Oswald. William Manchester, in his otherwise excellent book *Death of a President*, declared Oswald a superb marksman, yet the men who had fired next to him on the U.S. Marines rifle range in training sessions spoke of his ability as abysmal. There were times he was awarded "Maggie's drawers"—zero. Something did not add up.

Oswald did not "flee" from the Texas School Book Depository building. He simply walked out unchallenged, as others had. Some of the staff stood around watching the aftermath of the shooting, while Oswald made his way to his lodgings. He first boarded a bus, but it got bogged down in heavy traffic. Disembarking, he waited for a taxi, but when the first came along he courteously deferred to a little old lady who was also waiting, and he took the next. He left his taxi about a block away from where he lived and completed the journey on foot. His landlady, Earlene Roberts, saw him arrive and leave again shortly afterward. He had changed his shirt, put on a jacket, and, as we learned later, packed a revolver.

According to Roberts, Oswald left his lodgings in response to hearing a police car horn sounding twice outside her home. She looked through the window and saw the police car before it drove away. She also saw Oswald waiting for a moment at a bus stop before setting off on foot for his destination. He was next seen at the junction of Tenth Street and Patton Avenue, about a mile away, where he engaged in conversation with a police officer in what was probably the only police car not in downtown Dallas. The officer was J. D. Tippit, who got out of his car and slowly walked round to Oswald, fingering his gun. Then, Officer Tippit was shot dead and Oswald fled. Not long afterward, Oswald was seen entering the Texas Theater without having paid for a ticket. The cashier was said to have called the police, and the response was immediate. They turned out in force with sirens screaming, and after a scramble in the cinema, Oswald was arrested. He was not arrested for failing to pay at the box office. He was arrested for the murder of Officer Tippit. Much later in the day, he was accused of murdering President Kennedy.

If the police had been called out for a patron who had not paid his entrance to the theater, it was curious that the police turned up so fast and in such numbers to arrest such a dastardly scoundrel. Clearly, this was not so, and stories later circulated that police officers had lain in wait as Oswald entered the theater. Whatever the case, short of being clairvoyant, the police had information no one has ever unearthed. Long after, however, unsettling stories began to be told. One witness who believed he had seen Oswald being led from a side door into a police car was, some years later, astounded to discover Oswald had, in fact, been led through the front entrance to a police car. There is no information about a second man being arrested at the theater.

And Oswald's murder by Ruby opened up even more speculation about what exactly was going on when President Kennedy was murdered.

CHAPTER 13

Sounds Wrong, Sounds Right

Political language . . . is designed to make lies sound truthful.

—George Orwell

IN SPITE OF the confusion in the Dealey Plaza, the numerous critics of the Warren Report firmly held that shots had come from two directions: from behind and from in front of the motorcade. Many witnesses said this was the case, and an examination of the film taken by Abraham Zapruder served to support this amply to all able to view it except the Warren Commission, though it must be said the commissioners were shown a poor second-generation print. The fact that the people were not allowed to see the film made it easier for the Warren Report to be accepted and, generally, it was, particularly by loyal Americans who did not think of challenging what their government told them. It was ten years after the assassination that the Zapruder footage was screened on television, and the public at large were horrified. Not just by what they saw, but by the realization that their government had been so dishonest in the Warren Report. At last, they began to see that the critics of the report had been right all along and that there had been a conspiracy to kill President John F. Kennedy.

In 1979, the Senate Committee on Assassinations reexamined the assassination of President Kennedy and others who had been assassinated, notably Martin Luther King Jr. Taking a long time to set up, and having a deadline for reaching its conclusions, the short

time it had for real investigation was useful, though completely inadequate to the task undertaken. The direction taken by the committee created the feeling it would have been happier just to confirm
all that the Warren Report had said and leave it at that. Before the
committee's work was done, however, a bombshell of enormous proportions was dropped and compelling acoustics evidence to shatter
the Warren Report was given the credence is merited.

To reduce it to its lowest common denominator, the new evidence confirmed that there were at least two shooters in the Dealey
Plaza (and there were likely several more). Researchers knew what
had been going on long before there was any official acknowledg-
ment that Lee Harvey Oswald, if he was guilty, did not act alone.
The submission of acoustic evidence to the House committee was
"put on a peg," so to speak, when it was first introduced, but, left
until the end of the proceedings, the committee was obliged to consider it, and it was finally placed before its members. The impact of
this evidence was such that it compelled the committee to place on
record the significance it implied.

The sound recordings involved were derived from dictabelts,
that is, stored recordings made of police department conversations
via radio. One sequence of recording proved to be of special interest. The sounds had emanated from a police motorcycle transmitter
that had been stuck on "open" during the whole period of the
shooting in the Dealey Plaza. The Warren Commission had known
of the dictabelt recordings, but it decided the quality of recording
was too poor to yield any useful information. Ten years later, when
the dictabelt recordings were rediscovered by the researchers Mary
Ferrell and Gary Mack, technology had improved to the point
where the recordings could be made to bear witness to shots being
fired on Elm Street.

A detailed analysis of the tapes was carried out by a team at the
firm Bolt, Beranek, and Newman, under the leadership of Dr. James E.
Barger, and afterward honed by two scientists at New York University, Dr. Ernest Aschkenasy and Professor Mark Weiss. Shots were
identified as having been fired from two general locations, one in

front and to the right of the presidential Lincoln—in the direction of the so-called grassy knoll—and the other behind. The evidence was compelling: shots from two directions meant that two shooters were involved and that meant that a conspiracy had taken place. The House committee, perhaps reeling from the impact of this evidence, could not acknowledge the simple implication, but it did rule that a conspiracy had *probably* taken place when Kennedy was killed. The committee had done its best to shore up the disintegrating Warren Report, but in the end what had been known to researchers across the world for a long time was grudgingly admitted in the face of the evidence of the sound recordings.

Establishing the two general directions of gunfire did not preclude that snipers had not fired from other locations within the two general directions identified. In spite of what the Warren Commission had asserted, it was now established that shots had been fired from in front and to the right of the presidential Lincoln as well as from behind. Just two shooters were enough to confirm that a conspiracy had taken place, but there was, in fact, a team of shooters with their entourage—lookouts, radio contact men, and so forth—in the plaza that day. It was a well-planned operation.

Following the acceptance of the acoustic evidence, great efforts were made to discredit it, first with the police officer H. B. McLain revising his story by saying he was not in the plaza when the recordings had been made. He said he followed the presidential Lincoln to Parkland Hospital. A check through photographs taken in the Dealey Plaza after the president had been taken to hospital, however, revealed that McLain—with motorcycle—was where he first said he was, right there on Elm Street. The FBI pitched in with a report that was immediately shot down by the House committee chief counsel, Professor G. Robert Blakey, who denounced it as a "sophomoric analysis . . . superficial, shoddy, and shot full of holes." After that, it was the turn of the Justice Department, and it commissioned the tapes to be subjected to a completely fresh analysis—costing over $23,000, a fortune at that time—to be carried out by a panel of the National Academy of Sciences. Afterward, the panel announced that erroneous deductions had been made from the first analysis. But by that time, few were listening. The objections raised were generally recognized for what they were and did not reflect credit on the government. The whole sorry episode of attempts by one government department or another to shore up the fatally flawed Warren Report by discrediting the startling findings of the original dictabelt analysis was a dismal failure.

A more recent updated, totally independent analysis by Donald B. Thomas was published in 2001 in the *Journal of the U.S. Forensic Science Society*. The dictabelt recordings were freshly reanalyzed with advanced new equipment. Thomas also carefully examined the data the National Academy of Sciences panel had used in the Justice Department analysis. He found that the data the panel had used was not accurate and that it was the findings of the Justice Department analysis that were not valid. Further study revealed that the original analysis submitted to the House committee in 1979 was, in fact, correct and that the fatal shot was fired from the grassy knoll. Thomas contributed more, identifying one of the rifles used in the shooting in the Dealey Plaza, which was not a 6.5 Mannlicher-Carcano, the rifle the Warren Report said was used by Oswald. The rifle identified from the new acoustics analysis carried out by Thomas that was responsible for the final and fatal shot was a .30 caliber weapon. Remarkably, records show that immediately after the shooting, Police Inspector Herbert Sawyer, who was on duty in the Dealey Plaza, had radioed in a description of a man he wanted to detain. It ran, "The wanted person in this is a slender white male about thirty, five feet ten, one sixty five, carrying what looked to be a 30-30 or some kind of Winchester." The man was never identified and the rifle never found.

And as time has progressed, more and more evidence has been produced to support that Oswald was not a lone nut and that he did not kill the president. But then, how many people really knew Oswald, who he really was and what he really did?

CHAPTER 14

Oswald

You see but you do not observe.
—Arthur Conan Doyle, *The Adventures of Sherlock Holmes*

LEE HARVEY OSWALD is the great enigma in the case of the assassination of President John F. Kennedy. To understand the role of Oswald is to understand how the murder of Kennedy was planned and organized. I have said this before: in fact I have said it ever since I picked up a pen to write on this subject, and I did not start writing until I had served a long apprenticeship by way of research.

There is clear evidence that Oswald lived a secret existence, an existence the government has never acknowledged, in spite of the weight of clear indications; an existence that clarifies his role in the plot to murder President Kennedy, for such there was. There is convincing evidence, quite apart from the acoustics evidence, that a conspiracy took place. For instance, the rifle that was said to have been used by Oswald did not show any of his fingerprints. With a push and a squeeze, the Dallas Police Department claimed to have identified one of his palm prints, though the circumstances in which this turned up were not convincing. As I said earlier, the chances of Oswald even being where he could shoot at the motorcade at all were extremely doubtful.

Then there were the other rifles. The first pronouncement from the sixth floor of the Texas School Book Depository, from where the shots were claimed to have been fired, was that a 7.65 Mauser had been found among the boxes of books. Discovered by Deputy Sheriff

71

Luke Mooney and witnessed by Deputy Constable Seymour Weitzman, the rifle was identified and affidavits drawn up documenting the find. This also included Deputy Sheriff Roger Craig, who was in on the discovery, and their find was regarded as definitive. Henry M. Wade, the district attorney, announced its discovery on television, but it seems this was very premature. Apparently, this was not the rifle that should have been discovered.

Collected by Lieutenant J. C. Day and taken to police headquarters, the rifle was booked in as a 6.5 Mannlicher-Carcano. Those who found the Mauser were prevailed on to admit they had made a mistake and that the rifle was really a Mannlicher-Carcano. The two principals obliged: Mooney and Weitzman changed their affidavits. Craig, however, refused, and this was said to be the cause of him being hounded out of his job, shot at, being driven off the road and receiving permanent injury to his back from the crash that resulted, and finally his suicide, if that was really what it was. Police Captain Willy Fritz also witnessed the finding of the Mauser and identified it, but there was no comment from him.

To distinguish between the two rifles was not difficult. All that was necessary to tell the difference between the two was to be able to read. The Mauser had its name printed on the barrel, while the Mannlicher-Carcano had "Made in Italy" printed on its butt. Quite separate and distinct from these, another rifle was filmed being brought down from the roof of the Texas School Book Depository building. Held aloft by the police officer who had discovered it, it was described as the assassin's weapon, even though it had no telescopic sight. When the weapon described by Donald B. Thomas, the presence of which was confirmed by Police Inspector Herbert Sawyer, is added to the list, rifles abounded in and around the school book depository.

Why Oswald had ordered a rifle by post to be delivered to his post office box, when it was certain to be easily identified as belonging to him, became a mystery. Had he just gone along to one of the many shops in Dallas that sold firearms, he could have bought a rifle and been near enough totally unidentifiable. It all became clear, however, when it was discovered that Oswald had been enlisted into the ranks of the CIA while he served in the U.S. Marines. He had either been told to order a rifle that way—and he would do as he was told—or else it was ordered to be sent to him by someone else. In the light of later discoveries, the implications of this were very clear: Oswald had been marked out to be a patsy.

× × ×

But how many have traced the real Lee Harvey Oswald to his enlistment in the U.S. Marine Corps and his choice of radar for a specialization? He did well, attaining seventh place in his class, and was eventually posted to the Atsugi Base in Japan, where he excelled in his work, got along with the other men and officers in his unit, and quickly climbed the ladder of trustworthiness. He eventually held the highest level of clearance in respect of access to the secret operations conducted from Atsugi. This is believed to have been known as Crypto or Cryptonym.

Oswald was a quiet man. He read a great deal and discussed important issues with the other men. At first, he did not drink and, though he did not mind watching the others play poker, he had no interest in gambling himself. He watched football on television, played chess, and was generally very friendly to those around him. Not interested in women and not a frequenter of bars, he did not seem to mind being called "Mrs. Oswald" or get angry when he was thrown, fully dressed, into the shower. He did not seem to be short of friends and was, generally, well liked by his fellows.

Oswald began to change, though. He joined the "poker school," began taking a drink, and also started to be interested in women. For him this was very strange. He went from having no interest in women to frequenting a club to see a certain hostess, who was almost certainly a communist spy. His quiet, retiring manner suddenly took on aspects hitherto foreign to him. He obtained a .22 Derringer pistol and managed to inflict a minor injury on himself. It was an offense for marines to possess private firearms and Oswald was duly charged. On another occasion, he was thrown into the brig for having poured a drink over the head of a sergeant in a club, a most unlikely thing for him to do. But it appeared he had been selected for recruitment into the ranks of the CIA, and a likely explanation of his misdemeanors was that it had become necessary for him to be taken out of circulation from time to time for briefing by his new CIA masters. After a spell in the brig, it was said that, on his reappearance, his nature had changed. It was noted that he was bitter and resentful, saying how he was fed up with the ways of democracy and imperialism. Clearly, his time "in the brig" had been well used to prepare him for his new work. The minor charges for indiscipline that he had attracted were useful in another context. They somewhat "colored" his character and marked him out to watchers linked to his communist hostess that he was no wimp. It was "clear" he was not at all averse to doing his own thing, regardless of the consequences.

In September 1958, Oswald's unit, which was known as "Coffee Mill," was assigned to a mission in Formosa. The unit was sent there to monitor a position in which a naval offensive appeared about to be launched against the Nationalist Chinese, who were supported by the United States and who were fighting against communist forces. Coffee Mill was also there to do what it could to support the local Nationalist China resistance. It was during this time that Oswald, while on guard duty, had a bad experience. Mysteriously, several shots were fired while he was on duty, attracting the attention of the duty officer, who lost no time in getting to where Oswald was. In a distressed state and shaking when the officer arrived, Oswald reported he had seen men in the woods who did not respond to his challenge. He had opened fire on them before the officer had arrived.

Whatever the reason for this reaction, Oswald was very badly shaken up, and he was soon airlifted back to Japan for unspecified "medical treatment," which was probably another slot created for further schooling by the CIA. After this, he went on to another unit at Iwakuni, and this was observed as a turning point for him. It was at this time that he began to take an interest in all things Russian, and even started to learn the Russian language, always a tough task for Westerners. The officers, to whom Oswald's puzzled fellow marines drew attention, were clearly not interested in hearing about these new trends. Some time later, when Oswald had returned to the United States, it is almost certain he was sent to a specialist language school to complete his language studies. We know he became exceedingly competent in Russian, and it became abundantly clear he had been schooled to take on a mission to Soviet Russia for the United States.

CHAPTER 15

The Secret Oswald

Its mystery is its life. We must not let in daylight upon magic.

—Walter Bagehot

LEE HARVEY OSWALD was very quickly released from the U.S. Marines to "look after" his "ailing mother," who did not need looking after. It was clear this was a convenient way to hustle him out of the service and into his new role as a CIA spy in Russia. Via London and Helsinki, he was on his way to Moscow, his target destination. By this time, the Soviets were well aware that the CIA had a program for sending young men behind the Iron Curtain as spies. CIA agents had previously become more easily identifiable because they were all graduates with academic backgrounds—college types. When the CIA realized this, it started selecting suitable candidates from elsewhere, so the Soviets would not recognize the type of young man being recruited to be sent in the guise of a defector. But the Soviets were not as stupid as the CIA believed, however, and they soon cottoned on to what was happening. Consequently, Oswald found himself distinctly unwelcome and it was not long before he faced being sent back to the United States.

Determined to carry out his mission in Russia, Oswald feigned a suicide attempt that resulted in him being hospitalized. Grudgingly, the Soviets permitted him to stay, though Oswald, by then, might well have given them "sweeteners" with which to ingratiate himself, by passing on data hitherto kept secret. Anything in this category would have been given him by the CIA for that purpose. It is thought quite possible, for instance, he might have given the Soviets details of the secret high altitude U2 spy-flights—some of which operated out of Atsugi—that they had not been able to counter. A U2 aircraft, the first ever, was brought down by the Russians soon after Oswald "defected." It might be added, however, that this was apparently a time when the United States had satellite means of spying ready to deploy. In other words, the U2 flights were on the point of becoming obsolete.

Oswald was sent to work at a factory in Minsk, where, compared to other workers, he lived like a lord. The problem for him was that he was watched all the time, though despite all the difficulties, he spent some time in Kiev. It was quite plain that the Soviets knew who he was and what he was doing, and surveillance prevented him doing whatever it was he was sent to do. He persevered for two years, however, obtaining much valuable intelligence, before calling it a day and assuming the role of a disillusioned defector, deciding he wanted to return to the United States. By this time, he had married a Russian, Marina Nicolaevna Prusakova, though it might prove, from the emerging pattern of such marriages to "defectors," to have been a case of Marina marrying him.

Marina later said she took him for a Russian, his language merely reflecting a dialect from another part of the Soviet Union. It would be surprising if she did not know his background, however, for it appears she was marked out for marriage to another American, who was too heavily involved with other women, before she took up with Oswald. The U.S. government wasted no time in arranging for the repatriation of Oswald and his pregnant wife, who was expected to give birth before they could depart from Russia. Oswald's repatriation took a certain amount of time, but given the circumstances it could not reasonably have been faster.

Having stopped off in Holland on his way home, it is likely he was debriefed there. Certainly, there was no one interested in him when his boat docked in the United States. Neither CIA agents nor

FBI agents were there to interview him. This was another instance in which it was made clear who and what he was. With assistance from Traveler's Aid charity, he made his way to Dallas, where his mother now lived. He and his family stayed with her until they found a home of their own.

Oswald had audaciously sat out two years with the Soviets, collecting what data he could in highly dangerous times. His return to the United States might well have been a triumphant one, but it seemed he considered he had a future with the CIA, and he was content to feel his way forward as a returned defector. He awaited his instructions from the agency and was quite prepared to try again in Russia. After a protracted stay in Dallas, he finally received a proposal to go back via Cuba, where he would ingratiate himself to Fidel Castro with information he would be given to pass on to him. Under instructions, he went to New Orleans. There, he was "sheepdipped"—prepared for a new mission—by agents including Guy Banister and Dave Ferrie, and then it was on to Mexico City to seek a visa to Cuba. What he did not know was that this was totally unknown to the CIA per se; he had been given no new mission.

Oswald had been selected by a group of fellow agents to be the patsy in an assassination attempt plotted by the agency rebels who sought revenge for the Bay of Pigs debacle. Having been unsuccessful in bringing the Kennedy dynasty down with the murder of Marilyn Monroe, they were still resolute in pursuing their intention to bring down the Kennedy dynasty. Even though Oswald was available himself, his application at the Cuban embassy in Mexico City was made by another agent who impersonated him. The application was made so clumsily it was not even seriously considered by the Cuban authorities, which was exactly what the conspirators wanted. The conspirators wanted him to travel to Cuba, but they had their own specific ideas about how they wanted him to get there. He returned to Dallas and was found work at the Texas School Book Depository, where he entered the final phase in playing the role of the president's assassin.

Indications are that, having "failed" to get a visa for Havana, he was told that a flight to Cuba would be arranged for him, taking off from a small airfield undercover of the president's visit on November 22. He was designated to leave the depository after the motorcade had passed and make his way to his lodgings, where he would change and pick up a revolver. He would meet a police officer at a designated rendezvous, whose task was to transport him in a police car to Red Bird Airfield, where his plane and pilot would be waiting for him. As far as the conspirators were concerned, he had only to take off to confirm to the authorities that he had been the president's assassin, sent by Castro, and to whom he was attempting to return. It did not matter whether he reached Cuba. The consequence was calculated to be a bloody war, likely to attract the participation of the Soviets, on the one hand, and the British, on the other hand, probably turning into a devastating nuclear war.

Thus, all the objectives of the conspiring parties would be reached. Kennedy would be dead by then, and a profitable war would be engaged in; that is, profitable to those who survived it. Although he did not realize it, Officer J. D. Tippit was the hero of the hour. He was the police officer meant to take Oswald to the small Red Bird Airfield, only about a fifteen-minute drive away, and he was entirely responsible for the "Cuba" part of the conspirators' plan going awry. Totally innocent of any part in the plot to kill the president, he had probably been listening to the APB put out while he was waiting to give a ride to this young CIA man who, he had been told, needed to get to the airfield at a time the traffic on the roads might prove troublesome. Officer Tippit began to think. Why had he been pressed to helping out when every other car had responded to instructions to proceed to downtown Dallas? What if this was all a cover for the president's killer to make his escape?

Certainly, no one was going to stop him and wonder who it was he had in his car as he made his way to the airfield. By sauntering around his car to find out more about his pick-up, he walked into bullets fired by a concealed man whose only function had been to report that the pick-up had taken place. Explanations would not have satisfied a suspicious Tippit. He now knew too much and had to be disposed of. After he was shot, the killer ran way, perhaps with an accomplice, and Oswald ran the other way.

It should be recalled that Oswald believed that his flight to Cuba was part of a genuine CIA mission. CIA agents were trained that if things went awry, the thing to do was to proceed to the nearest theater, where contact would be made by the agent's "handler." By the time the police arrived in force, however, Oswald knew he had been set up: he had fallen into a trap from which it would be very difficult to escape. "Well, it's all over now," he cried as he was arrested. This remark linked with another he made at police headquarters during interrogation. He said, "Everybody will know who I am now," when he was identified by Deputy Sheriff Roger Craig. Ironically, it appears Craig was identifying an Oswald look-alike who had run from the back door of the depository building. The two remarks made by Oswald were highly significant, however. They entirely support that he was an agent and that he now had no future in the CIA.

Here was a young man entirely supportive of his country who had risked his very life in the service of it. In less than forty-eight hours he would be shot to death by those anxious he did not prove his innocence, and he would be confirmed a despicable killer by the country he had served so well.

He did not give up without a fight, though. When an agent knows he is exposed, he has nothing to lose by revealing who he really is. I am convinced he did so to his interrogator, Captain Willy Fritz. There is little doubt that Fritz would call CIA headquarters at Langley to be told they did not know a Lee Harvey Oswald. This is exactly what happens when agents get into trouble. They are disowned. Oswald wanted to reach a number in North Carolina, no doubt to reach the center from where naval intelligence ran its "defector" programs. It was likely he was trying to reach a personal contact who would vouch for him, but the Dallas police saw to it his call was never put through. We know about his attempt to reach a Raleigh, North Carolina, number because of two curious switchboard operators who were dying to know who he was trying to reach. The inquisitiveness of Mrs. Swinney and Mrs. Troon, the latter of whom recovered a discarded slip with the Raleigh number on it, served us well. They could not help Oswald, however, who was told his number, which had never been dialed, did not answer. And not a word of this was ever mentioned by the Dallas police.

The Dallas Police Department released details of an identity card found, it said, among Oswald's possessions. It bore his photograph and identified him as A. J. Hidell. Strangely, this did not happen during his arrest. The card bearing that name appeared to come to light the next day. It happened, however, that Lieutenant Colonel Robert Jones, who was the operations officer for the 112th Military Intelligence Group, wanted information about the assassination, and he contacted his own men in Dallas. They reported that "A. J. Hidell" had been arrested and was in the police department jail. There is no record of either police or press mentioning the name "A. J. Hidell" on the day of the arrest.

But military intelligence was, it proved, holding a file under the name "A. J. Hidell," which Lieutenant Colonel Jones, on hearing the report, went to consult. In a file that had recently been updated on Oswald's background, he found that "A. J. Hidell" was an alias for Oswald. The file was never made available to the Warren Commission, even though A. J. Hidell was the name under which Oswald was said to have purchased, by post, his rifle and revolver. By the time the House Investigation Committee was in session in the mid-1970s, military intelligence officials admitted the existence of the file, but by then, they said, it had been destroyed.

× × ×

A sequence of interrogation notes was released by the FBI, which did not really amount to very much. Researchers were far more interested in what Captain Fritz had taken down, but there was a severe disappointment to come. Fritz maintained he had taken no notes and that his interviews with Oswald had not been taped and that a stenographer had not been present. I have never believed this, and I was not surprised when, more than thirty years later, the Assassination Records Review Board announced it was releasing them. However, the scant notes released just about matched the details that had already been released by the FBI. In other words, in releasing his notes he was telling us nothing more than we already knew. What the board published is the sum and total of what we have been told to this day: that Captain Fritz interviewed Oswald for twelve of the hours he was in police custody.

It is most unlikely his interviews were not noted, and for that matter not recorded on tape. Why can we not have access to them? We have known all along that Fritz took notes. When asked again, during questioning, about the Hidell identity card, a tired Oswald was overheard snapping at Fritz, "I've told you all I'm going to about that card. You took notes, just read them for yourself if you want to refresh your memory." It is my belief the reason lies in Oswald identifying himself as a CIA agent. For that matter, as we later learned, he was also working for the FBI and likely for the Office of Naval Intelligence—and possibly even military intelligence—as well. This doubling and tripling of agencies was not uncommon. But the Dallas Police Department did not advertise that; neither did the Warren Commission. During Oswald's interrogation, Deputy Sheriff Roger Craig, who refused to change his affidavit concerning the discovery of a Mauser rifle, entered the room to identify Oswald. When he left, he made a curious comment. He said it looked as though Oswald was in charge of the proceedings.

Two days after Oswald's arrest, Jack Ruby dramatically stepped in to shoot Oswald at close range as he was being transferred from the police department to the county jail. Oswald died at the same hospital John F. Kennedy had been taken to, Parkland Hospital, on that day, November 24. Whoever sent Ruby hoped that would be an end to the matter.

It is a fair question to ask why the Warren Commission never became aware that Oswald lived a secret life and why his identity with both the FBI and the CIA was never brought to light. The commission was, in fact, made aware of his secret life, and it actually discussed indications that he worked for both the FBI and the CIA. This happened very early on in the proceedings, when

Waggoner Carr, the Texas attorney general, sent the commission details of Oswald receiving regular payments of $200 each month from the FBI. He said he was listed as "Informant 179" on the payroll, and the word was that this number had been "assigned to him in connection with the CIA." We would never have known about it if that stalwart researcher, Harold Weisberg, had not succeeded in securing the release of a top-secret transcript of the January 27, 1964, Warren Commission session that was not made available to the public. And what action did the commission take? What investigations did it set in progress? What was its reaction to such a profound report? There was none, on all counts: it ignored the information, and kept it secret.

The assassination and its aftermath have been investigated by private individuals ever since, and this work still, very much, goes on to this day. But the matter will not go away until it is fully and comprehensively investigated without bias by a government determined to find the truth.

CHAPTER 16

Spanner in the Works

Believe nothing of what you hear and only half of what you see.

—Proverb

OFFICER J. D. TIPPIT was the man who threw the entire plan of the conspirators off course. It is extremely unlikely that Tippit knew anything at all about a conspiracy to assassinate the president. It is believed that he was a friend of a conspirator who had persuaded him to carry out a vital part of the operation.

Roscoe White had been a CIA agent who had recently withdrawn from the agency. He had since applied to the Dallas Police Department and by the day of the assassination was enlisted, but had not yet been uniformed. It was White, I believe, who arranged the help of the unwitting Officer Tippit. As I see it, Tippit had been asked to help a young CIA operative to reach Red Bird Airfield to fly out on a mission at a time when the traffic would likely be in turmoil. Tippit had agreed but when the assassination of the president had occurred, he listened to instructions on his radio that all other mobile officers were instructed to make their way downtown to be available to help.

He must have wondered why he had become an exception. It was, no doubt, the fact the man he was picking up to take to Red Bird was a CIA man that persuaded him to stick with his agreement to provide transport, but, equally without doubt, he was uneasy about it since he realized he was the only officer not to comply with the instructions sent out. He had had a glimpse of the young CIA agent two days before this when, having breakfast at Dobbs Restaurant on North Beckley, he witnessed Oswald making a terrible fuss about the way his eggs were cooked. That was the Wednesday before the assassination, when Oswald, usually there between 7:00 A.M. and 7:30 A.M. each morning, was very late. It was about ten o'clock when he was there that day, the day Wayne January (see Chapter 22) said he was at Red Bird Airfield with two agents seeking to hire a light aircraft. The visit to the airfield may well have accounted for Oswald's lateness that morning, an unusual occurrence, but it may also have dovetailed with the need for Tippit and Oswald to have sight of each other.

Officer Tippit was thought by Earlene Roberts, Oswald's landlady, to have been in the police car that "pip-pipped" its horn clearly outside her house. This, she thought, appeared to signal to Oswald it was time to leave. Oswald had returned to his lodgings after leaving the Texas School Book Depository to change and collect a gun soon after the time of the assassination. Roberts said she only caught a glimpse of the police car number that, she thought, had a 1 and a 0 on it. Tippit's car was number 10. Immediately after the pips, she said Oswald left his apartment. He hung around outside a moment as though pondering whether to catch a bus, Roberts thought, then disappeared down the road, to be seen next with Tippit, about a mile away in the Oak Cliff district.

Meanwhile, as I have said, Tippit was sitting in his car listening to the APB put out on Oswald and likely was wondering what he had got himself into. It appears that after meeting up with Oswald and having a friendly conversation with him through the rolled down window of his car, he got out and wandered around the front of his vehicle, approaching the man he was to pick up. As he walked across to him, he fingered his gun, and it was likely that which proved fatal to him, since the next thing to happen was his brutal murder. He was shot repeatedly and, according to certain people who claimed to observe, died immediately. The killer was described variously by a number of people. Descriptions ranged from that phoned in at 1:22 P.M. by Officer R. W. Walker, who reported he was a white male, in his thirties, five feet eight inches tall, having black hair and of slender build, and wearing a white shirt and black slacks. Eight minutes later, Officer H. W. Summers, described the killer as a white male, twenty-seven, five feet eleven inches tall, 165 pounds, with black wavy hair and fair complected. Summers said he was wearing a light gray Eisenhower-type jacket, a white shirt, and dark trousers. The witness Acquilla Clemons said he was "kind of a short guy, kind of heavy."

Helen Markham, who had a lot to say about Tippit's murder, was featured prominently in Warren Commission deliberations, as we shall see in chapter 20. Her first description of the killer, given to Officer J. M. Poe, was that he was white, about twenty-five, five feet eight inches tall, with brown hair, and wearing a white jacket. Markham's statement was supported by Barbara Jeanette Davis. Though the white jacket was unacceptable, this could otherwise have been a description of Oswald. Later, however, when talking to an FBI agent named Odum, Markham changed her description to white, about eighteen, black hair, red complexion, and wearing tan shoes, a tan jacket, and dark trousers. Then, she changed her description yet again and told Mark Lane, a lawyer who had been hired by Marguarite Oswald, Oswald's mother, to defend him posthumously, that he was short, on the heavy side, and had slightly bushy hair.

Since there were several descriptions of Tippit's killer, it is likely there were actually two of them, or even three. Witnesses reported there was certainly more than one. Roscoe White answered to the general description of the killer: kind of a short guy, heavy set, and with black bushy hair—he wore a black bushy hairpiece—and there were more reasons than the description for believing White was involved. A diary surfaced many years after the assassination that was purported to have been written by White. The authenticity of it has been greatly disputed and it is not my intention of venturing here into whether it is genuine or not. In it, White claimed to have been one of the snipers in the Dealey Plaza who shot at Kennedy.

While I am somewhat skeptical of that in view of the fact that so many men made the same claim as time went on, I am more impressed by his claim to have also been Tippit's killer because of eyewitness descriptions that he matched. More than that, there is also the connection of him being a former CIA agent that makes this ring true. He is likely the kind of person who would have been brought in by the conspirators to make such an arrangement. This does not, in any way, rule out the presence of others at the scene of Tippit's murder. As I see it, White had arranged the "favor" of Tippit taking Oswald to Red Bird Airfield and was present to make sure all went well. When it did not, White shot Tippit to prevent him from blowing the whole thing wide open.

This was Oswald's signal to get away from the scene of the shooting without delay. He ran, no doubt, trying to piece together the events relating to his supposed pick up by Officer Tippit that had ended with bullets flying. I mentioned earlier that undercover operatives who found themselves in trouble or faced with exposure were to go to the nearest theater, where a handler would make contact. This is exactly what Oswald did. He made for the nearest cinema, the Texas Theater, where another set of odd circumstances overtook him. He entered the theater without paying and though it would have been far more likely the cashier, who saw him, would have dispatched a staff member to confront him, instead called the police. In turn, there was a curious response by the police answering a call about a man seen entering without paying. They arrived in a number of squad cars, including senior officers in their ranks. The lights went up in the sparsely attended matinee screening, and Oswald was quickly identified. He was arrested just before 2:00 P.M., less than 90 minutes after President Kennedy was shot.

There was reportedly something of a skirmish in the theater, and Oswald was accused of trying to use his gun. The volume of uncertainties, curious activities, and assorted anomalies surrounding the events in Oak Cliff was such that a charge of this kind would require substantial confirmation. Oswald did what a man with the knowledge of how to handle this situation would do. He yelled out, "I am not resisting arrest," drawing the attention of the patrons in the cinema and putting those arresting him in a position where they would not dare use excessive violence. He also was heard to say, "Well, it's all over now," no doubt thinking of the mission on which he believed he had been setting out for his CIA masters.

Putting aside the ludicrous suggestion of members of the police descending on the Texas Theater in number to arrest a man who had committed the dastardly crime of walking in without paying, there had to be an explanation for what happened. Another thing that would raise great doubts is the notion the police would respond to such a call from the theater on the off chance it might be Tippit's killer. To be more realistic, however, it has to be wondered if the operation was not being directed by someone at police headquarters who was in the know about the greater pattern of events, someone who also knew Oswald was an agent and was familiar with the "wait at the nearest theater to be contacted" instruction. This would explain a great deal. It might even explain a story that circulated that police officers were already in waiting near the theater—hiding in an alleyway—before Oswald ever arrived. At any rate, this makes for a more believable explanation than guesswork or clairvoyancy.

× × ×

Of the other witnesses to the Tippit murder, Frank Wright lived near the scene of the shooting and was at his front door as Tippit fell to the ground. He said he saw a man of medium height and wearing a long coat get into a gray 1950 or 1951 Plymouth and drive off fast, before the police arrived at the scene. Domingo Benavides was in the vicinity at the time, driving his pickup truck along Tenth Street in the direction of Patton Avenue. He was driving away from Tippit when he heard the shots and instinctively dived for cover when he heard them. When he peeped out, he saw the gunman discharging an empty shell and throwing away another before he left. Benavides was an important witness, for he soon went to Tippit's side. Not knowing how to operate the policeman's car radio, he engaged the help of a man named Bowley to make the vital call reporting what had happened.

It should be noted that, in describing the gunman, Benavides resolutely refused to identify Oswald as the man. For obvious reasons, he was not called to an identity parade, but he did succumb to pressure to identify Oswald when his brother was killed—he thought in mistake for himself—but here was another highly suspicious identification of Oswald. Certainly, no court would have accepted Benavides's lame and belated identification.

A gray Eisenhower-type zipper jacket that had been found nearby and that was brought forward as evidence of what the killer had been wearing, was the subject of considerable controversy and just a little hilarity. Helen Markham, having described his jacket as white, later said she believed the jacket to have been darker than the one produced in evidence, and William Scoggins, a taxi driver who was in the vicinity of the murder scene, agreed with this. With Oswald having changed his clothes when he reached his lodgings, Earline Roberts's evidence was more pertinent, however, and, looking at the light jacket shown her, she said it was not the one Oswald had been wearing, which was dark. Adding to the muddle, the Warren Commission, for whatever reason, claimed Scoggins's description to have been of a lighter jacket, and so the proceedings wandered on. Benavides, a broadly reliable witness, said the jacket worn by the killer was a light one, but, in a somewhat hilarious tangle, the jacket produced at the hearing for him to identify was the wrong one, and Benavides, anxious to oblige, identified it as the one he saw, anyway.

Barbara Jeanette Davis said the jacket she saw was white. When she was shown the gray zipper jacket, she said it was not the one she saw. Another witness, Warren Reynolds, said the the man running away wore a bluish jacket. Only Officer H. W. Summers agreed that the man he had seen was wearing a gray Eisenhower-type jacket, though the commission would not be interested in his description since everything else he had to say about the killer was distinctly not describing Oswald. Instead, the commission relied on the testimony of Marina Oswald, who was totally unreliable because of the circumstances of her anxiety to escape deportation. Having obliged with an identification of the jacket, however, she volunteered that Oswald never had his jackets laundered, which left the mystery of laundry tag B9738 unexplained. Remarkably, the FBI, if it ever tried, was unable to find the laundry to which the number belonged. The discovery of the jacket in question was credited to Police Captain W. R. Westbrook, though he totally denied having found it. Notwithstanding Westbrook's denial, the police produced records showing that Officer 279 had reported the find just a few minutes after the murder of Tippit, but to add mystery to mystery, no officer—or FBI agent—with the number 279 was ever identified.

The evidence provided by Scoggins was sketchy and unreliable. The trouble was that from where he observed a bush impeded his vision. Though he was close enough, he simply did not have a clear view of what happened. He was prepared to identify Oswald as Tippit's killer, however, and that made his testimony acceptable to the Warren Commission. Scoggins attended an identity parade in which he identified Oswald as the man he saw. At the same lineup was another taxi driver, William Whaley, who had driven Oswald from downtown Dallas to his lodgings. Afterward, Whaley spoke scathingly of the identity parade in his testimony to the commission. He said:

> Me and this other taxi driver who was with me, sir, we sat in the room awhile and directly they brought in six men, young teenagers and they were all handcuffed together. . . . You could have picked [Oswald] out without identifying him by just listening to him because he was bawling out the policemen, telling them it wasn't right putting him in line with these teenagers. . . . He told [them] what he thought about them. . . . They were trying to railroad him and he wanted his lawyer. . . . Anybody who wasn't sure could have picked out the right one just for that.

A striking confession from Scoggins while he was giving testimony still did not change his status with the commissioners. He told them how a policeman had given him some pictures to look at and he admitted, "I think I picked the wrong picture. He told me the other one was Oswald."

The favor of giving Oswald a ride to Red Bird Airfield was the only sense ever made of Officer Tippit being in the Oak Cliff district of Dallas, where he was shot. Officially, the dispatcher had supposedly sent him there to "be at large for any emergency," though this instruction could not be found in the radio log until it appeared some five months later. When it appeared, it was linked to a similar instruction to Officer R. E. Nelson. Enquiries revealed that Nelson apparently received no such instruction and went downtown to the area of the assassination.

This was not Tippit's beat, and every other police car had at that time been directed to proceed to the Dealey Plaza area. It raised the question of what kind of emergency was so likely to turn up in the quiet suburb of Oak Cliff that it took precedence over the assassination of the president? Or was that merely a cover for Tippit providing the favor of transport for White's friend, which would never have come to light if the officer had not been killed? Had he taken Oswald to Red Bird, he would never have been likely to admit the role he played when he found out in what he had become involved, no matter how unwittingly.

Considerable dispute surrounded establishing the exact time of Officer Tippit's shooting, though the problems tended to be driven by the Warren Commission's anxiety to establish that Oswald had had time to reach the scene of the killing, which some timings did not allow. Estimates were given of the shots being fired as early as one o'clock, when it was impossible for Oswald to be there, since he had only just left his lodgings at that time. But the accounts rendered by witnesses provided various timings. Helen Markham gave evidence it was 1:06 P.M., only to be told that it was that part of her testimony that was "unreliable." The problem with 1:06 P.M. was, as I have said, it did not give Oswald time to reach Tenth and

Patton. The time Bowley managed to radio in to police headquarters for Domingo Benavides was recorded as 1:16 P.M., and this was a much more acceptable time scale to the commission, even though it was clear some time had elapsed since the shots were actually fired.

The fact the Warren Commission ever put a case together pinning the murder of J. D. Tippit on Oswald was remarkable in many respects. It will be recalled that Benavides saw the killer throw away spent shells, and these were sought as evidence. The officer had been shot four times, and four shell cases were duly recovered. Benavides picked up two of the shell cases and put them in a cigarette packet before handing them over to the police. The other two were picked up and handed over by bystanders, Barbara Jeanette Davis and Virginia R. Davis. Two of the cases were Remingtons and two Winchesters. Oswald's revolver, a 3.8, did not eject empty cases, so we are faced with another conundrum: If Oswald was the killer, why would he stay behind to empty his gun, carefully presenting evidence to the police? This is even more mysterious because his weapon, when emptied, would have dropped out not only the spent shells, but also the two remaining live rounds, which were not found. In fact, when Oswald was later arrested his gun contained six rounds of live ammunition. The fact the gun was fully loaded was not enough to exonerate Oswald, for he could have reloaded it. This, however, would leave an extremely unlikely situation in which he had brought only four spare bullets with which to shoot Tippit, for there were no spares on him when he was taken into custody.

Benavides handed over the cigarette packet containing the empty shells to Officer J. M. Poe, who was instructed by his sergeant to inscribe his initials on them so that he could later identify them. Presented with the four empty shells at a later date, Poe could not find his initials. For that matter, his sergeant, W. E. Barnes, had also scratched on the initial B, but he could not find his marks either. Therefore, the Warren Commission had four spent cartridge cases that no member of the Dallas Police Department could identify.

Confusion involving the bullets that killed Officer Tippit had not yet reached its peak, however. When the bullets were extracted from the body, they were identified as three Western-Winchesters and one Remington-Peters, which were at odds with the four empty shell cases. This was followed by more confusion when the report came back from Cortlandt Cunningham, the FBI expert who was expected to confirm the connection between the retrieved bullets and Oswald's gun. He reported, "Well, it is my understanding that the first bullet was turned over to the FBI office in Dallas by the Dallas Police Department. They reportedly said this was the only bullet that was recovered, or that they had. Later at the request of this Commission we went back to the Dallas Police Department and found in their files that they actually had three other bullets."

"What proof do you have though that these are the bullets?" asked Congressman Hale Boggs. Nobody answered, and nobody took the police department to task for apparently misleading the FBI. Cunningham reported it was impossible to tell from the distorted bullets which gun they had been fired from. A second opinion sought from Joseph D. Nichol, superintendent of the bureau of criminal investigation for the State of Illinois Police Department obtained that "he found sufficient individual characteristics to lead him to the conclusion that the projectile was fired from the same weapon that fired the [test] projectiles," which were, one assumes, from Oswald's gun. But this somewhat shaky result was the best the commission could do in establishing a link between Oswald and the bullets that killed Tippit.

At best, the evidence against Oswald being Tippit's killer was extremely tenuous. There was no open and shut case here, and the bias against Oswald, as elsewhere in the commission's case, was suspect at every level. But the idea that Oswald had killed Tippit and had attempted to kill General Edwin Walker was necessary, as the Warren Commission saw it, to support the case against Oswald as the lone killer of President Kennedy.

CHAPTER 17

Ruby

With the Addition of a Grain of Salt.

—Pliny the Elder

WHEN JACK RUBY stepped forward and shot Lee Harvey Oswald, he knew what he was doing. It was not to spare Jacqueline Kennedy the ordeal of attending the trial of Oswald, as he first claimed. He later admitted his lawyer had told him to say that. He was silencing the man who could have blown the conspiracy to kill President John F. Kennedy wide open. He had been sent to do that. It was not his own idea.

Ruby, who ran the Carousel Club in Dallas, was also a small-time Mafia operative: a peanut. He drifted to Dallas from Chicago at a time when it was profitable to do so. Even in Mafia terms his credentials were not spectacular. He ran errands for Al Capone, if that is a recommendation. He was involved in the murder of a union official and given a short jail sentence for that. But he had ambition. He wanted to be accepted as a big-time operator. But in spite of his gun running to Cuba, the women he "provided," the drugs, the gambling, and other assorted objectionable activities, he remained a peanut. Why he was ever called in to silence Oswald is something of a mystery, other than he was available. He was not a man to trust with secrets: he was wrapped up in his own considerations. But he had a gun and he was not afraid of using it. Whether he did so because of promises of rewards made to him if he killed Oswald or threats if he did not we will never know.

Flanked by his lawyer who, amazingly, was there at the time to witness what happened, Ruby stepped forward and shot Oswald with great deliberation. Ruby was soon overpowered and taken into custody, while Oswald was taken to the hospital, where he died at 1:07 that Sunday afternoon. Ruby had achieved what he set out to do; it is my belief he had no option. I cannot see Ruby volunteering for the killing he carried out, which takes us deeper into the conspiracy that resulted in the death of President Kennedy. Make no mistake: Ruby had been sent to police headquarters to kill an innocent man who would have blown the conspiracy wide open, and it is not surprising there has been much study devoted to who it was who could have sent him. Some said the Mafia, but this did not stand up. Some said big business, but this had to be qualified.

A story circulated that an influential Dallas businessman sent his lawyer to the Dallas Police Department with the task of assessing how well Oswald was protected. He came back telling how he had taken the elevator only to find Oswald, handcuffed to a police officer, standing next to him. In other words, security was lax. The next part of the story tells of how Ruby was summoned to the businessman's office, and the rest is open to conjecture. This story is highly believable in view of other tales involving the businessman in question.

Whatever was the case, Ruby prevented the world from learning the truth behind the assassination of President Kennedy. Whether, in fact, he did it under duress or from dreams of profit we will never know. But whatever he was promised—and I believe he would be promised a great deal—I cannot see it being his choice. However, even though he pulled the trigger, it has been strongly suggested he did not do it without the cooperation of members of the Dallas Police Department. If there is any kind of defense for Ruby, it may be said that it is believed anonymous telephone calls made before he killed Oswald were made by him. These were calls that might have delivered him from having to murder Oswald if they had been acted on.

Perry McCoy, a sheriff's officer, reported:

At approximately 2.15 A.M. I received a call from a person that . . .
he was a member of a group of one hundred and he wanted the sheriff's office to know that they had voted one hundred per cent to kill
Oswald while he was in the process of being transferred to the
county jail and that he wanted this department to have the information so that none of the deputies would get hurt. The voice was
deep and course [sic] and sounded very sincere and talked with ease.
The person did not seem excited . . . he seemed very calm about the
whole matter.

He said later in his statement, "I received one other call regarding the transfer of Oswald and when I answered the telephone a
male voice asked if this is the sheriff's office and I said it was, he
said just a minute and another male voice stated that Oswald
would never make the trip to the county jail. I could not determine
whether or not this was the same voice that had called earlier."

Lieutenant Billy R. Grammar took a call in Police Chief Jesse
Curry's department saying that Oswald was going to be killed. The
person calling knew the details of the plan for moving Oswald, including plans for a decoy car, and warned that if Oswald was to live
the plans had better be changed. As with the other calls, the details
were written up for Chief Curry, who was well warned. To
Grammar the voice sounded familiar, but it was not until news
reached him on the Sunday morning that Jack Ruby had shot
Oswald that the lieutenant realized whose voice the caller had reminded him of. It was Jack Ruby. It was not that it was thought
that Ruby was conferring a kindness on Oswald in making telephone calls. Rather, it was thought that he was trying to wriggle out
of shooting Oswald. If all the arrangements had been changed,
Ruby could hardly have been blamed if he found it impossible to
carry out the murder.

The story of the businessman despatching Ruby to carry out the
killing may well be true. It is just as likely, however, that pressure
was brought to bear on him by a knowledgeable CIA agent. Ruby was
hardly the type to be involved in a high-powered assassination plot.

Rather, he was a fetcher and carrier type. He was likely to know nothing more about the assassination of Kennedy than the identity of whoever it was who had sent him to kill Oswald. This information, however, could possibly have provided the key to the solution of who was behind the conspiracy, but, incredibly, indications by Ruby that he would tell what he knew if Chief Justice Earl Warren, the chairman of the investigatory body set up by President Lyndon B. Johnson, would send him to Washington, far away from his Dallas cell were resolutely ignored. In his various statements, he involved Johnson in the conspiracy, but this was never investigated.

The Warren Commission was selective in what it put in its report regarding Ruby. Questioning him, counsel asked a witness, Nancy Perrin Rich, who worked for Ruby at the Carousel Club, if he had given orders that any member of the police department appearing at his club was to be provided with hard liquor.

"That is correct," responded Rich.

"Did they pay?" asked counsel.

"Oh, no, of course not," came the reply.

"Was that an order, too, from Mr. Ruby?" asked counsel.

"That was," said Rich.

None of this was mentioned in the report, which claimed that Ruby had no connections with the police department. The Warren Report stated, "There is no credible evidence that Ruby sought special favors from police officers or attempted to bribe them."

But Rich's assertions were confirmed by several others who were questioned, including the Carousel hostess Mrs. Edward J. Pullman, who told the FBI that "most of the officers of the Dallas Police Department" were seen at the club, that she "felt certain that Ruby knew most of these officers on a first-name basis," and that "the police officers . . . were never given a bill in connection with their visits there."

Ruby was well treated by the police. There is no record in the police files that Ruby was once arrested for carrying a concealed gun and that he had been brought in for other violations of the law. The Warren Commission listened to evidence that Ruby had "brutally beaten twenty-five different persons either as a result of a personal encounter or because they were causing disturbances in his club."

Yet when the Warren Commission's report was published, none of this was mentioned. Similarly, when it came to his Mafia, underworld, and criminal connections, the commission wore its blinkers again. To place on record that Ruby was not involved in illicit operations, it sought the advice of—unbelievably—his "Chicago friends," who, naturally, stated that "he had no close connection with organized crime." The commission stated further, "unreliable as their reports may be, several known Chicago criminals have denied any such liaison." It must be asked: Would they have said otherwise? To say the least, this is tantamount to asking one fox to clear another fox of raiding the chicken house. The report stated, "There is no evidence that he participated in organized criminal activity."

Where was the commission looking? And why? The objective, as far as the Warren Commission was concerned, was clearly one of preventing Ruby's action in killing Oswald from "confirming" that a conspiracy had taken place. At all costs, the commission was determined to attribute Kennedy's murder to Oswald, and Oswald alone. And this included being prepared to identify Ruby as another "lone nut" who had killed "lone nut" Oswald.

Of Ruby, the Warren Report baldly stated, "Ruby's background and activities yielded no evidence that Ruby conspired with anyone in planning or executing the killing of Lee Harvey Oswald."

If Chief Justice Warren knew of no evidence indicating that Ruby conspired with others to kill Oswald, it was because he chose not to seek it. The trouble all along was that uncovering a conspiracy to kill Oswald might lead to the uncovering of a conspiracy to kill President Kennedy, and Warren gave every impression he was dedicated to uncovering no such thing.

Ruby was very apprehensive of occupying a cell in a jail in or anywhere near Dallas. For those prepared to consider it, this was a clear indication that, even if he was not part of a conspiracy to kill the president, he was involved with the conspirators. The Warren

Commission was most certainly not prepared to consider it, however. At the end of a three-hour-long session with the commissioners, Ruby dropped something of a bombshell when he said to Warren, "You can get more out of me. Let's not break up so soon. . . . Is there any way to get me to Washington?" The conversation that followed was equally astounding:

Warren: I beg your pardon?

Ruby: Is there any way of you getting me to Washington?

Warren: I don't know of any. I will be glad to talk to your counsel about what the situation is, Mr. Ruby, when we get an opportunity to talk.

In other interviews, Ruby returned to what he saw as his desperate need to get away from Dallas. The following excerpts allow a clear picture to be seen:

Ruby: I would like to request that I go to Washington and you take all the tests that I have to take. It is very important. . . . Gentlemen, unless you get me to Washington, you can't get a fair shake out of me. If you understand my way of talking, you have got to get me to Washington to get the tests. . . . Gentlemen, if you want to hear any further testimony, you will have to get me to Washington soon, because it has something to do with you, Chief Warren. . . . When are you going back to Washington?

Warren: I am going back very shortly after we finish this hearing—I am going to have some lunch.

Ruby: Can I make a statement?

Warren: Yes.

Ruby: If you request me to go back to Washington right now, that couldn't be done, could it?

Warren: No; it could not be done. It could not be done. There are a good many things involved in that, Mr. Ruby.

Ruby: Gentlemen, my life is in danger here. . . . You said you have the power to do what you want to do, is that correct?

Warren: Exactly.

Ruby: Without any limitations?

Warren: Within the purview of the Executive Order which established the Commission. We have the right to take testimony of anyone we want in this whole situation, and we have the right, if we so choose to do it, to verify that statement in any way that we wish to do it.

Ruby: But you don't have a right to take a prisoner back with you when you want to?

Warren: No; we have the power to subpoena witnesses to Washington if we want to do it, but we have taken the testimony of 200 or 300 people, I would imagine, here in Dallas without going to Washington.

Ruby: Yes; but these people aren't Jack Ruby. . . . Maybe something can be saved, something can be done. What have you got to answer to that, Chief Justice Warren? . . . I want to tell the truth, and I can't tell it here. I can't tell it here. . . . Now maybe certain people don't want to know the truth that may come out of me. Is that plausible?

It seems that Warren, for one, was not anxious to hear what Ruby had to say, in return for the small inconvenience of taking him to Washington. The last time Ruby spoke to Warren he said, "Well, you won't ever see me again. I tell you that. . . . A whole new form of government is going to take over the country, and I know I won't live to see you another time."

Ruby was right. From prison he was taken to the local hospital suffering from cancer. He was convinced that a "visiting" doctor had injected him with whatever caused the cancer, and the jailer Sheriff Al Maddox supported this. In 1982, Maddox said:

We had a phony doctor come into [the jail] from Chicago, just as phony . . . as a three dollar bill. And he worked his way in through— I don't know, whoever supplied the county with doctors . . . you could tell he was Ruby's doctor. He spent half his time up there talking with Ruby. And one day I went in and Ruby told me, he said, "Well they injected me for a cold." He said it was cancer cells. That's what he told me, Ruby did. I said you don't believe that shit. He said, "I damn sure do!" I never said anything to (Sheriff Bill) Decker or anybody . . . [Then] one day when I started to leave, Ruby shook hands with me and I could feel a piece of paper in his palm. . . . [On it] he said it was a conspiracy and he said . . . if you will keep your eyes open and your mouth shut, you're gonna learn a lot. And that was the last letter I ever got from him.

What he believed to be tantamount to a lethal injection appeared to be no flight of fancy on the part of Ruby. Police Officer Tom Tilson said, "It was the opinion of a number of other Dallas police officers that Ruby had received injections of cancer while he was incarcerated in the Dallas County Jail."

Ruby had been sentenced to death, but he appealed his sentence and some three years afterward a retrial was granted away from Dallas. It is believed that Ruby would have obtained his release, telling all he knew about the conspiracy to kill Oswald and underscoring the conspiracy to murder President Kennedy. But this was not to be. Ruby never saw freedom and never told what he knew. He died in the hospital soon after his retrial was granted.

Chief Justice Warren apparently had had no second thoughts about Ruby's conviction that he was in danger in the Dallas jail. Neither did he appear to be interested in learning what Ruby could have told him. Warren had, however, given Ruby a piece of advice. Quite remarkably, he said he should say nothing if he believed speaking out would endanger his life.

Comment from me is not necessary.

CHAPTER 18

Absent

The absent are always in the wrong.

—Philippe Nericault Destouches

I RESPECT PATTERNS created by evidence, sometimes even more than witnesses, who can, on occasion, be mistaken about what they see or hear or be even biased. A pattern *exists*. It bears witness only to what it is. It cannot be wrong; either it exists or it does not exist. And it points an unerring finger to the truth. This chapter is dedicated to the readers who are still unconvinced of the existence of a conspiracy to kill President John F. Kennedy.

A pattern of sudden death soon began among those connected to the assassination in one way or another. There was Lee Harvey Oswald's landlady, Earlene Roberts, who died of a heart attack, as did Tom Howard, Jack Ruby's lawyer. Incredibly, Howard was at Ruby's side when he shot Oswald, as though on cue. Attention had been drawn to this by the journalist Bill Hunter, who died in a shooting "mishap" in a police station. Hunter had interviewed Howard with a journalist friend, Jim Keothe, who also died suddenly. He was killed after stepping out of his shower by an intruder who delivered a karate chop to his throat.

William Whaley, the cab driver who brought Oswald to his lodgings from downtown Dallas when his bus became traffic bound, was killed in a traffic accident while driving his cab, which was unusual. A cab driver being killed in a road accident was (and still is) an extremely rare event. Hank Killam, whose wife worked for Ruby, believed he knew a link between Oswald and Ruby. "I am a dead man, but I have run as far as I am running," he told his brother. His throat was cut in an alley. Another man who said he knew of a link between Oswald and Ruby was the businessman Bill Chesher. Chesher was another of those who had a heart attack. On the Wednesday before Kennedy died, twenty-three-year-old Karen Kupcinet was hysterical as she phoned a long-distance operator and screamed the president was going to be killed. By the day Oswald died, Karen Kupcinet was also dead, cause unknown to this day.

It will be remembered that Deputy Sheriff Roger Craig, the man who refused to change his affidavit regarding the discovery of the 7.5 Mauser rifle on the sixth floor of the Texas School Book Depository, lost his job, was shot at more than once, and was injured when his car was run off a country road. His wife left him and his life was in ruins. He was said to have shot himself at his father's home, but if this is really what happened, it does not alter that he lost his life because of what he knew about the assassination.

The name Dorothy Kilgallen might well be remembered by some readers. She was a well-known radio and television journalist who became a star celebrity, working also for a newspaper in Chicago and later in New York. Readers of my books on the death of Marilyn Monroe will recall she was another who believed Monroe had been murdered. Kilgallen interviewed Ruby and was given special treatment for her talk with him. In other instances, Ruby was interviewed either in his cell or later at the hospital in which he became a patient, and where, no doubt, in both cases, the whole proceedings were monitored and recorded. Kilgallen was allowed by Judge Joe B. Brown to interview him after a court hearing in a room behind the courtroom, by herself, with no prying cameras or microphones. She left, telling her friends, "I'm going to break the real story and have the biggest scoop of the century," but just a few days afterward she was found dead. It was a heart attack, the medical examiner said at first, but this was later changed to her having committed suicide, then later still she had died from "circumstances undetermined." The only close friend in whom she might have confided what she had learned was Mrs. Earl T. Smith, who was found dead two days after Kilgallen, the cause not determined. She, too, had taken her own life the medical examiner said.

Four showgirls who worked for Ruby at his Carousel Club died violent deaths. They were Nancy Jane Mooney, Marilyn Magyar, Rose Cherami, and Karen Bennett Carlin. Warren Reynolds worked at a car lot near to the junction of Twelfth and Patten, where Officer J. D. Tippit was killed. He witnessed a man running away from the scene who, he said, was not Oswald. Reynolds was shot by Darrell Wayne Garner, it was claimed, but Garner was given an alibi by Mooney. Mooney was later arrested for an unrelated minor offense and about an hour after being locked in a cell she was found hanging by her toreador trousers. Magyar's husband was convicted of murdering her, but doubts arose because of her intentions to write a book on the assassination. Cherami was the victim of a hit and run driver, and Carlin was shot to death in a hotel room in Houston.

Lee J. Bowers worked at the railway yard behind the Texas School Book Depository. From his vantage point on the railyard tower, he was witness to three cars that circumnavigated the car park behind the fence on the grassy knoll, where they should not have been. He was cut short when telling Warren Commission counsel he also saw "some unusual occurrence" behind the picket fence: "a flash of light or smoke or something." Bowers made no secret of what he had seen. A few weeks later his car went off the road. When he was found, he was dead. The doctors who attended him commented he appeared to be in a state of "strange shock" when he died.

Gary Underhill was a CIA agent who said he had inside knowledge about the assassination. He was found dead with a bullet in his head, having taken his own life, it was claimed. On the day of the assassination, when the shooting ceased in the Dealey Plaza, James Worrell witnessed a man—definitely not Oswald—running away from the rear door of the Texas School Book Depository. This man wore a dark coat. Worrell died in a road accident. Harold

Russell witnessed the escape of Officer Tippit's murderer. It was two years later, in July 1965 when, attending a party, he became hysterical. The concerned partygoers thought the best thing was to call the police, but when they arrived, an officer struck Russell on the head and he died soon afterward.

The case of Albert Guy Bogard is quite macabre. He worked as a car salesman at the Lincoln-Mercury dealership in Dallas when a man who identified himself as Lee Harvey Oswald came to look around with a view to buying a car. This was November 9, less than two weeks before the assassination. Oswald told him he was expecting to come into a lot of money, but later admitted he did not have the down payment for the car he had taken out on the freeway for a test-drive. He emphasized that workers in Russia did better, and it was this that drew attention to him. Hearing about this, the Warren Commission conducted an investigation into the event, the result of which was that whoever had been to the Lincoln-Mercury dealership that day was not Lee Harvey Oswald. It was confirmed that he was in Irving, Texas, on that day. This was one of a series of "sightings" of Oswald just before the assassination, which the commission was able to denounce as false. When Bogard saw pictures of Oswald, he categorically denied it was the "Lee Harvey Oswald" who had test-driven the car. Furthermore, the conspirators had made a blunder here. They apparently did not know that Oswald could not drive a car. Regardless, Bogard paid a heavy price for his involvement with the false Oswald. He was found dead in a car parked in a cemetery, gassed by exhaust fumes from a hosepipe stuck in a window that was left slightly ajar. It should be noted that while the Warren Commission confirmed that Oswald had been impersonated at several locations, it did not try to find out who was pretending to be him. Neither did it establish why.

As though to underline the reason for the series of deaths that occurred immediately after the assassination, a whole crop of others with connections of one kind or another to the killing of the president began to die when another investigation began in 1967. This was the investigation undertaken by the New Orleans district attorney, Jim Garrison, who was featured by Oliver Stone in his film *JFK*. He brought a case against Clay Shaw, a New Orleans businessman said to have CIA connections, for his links to a conspiracy, without exactly specifying it was the conspiracy to assassinate President Kennedy. Shaw had definite links with Dave Ferrie, a former Eastern Airlines pilot who had flown many times into Cuba after Fidel Castro came to power. Ferrie lost his job as an airline pilot because he was exposed as a homosexual, and homosexuality appears to have been an additional bond between him and Shaw. Ferrie, of curious appearance, suffered from alopecia and, therefore, had no hair on his head or elsewhere on his body. He was ridiculed for wearing a red wig and for painting on "eyebrows" at times. As an instructor, he had encountered Oswald as a very young man when he joined the Civil Air Patrol. Oswald met Ferrie again in New Orleans when he was being "sheepdipped" by agent Guy Banister for his new mission with the CIA.

Former FBI agent Banister, then a private detective with strong links to the CIA and the FBI, was the connection between Ferrie and Oswald in New Orleans. He operated from an office block in which Oswald had rented an office. Oswald purported to be a supporter of pro-Cuban activities, while at the same time having involvement in anti-Cuban activities. He later operated out of Banister's office, which tended to reveal his affinity to the nest of CIA-FBI operatives. The Reverend Clyde Johnson knew something useful, testified before Garrison, and was later shot to death. Ferrie was said to have taken his own life as the Garrison net drew in, and his friend, Eladio del Valle, was shot through the heart and had his skull split by an axe. Garrison wanted Nancy Perrin Rich's husband, who had been questioned by the Warren Commission, to give evidence, but Robert Perrin died of arsenic poisoning before Garrison reached him.

Another witness, Dr. Mary Sherman, was shot to death and had her bed set on fire. Coroner Nicholas Chetta, who ordered autopsies on the bodies of Ferrie, Sherman, and Perrin, died of a heart attack, while his assistant, Dr. Henry Delaune, was murdered a few months later. It was small wonder Garrison lost his case against

Shaw. Ironically, Shaw's link with the CIA, which was fundamental to Garrison's case, was confirmed some years later by no less than the CIA director himself.

Next, it was the opening of the Senate Assassinations Committee in 1976 and yet another sequence of related deaths began to occur. George de Mohrenschildt had links to the CIA and military intelligence and had a long background in intelligence work. He was almost certainly the agency's appointed "babysitter" for Oswald after his return from the Soviet Union. The House committee decided it wanted to question him and sent an investigator to arrange a date for his appearance to give testimony, but on that very day Mohrenschildt was found dead from gunshot wounds. He was listed a suicide, but his wife, Jeanne, who was closely associated with her husband's work, would not accept this and began to have fears for her own safety.

Six highly placed FBI officials died within six months in 1977. One of these was William Sullivan, Director J. Edgar Hoover's head of Division Five—his right hand man—who died before the House committee could question him. Sullivan, who was closely linked to the assassination investigation, died, medical examiners said, from an early morning hunting accident.

The two Mafia bosses, Chicago's Sam Giancana and his henchman, Johnny Roselli, were both required to testify before the House committee. They were the two who collaborated with the CIA in planning the assassination of Castro, and House committee staff were investigating a theory that the Castro assassination not having been achieved, the plan may have been changed into one in which Kennedy would be killed. To a large measure, this might have achieved those objectives in which the Mafia was particularly interested. Giancana was shot in the head and bullets were fired in a circle around his mouth, indicative of an execution to keep his mouth shut. However, there were distinct doubts that this was the work of the Mafia, in spite of the "signature" of the shooting. It was thought he might have been killed by others who wanted to convey the impression it was an internal Mafia slaying.

Roselli's body was found floating off the Florida coast in an oil drum before he could testify. Also, the body of another of Giancana's hit men, Charles Nicoletti, was found in a blazing car, having been riddled with bullets. To all this might be added that Teamsters' Union leader, Jimmy Hoffa, who had finally been locked away, was pardoned by President Richard Nixon. Hoffa, when released, disappeared and was never seen again. Believed to have been murdered, Hoffa had very close connections with Giancana.

Banister, who was highly involved with events in New Orleans, died in 1964, and not long before the House committee was convened, in 1974, Clay Shaw died in curious circumstances. One of Shaw's neighbors witnessed the arrival of an ambulance from which a stretcher was taken, carrying a figure covered up by a sheet. The stretcher was carried into Shaw's house where, later that same day, he was reportedly found dead. Since he was said to have died of cancer, no autopsy was carried out.

Oswald and his killer, Ruby, who died of cancer in the hospital while serving his sentence for murder, must also be added to the list. The House Assassinations Committee appointed its chief of research, Jacqueline Hess, to investigate the "mysterious deaths project." She looked at the circumstances surrounding twenty-one witnesses who died and concluded "the available evidence does not establish anything about the nature of these deaths which would indicate that the deaths were in some manner, either direct or peripheral, caused by the assassination or by any aspect of the subsequent investigation."

Once again, comment from me is not necessary.

CHAPTER 19

Scandals

It's ill waiting for dead men's shoes.

—Proverb

THE NIGHT BEFORE the assassination, Clint Murchison threw a party at his Dallas residence. Murchison was a wealthy man; he was an oil man and had interests also in banking and publishing. He knew many influential people, including several politicians, and was also acquainted with a few underground figures.

The guest list for the Thursday night party was impressive. It included Richard Nixon, who had been conducting law business for the Coca Cola Company that day, Texas Senator John Tower, and John McCloy, a banker with Chase Manhattan. McCloy would become a member of the Warren Commission. Oil billionaire H. L. Hunt was present, as was the FBI director J. Edgar Hoover, who was a particular friend of Murchison. Another special guest was Vice President Lyndon B. Johnson, who drove from Fort Worth, where the presidential party was accommodated in the Hotel Texas, to attend. Among many others at the party was Madeleine Brown, one of Johnson's mistresses, and she is also the person who gave me firsthand information about that night.

She told me that at one point a group disappeared into a private room. The group included Hoover, Nixon, and Johnson, and when they emerged, Johnson was extremely uptight. She told me something like, "Smoke was coming out of his ears." He left immediately, and she left with him. What he had been told she was not certain of until early the next morning, when he rang her from Fort Worth. During their conversation, in irritation he said to her, "Those damned Kennedys will not be poking fun at me after today." When John F. Kennedy was assassinated later that day, the whole thing became clear to her. He had been told this at the meeting held during Murchison's party the night before. No doubt, Nixon was also told, as were a few others. On balance, it would seem the most likely person to have brought this news was Hoover.

Hoover, of course, was no friend of the Kennedys, and it was an open secret the president was looking for the first opportunity to get rid of him from the directorship of the FBI. Hoover knew this well. It is known that, apart from any other intelligence to which he was privy, details of a plot to assassinate Kennedy in Dallas had been received by him. A copy of this warning was sent by telex to FBI man, William S. Walter. Walter was on duty as night clerk at the New Orleans FBI office when the message came through. It was dated November 17, which gave plenty of time for the alarm to be raised, but it appears no action was taken.

There is here no veiled inference that any of those at the Murchison party were part of the conspiracy to kill President Kennedy, but anyone present who received news of an assassination plot and did nothing was, indeed, guilty of treason. Some have claimed Johnson was part of the conspiracy; Ruby made this assertion, for one, but there is no hard evidence that Johnson was involved. It would appear he knew in advance it was going to happen, however. His actions at the time of the assassination did nothing to allay suspicions, either. When the shooting started, and people in the motorcade looked around asking who was letting off the firecrackers, Johnson dived to the well of the car in which he was traveling.

On his own account, Johnson was caught up in a top-level scandal that was reaching its culmination during the presidential visit to Texas. It concerned Bobby Baker, Johnson's protégé and close associate. He was charged with influence peddling and irregular financial manipulation. The Bobby Baker storm was about to break, and there was nowhere for Johnson to run. The day President Kennedy was killed there were as many as three stories in the *Dallas Times Herald* alone concerning the growing crisis. And this was by no means all. Billy Sol Estes, Johnson's close and very shady friend and associate, was in deep trouble and another scandal was rapidly brewing over Johnson's head.

The Billy Sol Estes affair was particularly nasty. In the first place, he was under investigation for malpractices relating to government contracts for the storage of grain and federal cotton allotments. When Henry Marshall, a government agricultural agent, ventured to Texas to investigate the irregularities in 1961, he died from gunshot wounds. Notwithstanding that there were five bullets fired into his body, which was found in a ditch, he was declared a suicide. Since there was no autopsy on the body, the whole affair was conveniently hushed up.

The matter had not entirely been forgotten, however, and some years later it finally surfaced in Washington. An exhumation and autopsy was ordered, and Marshall was found to have received a blow to the head and had suffered carbon monoxide poisoning before being riddled with bullets. The true verdict now reached was that of murder, and an investigation was set in motion.

It was at about this point that Kennedy was killed. The gathering clouds had grown darker and darker over Johnson's head and he was close to being deluged when he suddenly became president. There was no way he could have survived in politics under the intense pressure exerted by the combined Baker and Sol Estes scandals. But he was now rescued. It is my belief that the reason Johnson, in unseemly haste, had himself sworn in on Air Force One with the dead president's body in the same aircraft was to make himself safe; to become president before anything could possibly prevent it. Whether such haste was necessary I am not sure, but at that point the scandal stories ceased. He could forget about yesterday's news—even today's news—and in particular two stories run by *Time Life*, one as recently as November 9, THE BOBBY BAKER BOMBSHELL, in which he was pictured next to Baker, and the second on November 22, the very day Kennedy died, SCANDAL GROWS AND GROWS IN WASHINGTON.

The case against Sol Estes continued, even though the federal charges laid against Johnson were dropped after he became president. The state of Texas continued to pursue Sol Estes, however, and though the charge of murder was not pressed, he received a fifteen-year sentence for his part in the affair. Some years later, after Johnson was dead, the investigation into Marshall's death was resumed by a grand jury. Wanting Sol Estes's input, it granted him immunity from prosecution. His input was, indeed, explosive. He claimed Johnson had ordered the killing of Marshall to protect the exposure of his association with Sol Estes. Sol Estes was also linked to three other deaths. It is interesting to note that he lived right next door to Johnson.

The Bobby Baker scandal was eventually resolved. Baker was indicted on seven charges of income tax evasion, as well as on charges of larceny and conspiracy, and was brought to trial in 1967. If Johnson had not become president at that particular moment in November 1963, he would have been totally obliterated.

Sometime after Kennedy's death, Madeleine Brown was in conversation with Johnson on the subject of the assassination secrets locked away by the Warren Commission, not to be opened until 2039. Johnson said to her, "Remember box 13? There'll be no information there to hang LBJ, that's for sure." The saga of box 13 related to another scandal surrounding Johnson. That time it involved nonexistent votes cast for his election to the U.S. Senate.

It was a close-run election, and the outcome hung in the balance. It all depended on the count of votes cast in ballot box 13. When the last vote was counted, Johnson's opponent, Coke Stevenson, was credited with sixty votes. The votes for Johnson were announced as 765, not quite what he wanted. Then the number became 965, which saw Johnson the victor. Since only 600 ballot papers had been issued for box 13, questions were inevitable, and Johnson set his face against any investigation being carried out. At all costs, he had to defuse this budding scandal. The suspected irregularities were questioned in a state court case and later in a case at the federal court level. Johnson dug in his heels and obstructed an investigation by every means he knew. The court even ordered a reexamination of all the votes cast in southern Texas, but Johnson once again wriggled out of it. So he went to Washington as the elected candidate for the Senate. Box 13 involved deep skulduggery; but Johnson was an ambitious and determined man.

Perhaps the greatest scandal in which Johnson was involved occurred immediately after the assassination. President Kennedy was keeping tabs on what was happening in Vietnam. The American personnel were not, as yet, involved in the fighting. They were officially there as noncombatants, but for such a role as that which they purported to fill, their strength, though not huge, was significant enough. Kennedy made a decision to withdraw 1,000 of the personnel there, and it is believed that this was just the first withdrawal and that the United States would withdraw from all involvement in Vietnam. The letter of October 11, 1963, on White House notepaper and signed by McGeorge Bundy (see photo insert) evidences the decision to withdraw the 1,000 men. Kennedy reiterated this, saying on October 31, less than a month before his death, "I think the first unit or first contingent 250 men who are not involved in what might be called front-line operations."

On November 14, just a few days before he was shot, the *New York Times* reported him as saying, "We are going to bring back several hundred before the end of the year. But I think on the question of the exact number, I thought we would wait until the meeting of 20 November."

Those most senior in directing the operation in Vietnam met in Honolulu on November 20, two days before the president died. Dean Rusk was there, as was Robert McNamara, McGeorge Bundy, Admiral Harry D. Felt, Lieutenant General Paul D. Harkins, and Henry Cabot Lodge, who was the U.S. Ambassador to South Vietnam, and as a result of this meeting, the number of men to be withdrawn was increased from 1,000 to 1,300.

On December 3, 228 men were, in fact, withdrawn, and those

lucky ones included in the larger number were brought home before Christmas 1963.

But when President Kennedy was gunned down on Friday, November 22, the Vietnam policy was reversed at a truly remarkable speed. It at first appeared that on the day after his death, if not the same night he died, notices went out to most of those present at the Honolulu meeting, and some others besides, that the new president had called a meeting to take place in Washington on Sunday, November 24. The meeting did take place, but the decisions taken, evidenced by a letter issued on White House notepaper on November 26, were, as was revealed in 1991, *actually made on November 21, the day before President Kennedy died.* How this occurred it is not known, but the decisions taken on November 21, in spite of appearing, at first glance, to continue Kennedy's policy, did not at all. Effectively, they canceled his policy; as late as October 1963, Kennedy was refusing to commit the United States to the "overriding objective" of "denying" Vietnam "to communism." In other words, there was no commitment to war. NSAM 273 issued by Johnson reversed this and spoke of winning such a war as the central objective. It was a deceitful document, and it would be interesting to know how and why the decisions featured in it were reached the day before President Kennedy died. It was anticipatory. It brings into question whether Johnson knew about the plot to kill Kennedy even earlier than was detected. As a consequence of NSAM 273, decisions to step up the war with Vietnam, as we know, were made. It should also be noted this decision to reverse Kennedy's policy was deemed so urgent that the meeting called by Johnson took place the day before Kennedy was buried, which was on Monday, November 25.

There is little doubt that the families of the over 58,000 men and women who perished in Vietnam would rate this scandal as the greatest of all the scandals in which Johnson was involved. Not everyone was displeased with Johnson's new policy, however. The Vietnam War generated enormous business for the military-industrialists, those who made the bombs, the guns, the planes, and everything else needed for such a war, the scale of which was periodically "topped up" with more and more troops. To them, the war was worth $200 billion.

It must be remembered, also, that while the loss of over 58,000 represented an enormous sacrifice to the United States, the sacrifice of the Vietnamese killed was numbered in the millions.

CHAPTER 20

Hocus and Pocus

The cruellest lies are often told in silence.
—Robert Louis Stevenson

THE WARREN COMMISSION was a strange body in many respects. It honored those who said what it wanted to hear, no matter how feeble their offering, and it ignored or, worse still, discredited those whose voice rose up against the story it wanted to tell.

Perhaps one of the most blatant examples of the manipulation of evidence, adding up to plain lies, was to be found in the data provided by the Dallas City surveyor Robert West and Chester Breneman, another prominent surveyor. The two were commissioned by the FBI to match distances and elevations to the relevant terrain featured in the Zapruder film. This meant large areas of the Dealey Plaza. When their work was completed, it was submitted to the FBI, which was carrying out investigations for the Warren Commission and the U.S. Secret Service. Not surprisingly, it was made available to the commission and was duly published in the Warren Report.

To the utter amazement of the surveyors, they found that some of their data had been changed. Breneman charged, "these figures were changed just enough that the Warren Commission could come up with the idea that another shot came from the same direction as the first." I can confirm without doubt that their data was falsified. In researching the Smith-Vidit study, I came by a photograph of the West and Breneman original survey that was submitted to the FBI and Secret Service and that was supposedly quoted in the Warren

Report. After painstaking enlargements, I was able to compare the accompanying data with that shown in the Warren Report and found that Zapruder frame 161 had been substituted for frame 168, 166 had taken the place of 171, and frame 210 was where they had placed 208. One slip might have been accidental, but three were clearly intended to deceive.

As a result of the work they had carried out, both surveyors were convinced that shots had come from at least two different directions, something the Warren Commission was dedicated to oppose. Before they had undertaken the work for the FBI, West and Breneman had carried out an investigation for *Life* magazine that also involved matching the Zapruder film frames. That the Zapruder frames were available for matching so quickly after the assassination was remarkable, for the findings of the surveyors were published in the magazine on the Monday following the assassination (which took place on the Friday before). As a consequence of their work, the *Life* investigator handling the story was convinced the bullets fired could not have come from the same rifle.

During the work they carried out in the Dealey Plaza, West and Breneman identified a mark clearly made by a bullet on the Stemmons Freeway sign. The Warren Commission members who must have walked the Dealey Plaza in the course of conducting their enquiry, apparently never noticed that the sign, which featured so frequently in pictures taken at the time of the assassination, very quickly disappeared. It must be said that the Warren Commission would have found evidence of yet another bullet fired during the assassination extremely embarrassing and impossible to explain without enormous and far reaching changes to its submissions. I myself looked into the whereabouts of the original sign and was told that it was placed in the basement of the Texas School Book Depository building at first, but where it was taken to afterward nobody knew.

The witness Caroline Walther was present on Houston Street when the president was killed. She looked over toward the Texas School Book Depository and saw two men in a window there, just before the motorcade arrived and the shooting started. One wore a white shirt and had light colored hair, she said. He was holding a rifle and she took him for a guard. The other wore a brown suit-coat. They were both visible in a fourth- or fifth-story window to the right side of the building. This information attracted the attention of the world media, but the Warren Commission ignored it. Had she not identified the presence of *two* men—which, to the Warren Commission, would have represented a conspiracy—it might have been more interested. The commission, however, had set its face against the possibility John F. Kennedy had been killed as a consequence of a conspiracy having taken place. The commission had decided that the president was killed by Lee Harvey Oswald, alone and unaided.

Sam Holland, a railroad worker, was another whose evidence was falsified in the Warren Report. He gave evidence that while he and other railroad workers watched the motorcade from the railway overpass, he saw a puff of smoke rise from behind the picket fence on the grassy knoll at the time the shooting started. He also said he and his fellow workers ran down to the place behind the picket fence to see what they might find. This took them some two minutes, Holland said, and they did not expect to find a sniper lingering. They did find cigarette butts and footprints, however, clear evidence that someone had been at the spot, and a car facing the fence with a muddy bumper suggested to them someone had stood up on it to see over the fence. The group acted together and was in agreement on what Holland submitted in evidence to the commission. Holland also stated he had heard four shots fired.

The commissioners were obviously not minded to accept indications that a sniper fired from the grassy knoll, for this would have totally undermined their lone nut killer theory, which they were anxious to promote. The entire evidence submitted by Holland was completely distorted in the account that appeared in the Warren Report. Instead of publishing what would clearly have supported that there was a shooter behind the picket fence, the commission changed Holland's evidence so that it now supported the opposite to what he had said. The Warren Report stated, "Holland . . . immediately after the shots, ran off the underpass to see if there was anyone behind the picket fence on the north side of Elm Street but he did not see anyone behind the parked cars."

Since the commissioners' whole thesis depended on no more than three shots having been fired, they also blatantly changed Holland's evidence to read that he had heard *three* shots. Holland was given a transcript of what he was supposed to have said before the publication of the report, and, accompanied by his lawyer, he went to straighten them out. "We red-penciled that statement from beginning to end but it made no difference," said a furious Holland. "They simply ignored the corrections and published what they wanted."

Holland's assertion that a puff of smoke was visible rising from behind the picket fence was also supported elsewhere. Ed Johnson, who was a reporter for a Fort Worth newspaper, wrote an article that stated, "Some of us saw little puffs of white smoke that seemed to hit the grassy area."

The Fort Worth newspaper featured the article the day after the assassination took place, but if the Warren Commission members ever saw it they ignored it.

Jean Hill, watching the motorcade opposite the grassy knoll, was the closest of all the witnesses to what happened. She was located only feet away from the point at which the president was fired on, and she said that looking across the presidential car she saw a sniper on the knoll fire at the president and that smoke was seen to be rising from his rifle. Once again, the Warren Commission stoically ignored Hill. Hill stood next to Mary Moorman, who took a Polaroid picture that became one of the most celebrated of all those taken in the Dealey Plaza. It showed a sniper toward the corner of the picket fence, dressed in what looked like a policeman's uniform, and for that reason this image of the sniper attracted the title of "the badgeman." Again, the photograph was not sought by the Warren Commission: the identification of a sniper on the grassy knoll would have totally destroyed its case against Oswald being the lone killer.

It is interesting to note that totally independent researches have indicated the presence of a sniper at the location photographed by Moorman. The computerized Smith-Vidit study, which I carried out with the brilliant German computer programmer Joachim Markus, demonstrated in most striking terms that a sniper was present at exactly the spot photographed by Moorman. He was the one who fired the shot that hit the president in the throat, a front entry wound. Identified as such by the doctors at Parkland Hospital in Dallas, to where the president was taken, it was later reidentified as an exit wound to please the autopsy doctors. There is no doubt the first identification was correct and that the bullet came from where "the badgeman" stood.

About half an hour before the motorcade was due, Julia Ann Mercer drove down Elm Street and had to wait to pass a pickup that was parked half on and half off the pavement. This was just at the foot of the grassy knoll. A man wearing a gray jacket, brown trousers, and a stocking cap took from the pickup a case that looked very much like a rifle case and carried it up the grassy rise. Mercer's reaction was that she had seen a Secret Service man move into place. As she passed the pickup, she took a long look at the driver, still sitting in the vehicle. She noted he was white, fair-haired, about forty years of age, heavy set, and wearing a green jacket. When she heard about the shooting of the president, she contacted the sheriff's office to report what she had seen. Interviewed by FBI agents on Saturday, the day after the assassination, she answered their questions and went on to examine about two dozen photographs they had brought with them. Having identified the man she saw in the truck, the matter was left there.

While watching television the following day, she was thunderstruck when she recognized the man who shot Oswald in the basement car park of police headquarters. It was Jack Ruby, the man she saw in the truck the previous day, though she did not know his name. Mercer was another who complained when she saw a transcript of what she was supposed to have said. Added to the description she had given the police, the truck in question was said to have had a sign that was not present on the pickup: AIR CONDITIONING. This would completely mislead those seeking the vehicle and it would also certainly have put private researchers who tried to find the truck off the scent. Also, the date of her searching through the photographs had been changed. It was now made to appear that she had examined them some days after it really happened, and, unbelievably, it was recorded that Mercer could not make an identification from the pictures she looked at. She also complained that an affidavit she had signed had been altered. It needs hardly be mentioned the Warren Commission did not call Mercer to give evidence.

In the case of the opposite happening, where the commission embraced exceedingly unreliable evidence because it favored the case it was building against Oswald, Helen Markham is a prime example. She was standing waiting for a bus near the junction of Tenth Street and Patton Avenue in the Oak Cliff area when, she said, she saw Oswald shoot Officer J. D. Tippit and then run away. She was questioned by Joseph Ball, the senior counsel to the Warren Commission, and her evidence ran as follows:

Ball: Where was the police car when you first saw it?

Markham: He was driving real slow, almost up to this man, well, say this man, and he kept, and this man kept walking, you know, and the police car was going real slow now, real slow, and they just kept coming in to the curb, and finally the [*sic*] got a little way up there a little ways up, well, it stopped.

Ball: The police car stopped?

Markham: Yes sir.

Ball: What about the man? Was he still walking?

Markham: The man stopped. . . . I saw the man come over to the car very slow, leaned and put his arms just like this, he looked over in this window and looked in this window. . . . The window was down. . . . Well, I didn't think nothing about it; you know, the police are nice and friendly and I thought friendly conversation. Well, I looked, and there were cars coming so I had to wait. . . . This man, like I told you, put his arms up, leaned over, he—just a minute, and he drew back and he stepped back about two steps. . . . The policeman calmly opened the door, very slowly, wasn't angry or nothing, he calmly crawled out of this car, and I just thought a friendly conversation.

Markham told how the policeman, while walking around the front of the car, was shot four times by the man he had been talking to. She described him as about twenty-five years of age, five feet eight inches tall, and having brown hair. He was wearing a white jacket, she also said. It should be remembered that Earlene Roberts, Oswald's landlady, gave evidence that Oswald had changed into a dark coat before he left her boarding house, about fifteen to twenty minutes before this time, and this was in direct conflict with Markham's description.

By the time Markham had finished her description of the killer, she was in hysterics and had to be sedated before being taken to the police department to an identity parade. Curiously, Markham brought into her testimony that she had put her shoes on top of Tippit's car.

After the identity parade, she was questioned further by Ball:

Ball: Now when you went into the room you looked these people over, these four men.
Markham: Yes, sir.
Ball: Did you recognize anyone in the line-up?
Markham: No, sir.
Ball: You did not? Did you see anybody—I have asked you that question before—did you recognize anybody from their face?
Markham: From their face, no.

This must have been a very bad moment for Ball. He continued:

Ball: Did you identify anybody in these four people?
Markham: I didn't know nobody. . . . I had never seen none of them, none of these men.

Ball: No one of the four?
Markham: No one of them.
Ball: No one of all four?
Markham: No, sir.

By this time, Ball would have been forgiven for walking away from it all, but he had to get from her an identification of Oswald. A policeman present at the identity parade told later that in her first attempt at identification she picked out a policeman from the line-up. With Markham being totally unresponsive to him, Ball, unthinkably, fell into the trap of prompting her:

Ball: Was there a number two man in there?
Markham: Number two is the one I picked. . . . Number two was the man I saw shoot the policeman. . . . I looked at him. When I saw this man I wasn't sure, but I had cold chills just run all over me.

Not only do we have on record an unprofessional and unethical maneuver on Ball's part, we have to note it drew, at best, a very shaky answer from Markham. It may be wondered what would have happened in a court of law. Undoubtedly, any defense attorney worth his or her salt would have had the testimony thrown out. But this was not a court of law, and with the Warren Commission investigation there was no defense at all. Also, it clearly revealed that the commissioners were hungry for anything at all that might tie Oswald into their scenario, even if the rules had to be stretched.

Mark Lane was a lawyer who had been engaged by Marguarite Oswald, Lee's mother, to posthumously defend him. He telephoned Markham to discuss the evidence she had given. The content of the tape recording was sent to the Warren Commission, which heard Markham now describing Officer Tippit's killer as short, on the heavy side, and having somewhat bushy hair. Here, she was decidedly not repeating the description she had given to the Warren

Commission. Markham was, unsurprisingly, summoned to appear before the Warren Commission again to answer further questions.

> *Counsel:* We have a tape recording of a conversation that purports to be a conversation between you and Mark Lane on the telephone.

The tape was played, and soon after it started Markham began to shake her head.

> *Markham:* I never talked to that man.
> *Counsel:* Is that not your voice on the tape?
> *Markham:* I can't tell you about my voice, but that man . . . and those words that he's saying—that's nothing like the telephone call I got—nothing.

The tape playback continued and the description of Tippit's killer as given to Lane was heard. Markham floundered.

> *Markham:* This man . . . this man that called me like I told you, he told me he was from the city hall, the police department, the police department of the city hall.
> *Counsel:* Well, now, do you remember having this conversation with somebody?
> *Markham:* Yes, I do, but he told me he was from the police department of city hall and he had to get some information.

Lane correctly pressed that his tape contained none of Markham's assertions relating to him saying he was from "city hall" or the Dallas—or any other—Police Department. Markham continued to make such assertions, however, and eventually argued that the woman's voice on the tape recording was not hers. Finally, she accepted the voice as hers, but continued to say the man said he was from the city police. The tape recording was finally accepted as a conversation between Lane and Markham, and, with enormous difficulty, Lane established that Markham's description of Tippit's killer was totally unreliable.

Markham asked if she would get into trouble over her untruths in regard to the telephone conversation and was assured she would not. On the contrary, Lane had previously been threatened with prosecution if he so much as submitted the tape to the commission. Markham had given evidence saying that the right window of Tippit's police car was rolled down, though this was demolished by evidence from other witnesses and photographs taken at the time. Markham asserted that she spoke to the dying Tippit for some twenty minutes before he was taken away in an ambulance, which was in direct contradiction to the evidence of other witnesses who said that Tippit collapsed after four bullets were fired and that he died immediately.

Finally, when Markham's sworn testimony that the shooting took place at approximately 1:06 P.M. was offered, as I said in an earlier chapter, it was immediately brought into question. The trouble was that if she was right, Oswald could not have been Tippit's assailant. The commission considered this and decided that on this score Markham *was* unreliable.

The commission decided that "in her various statements and in her testimony, Mrs. Markham was uncertain and inconsistent in her recollection *of the exact time of the slaying*" (emphasis added).

However, this did not stop Markham continuing to claim that the time of the killing was 1:06 P.M. Neither did it prevent the Warren Commission from quoting her on this in the Warren Report. When push came to shove, it appeared that the only person prepared to cast Oswald in the role of Officer Tippit's slayer must have that part of her testimony honored, no matter how shaky or unreliable she was as a witness. So the Warren Commission accepted those parts of Markham's evidence that supported the guilt of Oswald and rejected the parts which supported his innocence.

Markham was neither a stupid woman, nor the "nut case" she was called. On the day in question, she was doing her best to cope with the demands of a police department anxious to find the murderer of the president and the murderer of a fellow officer. It appeared that the police and the commission were simply far too demanding of her. Detective James R. Leavelle, who saw her being hustled to make an identification, said she was, "suffering from shock." She "was in such a state of shock she had been unable to view the line-up." But Captain Willy Fritz, who was in charge of the line-up proceedings, was not accepting delays for any reason. Incredibly, he explained, "we were trying to get that showup as soon as we could because she was beginning to faint and getting sick." It is small wonder that she was not up to what was being thrust on her. The tragedy is that in the long run it did not seem to matter. And this was not the only instance where the rules were stretched in relation to so-called evidence against Oswald.

Just as it suited the book of the Warren Commission to cast Oswald in the role of the killer of Officer Tippit, it similarly suited its book to cast him in the role of the man who had taken a shot at General Edwin Walker. Walker, a Dallas citizen and avid right-winger, had been dismissed from his post as commander of the Twenty-fourth Division of the U.S. Army in West Germany for circulating anti-Kennedy literature among the troops. He was on the scene when Kennedy faced the famous confrontation over his desegregation program at the University of Mississippi.

Not surprisingly, Walker needed the assistance of aides when it came to protecting himself, and it was one such aide who drew attention to suspicious activities in the proximity of the general's house on the night of April 8, 1963. It was not until two days later, however, that a shot was fired through Walker's window in Dallas, narrowly missing him. There was no suggestion at the time that Oswald was involved in the incident. After the assassination, however, when the Warren Commission was in session, it was decided that he was involved and that this demonstrated his predisposition to violence. The evidence, such as it was, was produced primarily by Marina Oswald, Oswald's wife. It must be said that Marina was putty in the hands of the authorities since if she was difficult she would be sent back to the Soviet Union, her home, where she would receive a cold reception indeed. She was the sole source of the Warren case for Oswald's involvement in the Walker shooting. She provided bus timetables for the route, since Oswald could not drive a car, showing his interest in the district. She claimed her husband had taken photographs of General Walker's house, one of which she was said to have passed to the police, and testified that he was not at home when the incident occurred. She also said that he had told her he had fired the shot. The police department supported this with evidence that the remains of a 6.5 bullet was recovered from the scene, the same caliber as that claimed by the commission that had killed President Kennedy.

Unhappily, for those who went further than the Warren Report, the truth was not at all what the commissioners led us to believe. In the first place, the man involved in the shooting had driven off in a car, clearly witnessed by a sharp-eyed boy of sixteen who lived next door to Walker. Remember that Oswald could not drive a car. Second, the items supporting Marina Oswald's assertions had, by this time, all been destroyed, and there was no evidence other than her word that Oswald had said he had fired a shot at Walker. One piece of evidence appeared to survive scrutiny: the photograph of the rear of Walker's house she had supposedly handed to the police. "Supposedly" is a pertinent word here, because she later stated that she had been "shown it" by an FBI agent who had searched for her husband's possessions.

As it happened, there was a problem with this photograph. Sometime before being produced as evidence, a hole had been driven through the print at the very point showing the license plate of a 1957 Chevrolet parked behind Walker's house. The number was obliterated. The police argued it was like that when they had received it. However, we have Police Chief Jesse Curry to thank for being able to verify that this claim was false. Curry wrote a book in which a picture of Oswald's supposed possessions was reproduced. The picture now offered for evidence was there for all to see, and it had no hole driven through it. Unfortunately, the print of the print was too indistinct to reveal what the number was, apparently a number that someone at police headquarters was anxious to conceal.

But there was the evidence of a 6.5 bullet recovered from the scene of the crime that should have kept the accusation against Oswald going, but that was not to be the case. It is remarkable that no mention was ever made during the Warren proceedings that the remains of the bullet recovered had already been identified by the police as a 30.06 missile. This had not been missed by the press and was widely publicized at the time. Then the other "props" also fell apart. Marina Oswald had given evidence that on the night of the shooting her husband had returned home in a distressed state, telling her he had buried his (6.5) rifle and would dig it up "when the heat was off." She even confirmed that he did, later, dig it up and that he brought it home. This was completely shot down by two guests entertained by the Oswalds during the time the gun was supposedly buried. Russian-speaking friends, George de Mohrenschildt and his wife, Jeanne, were at the Oswald apartment, and they said they saw the rifle in question while they were there.

The Warren Report, 10 million words long and contained in twenty-six volumes, no doubt initially achieved what it set out to do. If we were told a straight tale, there was the threat of a war with both Cuba and Russia. This is why Chief Justice Earl Warren accepted the chairmanship of the Warren Commission, against his instincts, but in the face of intense pressure brought about by Lyndon B. Johnson. The Warren Report, we are told, took the pressure off, and the time passed. Nobody seemed to notice that Jacqueline Kennedy, in a poignant personal letter to President Nikita Khrushchev, probably achieved as much or more. The tone of her letter clearly indicated she knew her husband's death was not the work of communists. For that matter, that she wrote at all said this quite clearly. The fact the letter was not well publicized might be significant. Though she told Johnson about the letter before it was sent, she did not tell him what she was putting in it. She wrote:

White House, December 1, 1963

Dear Mr. Chairman-President:

I would like to thank you for sending Mr. Mikoyan as your representative to my husband's funeral.

He looked so upset when he approached me, and I was very touched by this. . . .

Therefore now, on one of the last nights I will spend in the White House, in one of the last letters I will write on this White House stationery, I would like to write my message to you. . . .

I am sending it only because I know my husband was concerned about peace [translator's note: the Russian word *mir* used here can mean either "peace" or "the world," but the context seems to indicate that she meant "peace"] and how important the relations between you and him were to him in this concern. He often cited your words in his speeches: "In the next war the survivors will envy the dead."

You and he were adversaries, but you were also allies in your determination not to let the world be blown up. You respected each other and could have dealings with each other. I know that President Johnson will make every effort to establish the same relations with you. . . .

I am sending you this letter because I am so deeply mindful of the importance of the relations that existed between you and my husband, and also because you and Mrs. Krushchev were so kind in Vienna. . . .

Sincerely,
Jacqueline Kennedy

Khrushchev replied warmly, unofficially inviting Jackie and her family to a holiday in Russia.

The Warren Commission has been said to achieve a great many other things as well. It achieved concentrating on Oswald as the lone killer, in the face of incredible evidence that the president's murder was the consequence of a conspiracy, thus diverting any serious efforts to look for a plot to kill the president, or even another individual, for that matter. Effectively, it sheltered the guilty. It allowed the trail to cool off for those who were determined to find the truth. It deceived the American people and, indeed the world, and those responsible for it stood by and allowed those early researchers—who began to expose it for what it was—to be scorned and abused by loyal, honest folk who, for so long, could not be convinced that their government would do such a thing to them: surely they would not conduct an enquiry of the sort the critics were stripping.

Whatever it was—or was not—the Warren Report was definitely not a beacon of truth.

CHAPTER 21

The Autopsy

To go too far is the same as not to go far enough.

—Confucius

THE BODY OF John F. Kennedy was taken from Parkland Hospital under protest. Those at the hospital spoke of breaking the chain of evidence if the body was taken away before autopsy. They spoke of the rights of the man who would eventually be charged with murder. They were adamant that an autopsy should be carried out in Texas.

But when a nasty scene began to brew, and Secret Service agents stood firm against them and *demanded* the removal of the body, and especially when people were getting edgy and a trigger was being fingered by a police officer located nearby, something had to give, and the Secret Service personnel won the day. They wheeled out the body in the best coffin the undertaker could provide in the time scale, regardless of permission being withheld or a release being signed. In fact, the release was signed and rushed to the departing group just before vehicle doors closed and the journey began to Air Force One at Love Field and then to Washington, D.C. The full-scale argument that had broken out makes an interesting study by itself. Why were the Texas authorities so anxious to follow the letter of the law, even when it related to the body of the president? And, for that matter, why were the Secret Service agents so rigidly determined the body would not stay in Texas for autopsy? Legally, the Texans were right, but how did it all culminate in a near brawl?

In view of what was to happen, many would concede it might have been better if the body had remained where it was. The official autopsy, carried out that same night at Bethesda Naval Hospital near Washington, has given rise to enormous uncertainty as to what, in fact, it revealed, and to add to that, the body, when delivered to Bethesda, reportedly bore clear signs of having being tampered with somewhere on the way.

The tampering with the president's body was primarily evidenced by the size of the major wound at the back of his head. This was the fatal wound, created by a bullet that blew out part of the rear skull and brain tissue, leaving no opportunity for recovery. It is part of medical routine to measure wounds, and the Parkland Hospital doctors recorded this as two and three-quarter inches in diameter. The autopsy doctors at Bethesda recorded the same wound as measuring five and one-eighth inches by seven inches. This kind of discrepancy cannot be attributed to mere haste, simple error, or any other kind of acceptable cause.

The person (or persons) responsible for this extraneous "surgery" remains a mystery to this day, but the result of the changes made to the wound are not difficult to understand. As a consequence of what they saw, the autopsy doctors felt able to declare that all the bullets that hit the president had come from behind. In fact, this was still putting a huge gloss on which direction the bullets had actually come from, but, one assumes, the wounds in their original state would have indicated bullets came from in front as well as from behind. It was absolutely essential to those who were desperately anxious to show that all the bullets had come from behind, from one rifle—the rifle of Lee Harvey Oswald—that the Bethesda doctors were able to say this. But who would carry out such an outrageously offensive—not to mention gruesome—act? One thing is certain however: a body as closely guarded as the body of President Kennedy could only be tampered with by the complicity of a person or persons in high places.

Neither of the two principals conducting the autopsy, Commander James J. Humes and Dr. J. Thornton Boswell, had ever conducted an autopsy before, nor had Army Colonel Pierre A. Finck, who was brought in as a consultant. None of the three was a forensic pathologist. Therefore, with this handicap the president's body was subjected to scrutiny that led to disbelief and uncertainty, but that satisfied those who sat like buzzards awaiting the outcome. By all appearances, the predetermined outcome had to support an investigation that would reach the conclusion there was no conspiracy to kill the president and that would build an indisputable case against Oswald as the lone, crazed killer.

Mystery surrounded the autopsy from the very beginning. Shocking stories that began to circulate about the president's body arriving at Bethesda in a common or garden pink-gray body bag inside a gray metal, nondescript shipping coffin have now been confirmed by several members of the Bethesda medical staff, who eventually felt they could reveal such a thing. The evidence the body arrived at the back door of Bethesda Naval Hospital in an unmarked decoy vehicle was provided by Lieutenant Richard A. Lipsey in a statement he made in 1979. Lipsey confirmed he was in attendance at the delivery of the coffin. The polished bronze coffin was admitted at the front door twenty minutes later, accompanied by Jacqueline Kennedy and her brother-in-law, Robert. One staff member recalls seeing the arrival of the ornate coffin as he was already taking X-ray plates of the president's wounds to another part of the building for development.

Questions relating to why the body had been taken out of one coffin and placed in another only serves to enhance the claims made that the wounds had been altered before autopsy so that they might be supportive to a single gunman having been responsible for them. The evidence of two FBI agents, James W. Sibert and Francis X. O'Neill, who witnessed the arrival of the body, also supported the claims that it had been tampered with. When they first saw the president's body being lifted from the coffin in which he arrived, they noted that "surgery of the head area" had occurred, much blood being in evidence. The doctors at Parkland Hospital, however, confirmed that they had carried out no surgery other than turning what they said was a front-entry wound to the throat, by extension, into a tracheotomy to help the president breathe.

The president's head was wrapped in a towel before it left Parkland Hospital in Dallas. From then on, blood would not flow except for a minimal amount. The "much blood" noted by the FBI agents could only have occurred if the wounds had been severely aggravated. The relevant page of the Sibert and O'Neill report is online at www.jfklancer.com, exactly as it was submitted to Washington. There is no doubt about what it says, and there is no doubt this was not as Parkland Hospital had dispatched the president's body.

Sibert and O'Neill made another important contribution to what we know about the autopsy. In another written report, they refer to the discovery of a "missile" that was removed from the president's body and handed to them by Commander Humes that completely disappeared, never to be seen again. It has been vigorously argued that what they really meant was a bullet fragment when they spoke of a missile. However, in another report they refer to "bullet fragments," so it is reasonable to assume that by stating "missile" this time they really meant a complete bullet.

The autopsy deliberations were there to be challenged. The first bullet fired was from the front right, as the Parkland doctors said, a second bullet came from behind, and a third and fatal bullet came from the front right again, blowing the rear of the president's head out. But the autopsy doctors pressed the Parkland Hospital doctors to revise their ideas on the first bullet, which they dutifully did. They agreed the throat wound could have been an exit wound from a bullet from behind, which, as we shall see, is nonsense. Then the autopsy doctors argued the fatal shot had also come from behind, which patently it could not have done.

The computer research I worked on with the German computer expert Joachim Markus, which became known as the Smith-Vidit study, confirmed that the first shot came from the front, just as the Parkland Hospital doctors had originally said. It also confirmed that the fatal third shot also came from the front, as researchers had long since claimed, and that has been supported on all sides, including by the acoustic evidence. At least two shots came from behind in addition to these two shots, however. One missed and hit the ground, throwing up a concrete fragment that injured James Teague, an onlooker. The other shot from behind hit the president in the back, immediately after the first wound to the throat, as can be seen in the Zapruder film. The Smith-Vidit study identified that the origin of the first and last shots was behind the picket fence on the grassy knoll. The idea of a bullet passing through the president's body, exiting and passing through Governor John Connally's body, exiting again to pass through the governor's wrist, and ending up in his left thigh was investigated as far as possible. The trouble was it did not fit the circumstances at any of the stages. Such a bullet would have gone in one direction, then another, changing direction in a bewildering number of ways. The single-bullet theory was clearly not true, as many researchers without the benefit of computer research have pointed out.

However, it would appear the Warren interpretation of the location of the bullet wounds was revised to fit the theory. Not only was the throat wound declared an exit wound to suit what the commission was claiming but also the bullet wound to the back was "raised" a few inches to allow it a degree of authenticity. The Smith-Vidit research showed that if a bullet had entered the president's back and exited his throat, the sniper would have been lying in the middle of the road, in the path of the outriders.

Governor Connally's wounds were clearly the result of two other bullets being fired: one was fired from behind, which hit him in the back and exited his chest, and the other was fired from the grassy knoll, which hit his wrist, exited, and came to rest in his thigh. But all this hacked at the roots of the single sniper idea. These shots patently advertised the presence of minimally two snipers, and there were certainly more.

The evidence of the X-rays, which should have been indisputable, has been called to question on a number of grounds. The many photographs taken during and after the autopsy should have provided sure confirmation of what was discovered. This is not the case. John Stringer, former U.S. Navy photographer, denied the pictures of the president's brain were taken by him: he could not recall taking shots from the angles in the pictures and, anyway, he used different film! In another case, a photograph showing a neat bullet hole in the back of the president's head, which was shown to be intact, was denounced as a fraud. Agent O'Neill witnessed the president's brain being removed. He told the Assassinations Record Review Board that when he later saw photographs they did not resemble what he saw. He told them, "I did not recall it being that large." There was, of course, controversy about part of the president's brain being blown away. There was also controversy about whether the brain identified really belonged to the president. The retained brain, in fact, disappeared and has never been seen since.

The Warren Report and the autopsy findings have been under severe attack on all sides from the findings of researchers determined to establish the truth. Remarkably, however, the U.S. government, as though wearing blinkers, has ignored this and officially still supports the findings of the Warren Commission.

CHAPTER 22

The Key to the Conspiracy

I transmit but do not create.

—Confucius

I HAVE TOLD this story in more than one of my books, but never before have I been able to tell it as fully as this. In the first place, I previously had to use a nom de plume for my informant, Wayne January: I promised him I would not reveal his name. I report with much sadness that January has now passed on, and his wife said I might now reveal his identity. Second, it took a long time for me to see the correct perspective in regard to January's most important story. I knew from the beginning it was important, but not how important. I do not think January realized the real importance in what he told me, either. January was a gentleman, and, indeed, a gentle man. It was a great privilege to know him. He became a minister of religion, a devout Christian, and an insightful man who regaled me with many wonderful and heart-warming stories. We became good friends as a result of his confiding in me, and I mourn his loss.

In November 1963, January was a partner in an aviation company based at Red Bird Airfield, close to the boundary of the city of Dallas. I learned much later that he was listed in a CIA booklet as a man on whom agents could trust and rely. That, of course, as far as January was concerned, would have related to anyone, but the CIA produced this booklet so that, wherever agents went, they had people they need not have fears or doubts about employing. January was not in the pay of the CIA, nor was he an agent at any level, but the connection he had with the agency explains, in part, the events of which he told me.

January first came to my notice in a footnote in a small but useful book by Richard H. Popkin titled *The Second Oswald*, which detailed the appearances of a false Lee Harvey Oswald. The footnote referred to a researcher interviewing Wayne January in regard to a possible sighting of Oswald—real or false—at Red Bird Airfield a few days before the assassination took place. For whatever reason, I filed this reference under genuine sightings and found it created a pattern of events that were impressive and, indeed, very revealing. Following up what promised to be a rewarding lead, I went to Dallas to meet him.

Our first meeting was in 1991, and we got along very well together. I had stopped off at the home of the legendary researcher Harold Weisberg in Maryland before my trip to Dallas, and he had invited me to make every use of his vast files of documents obtained under the Freedom of Information Act. Searching his files, I found an FBI account of an interview agents had conducted with January. The agents recorded that he told them his sighting of Oswald was the July before the assassination, making the significance fairly small, even worthless. January had told me on the telephone that the sighting was the Wednesday before the assassination, however, and I took this up with him at our meeting. I showed him a photocopy of the FBI report and he was bewildered. "I saw Oswald on television just a day or two afterwards," he said. "The memory of seeing him the previous Wednesday was fresh in my mind. How would I have recalled having seen him several months before?" There may have been reasons for the report showing the month it did, of course. My interest would have died immediately if January was claiming to have seen Oswald the previous July, and, no doubt, that would have also applied to anyone reading the report. A man on the CIA "vetted" list having recognized Oswald from two days before, however, would have commanded a great deal of attention and highlighted the story surrounding the visit that he had to tell.

The FBI report definitely capped any such prospect, which, as I have indicated, was the whole purpose of it.

The story relates to Wednesday, November 20, when January was approached by two "hippie" like young people, a man and a woman, who were seeking to hire a light aircraft for a flight to Yucatán. They arrived in an old black car, and, he saw through his office window, left behind them another passenger in the front seat. January described the man and woman well and carefully recounted what they said to him. They wanted to hire a plane to fly out of Red Bird Airfield two days later, on Friday, November 22. He wondered whether they could afford to rent a plane, then had misgivings they were heading for Cuba. When he finally drew the conclusion they might well want him to pilot the plane, he put up the shutters and refused them point blank. He told me he had a feeling he might take them where they wanted to go and never be allowed to return.

The car he saw them arrive in was an older model of a make he had once owned, and he was interested in it. He escorted his visitors to their car so that he could view it more closely. He also saw the young man sitting in the front seat at close quarters and, two days later, when the president was killed, he realized from pictures shown that it was Oswald.

Assuming that the young man in the front seat was really Oswald, the scenario becomes clearer. The couple who had approached January were CIA agents trying to set up an "escape route" for Oswald, the patsy, after the president's assassination. Having failed with January, presumably the two agents succeeded with another company, because it was well established that a small plane was ready for take-off and revving up for so long near the perimeter fence of Red Bird Airfield that complaints from nearby residents were made to the police, resulting in the aircraft being impounded by the FBI. There is no doubt about the complaints being made to the police: they were reported on local television during the afternoon of Friday, November 22. Oswald, the victim of a plot to incriminate him in the president's murder, failed to reach the plane and never made the flight to

Cuba that had been planned for him. Either way, he was a doomed man.

But during that week preceding the assassination of Kennedy, January was by the stealth of others—and without any knowledge of it himself—becoming drawn into the plot to kill the president.

× × ×

The Royal Air Service Inc., the aviation company in which January was a partner, owned a small fleet of what, for Red Bird Airfield, were larger aircraft. It had been obtained to carry out a fascinating top-secret government contract involving high-powered scientists being flown to develop radar mapping for low-level all-weather flying. This was being carried out to equip the black box of the F-111 fighter-bomber. When the company's contract ended, the larger aircraft were to be sold off. There was no difficulty in selling them, and eventually there was only one Douglas DC3 that was left on the books awaiting a buyer. This was finally sold by phone in mid-November by January's partner, to a buyer who turned up on November 18 to sign for it. He was, January told me, a well-dressed gentleman who turned up enquiring about the plane, for which he held the proper ownership papers. January described him as about six feet tall, fair complexioned, with brown hair, and late thirties to early forties. His haircut was a short, military type, and he wore slacks and a sports shirt. He had no particular accent, January said. He later discovered the man was an air force colonel who was a specialist in the kind of plane being bought.

The air force colonel brought with him an experienced pilot who would, with January, check the plane over before the transaction was completed. Not remotely like buying a used car, which might break down before the unfortunate purchaser had reached the end of the street in which it was bought, used planes are carefully checked out by a representative of the buyer with a representative of the seller before the deal is complete. January was celebrating his birthday on November 18, however, so he handed over the keys for the DC3 to the pilot, when they had been introduced, and arranged to begin work with him the following day. As January began this task the next day, the pilot confided to him a little of his background.

He was born in Cuba, he said, and had been a senior pilot in Fidel Castro's air force. Recruited by the CIA, he had flown for it at the Bay of Pigs, when the CIA-led invasion had been routed. He talked to January, and as the day passed, they became friends. The next day, Wednesday, November 20, the day January had the encounter with the "hippie"-type CIA agents, they became relaxed and even friendlier. It was the following day that the anti-Kennedy feeling in the air became apparent. January told me, "[There] seemed to be an air of anxiety because the radio and television were spending a lot of time [discussing] the President's visit to Dallas. Many people were displeased with the President's policies and with politics in general." It was about ten o'clock in the morning when a friend of January's drove up to the plane and stayed talking for over an hour. He added his own unhappiness with the president to what was going about. "I really didn't pay any attention," said January, "for I just considered him to be rambling with his mouth like everybody else."

After his friend left, January asked the CIA pilot if he would like to eat lunch. The pilot said he did but that he did not want to leave the plane, making the excuse that they were a little behind with preparations. January obligingly went over to the restaurant and bought sandwiches for them both. They settled down leaning against the plane's landing wheels and chatted. Then there was a pause, January told me.

It was now between 12:30 and 1:00 P.M. The CIA pilot looked at January and said, "They are going to kill your president."

"What do you mean?" January asked.

"I mean they are going to kill your president," replied the pilot.

"You mean President Kennedy?"

"Yes."

"What makes you think that? Why would anyone want to do that?"

January told me the CIA pilot, with a somber face, said, "I was a mercenary pilot, hired by the CIA. I was involved in the Bay of Pigs planning strategy which was operated by the CIA. I was there involved with many of my friends when they died, when Robert Kennedy talked John Kennedy out of sending in the air cover which he'd agreed to send. He canceled the air support after the invasion was launched. Many, many died. Far more than was told. I don't know all that was going on, but I do know that there was an indescribable amount of hurt, anger, and embarrassment to those that were involved in the operation."

"Is that why they will kill the President?" January asked.

The CIA pilot replied, "They are not only going to kill the President. They are going to kill Robert Kennedy and any other Kennedy that gets in their position."

January told me that the pilot did not say what that position was. He said to the CIA pilot, "To be honest with you—and myself—I take what you have said with a grain of salt. Not meaning to insult you or hurt you in any way, it's just too far fetched for me to believe. If I mentioned anything like that to the world, they would put me out of aviation as a nut, and ruin my reputation as a businessman." The pilot's only answer was, "You will see!"

"I have to say," said January, "I had no answer to that. I could understand his feelings for the friends he lost, but I could not understand the matter-of-fact statements he had uttered, neither the certainty that was in his voice." The conversation was dropped for a while, favoring small talk. Then the pilot came back with, "They want Robert Kennedy real bad."

"What for?"

He said, "Never mind. You don't need to know. Let's get this job done, time is running out. My boss wants to return to Florida: he thought we would be through today. I told him we would be finished tomorrow by early afternoon." Tomorrow was November 22, 1963.

Nothing else was said. We just worked late to finish our job.

Friday, November 22 was just as usual. We were buttoning up the inspection plates and latching the engine cowling and so forth, making ready to fuel up for flight. We were about complete with the plane except for fuel, when there was a lot of commotion going on in the terminal area. I noticed a friend of mine, a Texas Ranger captain, leaving the terminal area extremely fast. I made for the terminal, and was stopped by a friend in his car. He said, "Had I heard?" "Had I heard what?" I replied. "The President has been shot."

I just froze. I did not know what to say. I just listened to the radio until they announced his death, even though I knew he wouldn't make it from reports that were being broadcast. I was deeply saddened, but at the same time I sensed fear. By the time I walked back to the plane, the pilot had already fueled up, and he was in the process of loading up personal things, like baggage. I helped him load a few cases of oil to the baggage compartment.

I did not know how to handle the situation. I knew the pilot was not involved because he was with me. Then I could not help myself: I had to ask him if he knew what had happened. He told me the man on the fuel truck had said what had happened. There was a long pause, a sadness in the air, then he said, "It's all going to happen just like I told you."

We talked a few moments about the plane and its condition. My day was wrecked. I just wanted to go home to watch the television reports. I asked the pilot if there was anything else I could do. I shook his hand experiencing a mixture of friendship, confusion, and fear at the same time. I asked him were they leaving today, and the pilot replied, "Whenever the boss is ready."

Many thoughts ran through my mind. The day I was told all those things I did not believe what I was hearing. The next day I believed. I mentioned nothing of this except to my business partner. I didn't know if this incident had anything to do with anything. At times, my imagination would focus on certain facts, like the timing of the sale and the need for so many passenger seats. Maybe there were several agents that needed private transportation. How did this pilot know so much? Was he really involved and me so stupid? Did his boss's connection with the U.S. Air Force mean anything? Why was the make ready date for the plane so important? Why wouldn't this pilot go to the restaurant to eat? Where was the pilot's boss all the time? Why did the boss and his pilot not visit one another at any time they were here? And on and on.

It's tough, when you don't have anyone you can talk to about this for thirty years. Maybe I'm wrong, but it has certainly struck me with fear.

There is little doubt this DC3 flew out of Red Bird Airfield on Friday afternoon with the complete team that had murdered the president. It took them to safety, under the security accorded the CIA. I made enquiries about planes leaving Red Bird Airfield on the afternoon of November 22, and this plane was not logged out, another indication it was then under the auspices of the CIA. It would seem to me to be logical that the plane went to Houston, where it would have total CIA security. I can see how Dave Ferrie's few days' mystery trip at the time of the assassination—details of which came out of Jim Garrison's New Orleans prosecution—dovetails with this, with him likely piloting the plane from Houston to its ultimate destination, wherever that was to be. Ferrie did not drive hundreds of miles in a thunderstorm from New Orleans to Houston to ice skate, as he purported.

On hearing the Douglas DC3 story, I began my investigations, helped by January. He had the number of the plane, which was N-17888. At my request, he took this to the Federal Aviation Authority (FAA), asking for the details of the new ownership. FAA officials returned to say the number belonged to a plane totally different from a DC3, which was not a good start. "They said no such plane existed," said January. I asked him to press them and tell them they were wrong. He was told the answers lay in parcels of old documents in storage, examination of which would cost. He agreed to pay, and, after many phone calls, the FAA returned to confirm the number had originally belonged to a Douglas DC3, having later been transferred to another aircraft.

I next needed the advice of L. Fletcher Prouty, a retired U.S. Air

Force colonel who had been the Pentagon's liaison with the CIA. I asked him how often numbers were changed on aircraft and he told me never, except by the CIA.

I then awaited the results of the search January was carrying out for me with the FAA. It proved the plane had been bought by the Houston Air Center. The difficulty in establishing the buyer's details were complicated by the fact that aircraft companies did not enjoy paying taxes, and taxes due on the purchase of an aircraft if not paid immediately became due when the plane was resold. Having established the company that bought the DC3, I contacted a former CIA agent in Houston and asked him to check the Houston Air Center out. He eventually reported that it was a front for the CIA. I pursued it a little further before I realized I had gone as far as was necessary to establish the complicity of the CIA Bay of Pigs survivors in the president's murder. Take note: This did not involve the CIA per se. The Bay of Pigs survivors became a group of renegades, and they are the ones who were involved in the president's murder.

× × ×

Because January's evidence was of such importance, it was vital that I obtained a "second opinion." Not that I had any doubts, but if I was unable to publish my informant's name—as was the case in my first, guarded versions of this evidence—I had to provide a guarantee to my readers that what I published was genuine and reliable. I asked January if he would agree to be interviewed by Mary Ferrell, perhaps the most knowledgeable and discerning of all of the leading researchers. He agreed and a meeting was arranged. Afterward, Ferrell told me she had believed early on that January had evidence that he had never provided. She confirmed to me that I might rely on all he had told me.

× × ×

I confess to being slow in fully realizing the importance of the evidence I had acquired. I saw the implications at once, but it took time for me to appreciate the overall significance in what I had learned. I finally saw the complete picture in which the murder of Marilyn Monroe advertised itself as the first attempt on the part of the renegades to set Robert F. Kennedy up to take the blame for her death. Since he was innocent, they did not hope for him to be accused of the murder. It would have been enough for Kennedy, the U.S. attorney general, to be openly questioned by the police for their plan to succeed. Such an interrogation would have made public the affair he had conducted with Monroe, and would have led to the exposure that John F. Kennedy had also had a relationship with her. The attorney general's resignation would have been sought the day after a public denunciation, and the president's the following day. Thereafter, the Kennedy name would have been enough to prevent any member of the family from reaching the White House for generations to come.

But Police Chief William Parker, it appears, had a clear picture of what was happening, no doubt with the full details of the true events surrounding Monroe's death to support it. The cover-up was then successfully put in place to protect the Kennedys, but it did nothing to protect Monroe from the stigma of suicide that was placed on her.

All in all, I now had a clear picture of where we had come from and where we were going. It became clear that having failed by murder and intrigue to remove the Kennedys from power, they went on to join forces with certain Establishment members who saw the Kennedys as an enormous threat to their well-being and justified their hostility by fancifully identifying them as enemies of the United States. Without recognizing them, the renegades were those I had perceived long ago in a different context and from a totally different angle, collaborating with Establishment members to kill President Kennedy. I could hear those sad members of the Establishment, suffering from the greatest of all delusions, saying, "We will do this for the good of the country."

But not long after the president was dead, Robert Kennedy was making plans to follow in his footsteps.

Senator Robert F. Kennedy

CHAPTER 23

The Candidate

A Star for every State, and a State for every Star.
—Robert Charles Winthrop

ROBERT F. KENNEDY was certainly a star. Four years after the murder of John F. Kennedy he found himself, for the first time, outside of the shadow of his lamented brother. He had emerged as Robert F. Kennedy, not the brother of the late president, but a seasoned campaigner in the fight to get out of Vietnam and the defender of those minorities needing help and protection. He had fought and won the battle for the U.S. Senate, representing New York, and was now faced with encouragement to throw his hat into the ring as a contender for the presidency. The 1972 election would be soon enough, he reckoned, though it was felt he should drive home his feelings about the Vietnam War and run against Lyndon B. Johnson in 1968, an idea that was, at the outset, unthinkable to him. It goes without saying he was also blissfully unaware of the commitment of the CIA-Establishment alliance to make him their next target if he succeeded in winning the Democratic nomination.

However, his friend, Jack Newfield, writing in the influential *Village Voice,* said, "If Kennedy does not run in 1968, the best side of his character will die. He will kill it every time he butchers his conscience and makes a speech for Johnson next autumn. It will die every time a kid asks him, if he is so much against the Vietnam war, how come he is putting party above principle? It will die every time a stranger quotes his own words back to him on the value of courage."

This was not an easy issue for Kennedy, but he had by now seen Senator Eugene McCarthy of Minnesota engaging in battle with Johnson, with a following he would have expected as his own lining up behind the senator. He felt unable to support McCarthy, however, and he certainly could not have stood behind Johnson and the Vietnam War. He was between a rock and a hard place. On the one hand, he did not want to be seen as opposing Johnson out of spite. On the other hand, he was not enamored with the idea of splitting the party. His participation would have split the party three ways. To make matters worse, a valued advisor wrote Kennedy, "Your plunging in might be an act of conscience to some people. But it would likely also be political suicide for you." Regardless, his apprehension over a Johnson victory did not diminish.

Students at Brooklyn College had a finger on the pulse when they displayed a placard in front of Kennedy proclaiming: BOBBY KENNEDY, HAWK, DOVE OR CHICKEN? His potential support was already deserting him. He had to make up his mind. It was now or never as far as 1968 was concerned, and perhaps now or never for all time. One important statistic in the dilemma Kennedy faced was that the huge number of troops in Vietnam in 1964 was 23,000, and by 1967 it had risen, unbelievably, to twenty times that number. He was also anxious that Robert McNamara, a restraining influence in the White House, had been sacked and replaced by Clark Gifford, undoubtedly a hawk. Henry Kissinger was heard saying he had "a conviction that LBJ's resistance to negotiation verges on a sort of madness." Kennedy made a speech in which he gave voice to a growing anxiety in the United States over the legitimacy of the Vietnam War, concern for the massive loss of life in the conflict, and the demoralizing effect on the United States. He said:

Now we're saying we're going to fight there so that we don't have to fight in Thailand, so that we don't have to fight on the west coast of the United States, so that they won't move across the Rockies. . . . Maybe [the people of South Vietnam] don't want it, but we want it, so we're going in there and we're killing South Vietnamese, we're killing children, we're killing women, we're killing innocent people . . . because [the communists are] 12,000 miles away, and they might get to be 11,000 miles away.

Kennedy questioned the right of the United States to kill tens of thousands, including women and children, and make millions refugees. He continued:

Those of us [at home] we must feel it when we use napalm. . . . This is also our responsibility. . . . The picture last week of a paratrooper holding a rifle to a woman's head, it must trouble us more than it does. . . .

We love our country. . . . It is not just the land, it is not just the mountains, it is what this country stands for. And that is what I think is being seriously undermined in Vietnam.

The American people had gone through a phase in which they supported the war in Vietnam, then they began to have doubts but were prepared to tolerate it. For many, the doubts had increased and had become intolerable, and for some it had become a burden they could not live with. The sentiments being expressed by Kennedy were by now receiving growing acceptance, particularly among young intellectuals. Kennedy saw huge dangers in Johnson being elected to a second term. But his misgivings about splitting the Democrats, and his reluctance to be seen in opposition to Johnson were imponderables. He saw McCarthy developing his campaign, the campaign he knew should have been his, and yet he did not see McCarthy becoming the force to oust Johnson that would be needed. And all things being considered, not too far back in his mind, he could not face the prospect of being called on to endorse Johnson's bid for another term that he believed would be disastrous for the United States.

Not to mention, he knew that if he did so he would have faced being found politically dead in the water.

Kennedy finally made up his mind to run for the presidency when news broke of the Tet offensive, in which the North Vietnamese in a bold offensive had devastated thirty cities in South Vietnam and arrived at the gates of the U.S. embassy in Saigon. The Pentagon wanted to dispatch a further 200,000 troops to the war. He declared his candidacy and threw himself into an intensive campaign that marked him out as the leading peace candidate. Misquoting *The American Scholar*, he wrote to a friend, "They did not yet see, and thousands of young men as hopeful, now crowding to the barriers of their careers, did not yet see if a single man plant himself on his convictions and then abide, the huge world will come round to him."

To those who criticized him for belatedly entering the presidential race, he was able, in justification, to point out that the party had already been split by McCarthy and that the risk of a personality struggle with Johnson was a risk he now found he could not avoid.

His campaign was sparkling and energetic. The dynamism and exuberance displayed by the candidate and those who worked with him were reflected in the sheer enthusiasm that bred even more enthusiasm. It was catching. It not only could be felt; those involved said it could also be touched. This was the moment Kennedy stepped out of his brother's shadow. Above all, it was his message that brought him supporters in droves. He was compassionate, warm, and sincere. His listeners found him irresistible and compelling. And the main plank in his platform, peace in Vietnam, was by no means the only attraction to the people. People who were victims of the "system" were high on his list of those he wanted to help. Puerto Ricans, Indians, Mexican immigrants, and blacks were his concern, and the poor of America were not to be overlooked.

As his campaign grew, and the number of states in which he spoke grew, it was a speech in California that crowned his success. There, he said:

Our brave young men are dying in the swamps of South-East Asia. Which of them might have written a poem? Which of them might have cured cancer? Which of them might have played in a World Series or given us the gift of laughter from the stage or helped build a bridge or a university? Which of them would have taught a child to read? It is our responsibility to let these men live. . . . It is indecent if they die because of the empty vanity of their country.

The people were ecstatic. Here was someone who put their thoughts into words. Before he could get away, they mobbed him: they cheered, they pulled at his hair, they scratched his face and hands, and they stole his cuff links. He acknowledged this with the understatement, "I'm beginning to feel the mood of the country and what they want." He now knew he talked the language of the ordinary American.

None of the contenders were ready for the shattering announcement that came on March 31, 1968. Johnson told the nation he would not be running for reelection. He privately said he "could not function" under the strain of daily attacks by his Republican opponent, Richard Nixon, and those who were opposing his reelection in his own party, especially McCarthy and Kennedy. Others, however, spoke of the deterioration in his health, including his mental health. In an interview with the author Doris Kearns Goodwin, he confided a recurring nightmare:

I was being forced over the edge by rioting blacks, demonstrating students, marching welfare mothers, squawking professors, and hysterical reporters. And then the final straw. The thing I feared from the first day of my Presidency was actually coming true. Robert Kennedy had openly announced his intention to reclaim the throne in the memory of his brother. And the American people, swayed by the magic of the name, were dancing in the streets.

He also spoke of another nightmare he experienced, "I would see myself tied to the ground in the middle of a long open space. In the distance, I could hear the voices of thousands of people. They were all shouting at me and running toward me: 'Coward! Traitor! Weakling!' "

Johnson's identification of Kennedy as "the enemy," Kearns Goodwin believed, hardened his determination not to let up in Vietnam. It was not until the end of his term that negotiations even found a place among his options.

Johnson's decision not to seek reelection had a profound effect on the fight between Kennedy and McCarthy. Their sniping at Johnson quickly became sniping at each other. McCarthy pitched his appeal to the American middle class, while Kennedy turned to the poor and underprivileged.

It was at this time that Kennedy found an ally in Martin Luther King Jr. King was opposed to the war in Vietnam and he and Kennedy more and more found themselves in harmony over the issues to which they were both committed. The "Poor People's Campaign" was Kennedy's, but it was the support it received from King that enlivened and invigorated it. Washington was targeted by vast numbers of the poor who marched through its streets to seek support from Congress.

Kennedy was designated to speak to the black poor in Indiana. Boarding his plane for Indianapolis, he received, ahead of the media, news that King had been shot, and when he arrived at his destination, the news was even graver: King was dead. The huge numbers involved in the march on Washington seemed to be the provocation for his murder. It appeared the Establishment was unnerved by this powerful maneuver. Against advice, Kennedy took the news to the black ghetto at Indianapolis himself. He climbed onto the back of a truck to speak to the people, "I have some bad news for you, for all of our fellow citizens, and people who love peace all over the world, and that is that Martin Luther King was shot and killed tonight."

His listeners were devastated. They could scarcely believe the news. Kennedy continued:

Martin Luther King dedicated his life to love and to justice for his fellow human beings, and he died because of that effort.

In this difficult day, in this difficult time for the United States, it is perhaps well to ask what kind of a nation we are and what direction we want to move in. . . . Considering the evidence there evidently is that there were white people responsible . . . you can be filled with bitterness, with hatred and a desire for revenge. . . . Black people among black, white people among white, filled with hatred toward one another.

Or we can make an effort, as Martin Luther King did, to understand and to comprehend, and to replace that violence, that stain of bloodshed that has spread across our land, with an effort to understand with compassion and love. For those of you who are black and are tempted to be filled with hatred and distrust at the injustice of such an act, against all white people, I can only say that I feel in my own heart the same kind of feeling. I had a member of my family killed, but he was killed by a white man. . . .

We've had difficult times in the past. We will have difficult times in the future. It is not the end of violence; it is not the end of lawlessness; it is not the end of disorder.

But the vast majority of white people and the vast majority of black people in this country want to live together, want to improve the quality of our life, and want justice for all human beings who abide in our land.

What we need in the United States is not division . . . not hatred . . . not violence or lawlessness, but love and wisdom, and compassion towards one another. . . . Let us dedicate ourselves to that, and say a prayer for our country and for our people.

When King died, Kennedy lost a powerful supporter. Kennedy firmly believed King would have declared for him. But, with the other minorities in the makeup of the American people, the cause of the blacks was undoubtedly Kennedy's cause. Late for a meeting with black militants, the group was unhappy with him, "Our leader is dead tonight, and when we need you we can't find you." Found in Kennedy's words to them that night are some that were not written by his speechwriter. They were his own. He said, "Yes, you lost a friend, I lost a brother, I know how you feel. . . . You talk about the Establishment. I have to laugh. Big business is trying to defeat me because they think I am a friend of the Negro."

In these personal remarks, Kennedy might almost have been revealing a knowledge of the powers set up to remove him if he got too close to the White House. He won the support of those in the group listening to him, but Arthur M. Schlesinger Jr., in his biography of Kennedy, said later, "Kennedy seemed overwhelmed, despondent, fatalistic. Thinking of Dallas, perhaps." Dallas was likely never far from his mind.

King's death sparked riots in over 100 U.S. cities. Thirty-nine people died and 25,000 were injured. Both the National Guard and federal troops were called out, and Washington itself was placed under curfew. King's funeral was well attended by white dignitaries, including McCarthy and Kennedy. Meanwhile, Britain's Roy Jenkins, a prominent politician asked where President Johnson was.

The campaign trail took Kennedy to the Indiana Medical School, where he condemned the failing health system. When he was asked where the money was to come from to finance his new proposals for a realistic health program, he did not spare his listeners:

> From you. . . . I look around this room and I don't see many black faces who will become doctors. You can talk about where the money will come from. . . . Part of civilized society is to let people go to medical school who come from ghettos. . . . You are the privileged ones. . . . It's our society, not just the government, that spends twice as much on pets as on the poverty program. It's the poor that carry the major burden in Vietnam. You sit here as white medical students, while black people carry the burden of fighting in Vietnam.

After Johnson's decision not to run for reelection, Vice President Hubert Humphrey, late in the day, joined battle with McCarthy and Kennedy for the Democratic nomination. The three-way contest in Indiana, however, was a great victory for Kennedy. He also took

Nebraska, South Dakota, and the District of Columbia. David Broder, who wrote of Kennedy's first appearances in Indiana in the *Washington Post*, said, "Kennedy's manner—the nervous, self-deprecating jokes; the trembling hands on the lectern; the staccato alternations of speech and silence; the sudden shifts of mood—all seem to betray an anticipation of hostility from the crowds." Broder did not understand how the American public perceived him, however. To them he appeared the honest politician, understandably nervous, and appreciative of the support his audience gave him.

Another *Washington Post* writer, Richard Harwood, at first a leading skeptic of Kennedy, fell victim to an unsettling change in his attitude to the senator from New York. He encountered something—with other reporters—listening to the candidate in Nebraska that threw the Broder image of an uncertain Kennedy into sharp relief. He wrote retrospectively, "We discovered in 1968 this deep, almost mystical bond that existed between Robert Kennedy and the Other America. It was a disquieting experience. . . . We were forced to recognize in [Nebraska] that the real stake in the American political process involved not the fate of speech-writers and fund-raisers but the lives of millions of people seeking hope out of despair."

The radical Paul Cowan said Kennedy was "the last liberal politician who could communicate with white working class America." The Reverend Hector Lopez, a community adviser, did not agree entirely with this. After the experience of a meeting Kennedy held in Oakland, where members of the Black Panther movement attended, he said Kennedy would not have liked being labeled the last of the great liberals. "I know he wouldn't," he said. "I guess I'd have to say he was 'the last of the great believables.' "

The whistle-stop that took Kennedy to San Francisco, San Diego, and Sacramento, California, brought him ever closer to his grand finale in Los Angeles. By now, the campaign had, as Charles Quinn in the *Stein Papers* put it, become a "huge, joyous adventure." Kennedy's support was still increasing. He was on a rising tide of popularity as he neared the City of Angels, where he would learn whether he had secured the last—and biggest—of the primaries. He was now the most seasoned of campaigners, and his personality was magnetic; he was bringing to the electorate what it sought most: A figure to unite the nation, with the poor and down-trodden, the blacks, and all other minority groups—the sick, the disabled, and the unemployed—featured in a presidential election manifesto as they had never featured before.

The Kennedy family had differing attitudes toward Robert as a presidential candidate. His wife, Ethel, was enthusiastic about it. Edward, asked if he had ideas about what Jack would have thought, replied, "I'm not so sure about that." Then he added, "But I know what Dad would have said . . . don't do it." Afterward, he said, "Jack would probably have cautioned him against it, but he might have done it himself." It was Jacqueline Kennedy who was prophet-ically morbid about it. "Do you know what I think will happen to Bobby? . . . The same thing that happened to Jack."

And outside of the family members of the press were also weigh-ing the pros and cons. One asked whether Kennedy had the stuff to go all the way. *Newsweek*'s John J. Lindsay gave the reply, "Of course he has the stuff to go all the way, but he's not going to go all the way. . . . Somebody is going to shoot him. . . . He's out there now waiting for him."

CHAPTER 24

Murder at the Ambassador Hotel

It is like writing history with lightning. And my only regret is that it is all so terribly true.

—Woodrow Wilson

EIGHTEEN HUNDRED PEOPLE crowded into the ballroom of the Ambassador Hotel in Los Angeles to hear the announcement that Robert F. Kennedy had won this all-important primary, becoming the front runner in the fight for the Democratic presidential nomination. It was not greeted by a collective sigh of relief: this result was expected by Kennedy's buoyant supporters. It was a cry of jubilation that echoed through the length and breadth of the hotel. Kennedy stepped forward on the ballroom stage to thank those who had helped him to achieve this great success, "Thank you very much. . . . You can't hear . . . [the sound system was having trouble coping with the noise of the crowd]. Can we get something that works? Just one moment. . . . I want to first express my high regards to Don Drysdale, who pitched his sixth straight shutout tonight and I hope we have as good fortune in our campaign."

He joked in the manner his brother had joked at that last breakfast in the Texas Hotel at Fort Worth before his tragic visit to Dallas, and everybody laughed. He thanked those who had wrought this great success for him, then their boisterousness simmered down as he began to speak seriously to them. He ended his speech by saying, "The division, the violence, the disenchantment with our society; the divisions, whether its between blacks and whites, between the poor and the more affluent, or between age groups or on the war in Vietnam, is that we can start to work together. We are a great country, an unselfish country, and a compassionate country. I intend to make that my basis for running."

He gave the victory sign, and when the cheering began to subside he added, "My thanks to all of you and now it's on to Chicago and let's win there."

There was a carnival atmosphere in the huge ballroom. The smiles were broad and there was a sense of enormous satisfaction. Those present were now determined to make it a night to remember, and the fun began. Kennedy wanted, most of all, to rest, but he had one more obligation before he could do so. He had to speak to the reporters who were gathered in a room waiting for him. To reach it he took the shortest possible route, through the kitchen pantry.

The pantry was, by pantry standards, fairly spacious. It was long and each side was lined with kitchen equipment. As Kennedy made his way through it, crowds of people engulfed him, a seething mass of well-wishers. They surrounded him to such an extent that he could hardly walk. He paused here and there to shake the hands of hotel staff even though he must have been totally exhausted. Noticeably, the senator was not surrounded by security staff. He had forbidden this. His former FBI friend, Bill Barry, who had taken leave of absence from his post as the vice president of a bank, was his lone protector, and even he was there under protest. Kennedy refused to be shadowed by "heavies." During the campaign, Barry had quietly engaged off-duty policemen to occupy the lobby of a hotel in which Kennedy was staying, but they were promptly dismissed when Kennedy found out. Barry said, "He only accepted as much protection as he got because he liked me. . . . He wouldn't have had anybody if really left to his own choice." In fact, he had only Barry. The hotel had its own security staff, hired that night from the Ace Guard Service. As Kennedy slowly pressed his way through the pantry area, Thane Eugene Cesar, an Ace security man, clutched the senator's arm, no doubt to his annoyance.

One fleeting shadow was that of fifteen-year-old Scott Enyart, who, with his new professional-quality camera that his dad had bought for him, had taken pictures while Kennedy made his speech, and was now following Kennedy through the pantry snapping away, jumping on top of the tables to get a better view. He was right there when the senator turned to his front again to continue his journey, and it was then that someone shouted, "Kennedy, you son of a bitch," and opened fire on him with a snub-nosed pistol.

Those who saw the gunman said he was smiling and had a peaceful look on his face. He was of medium build and had a Middle Eastern appearance, and had been seen hanging around farther down the pantry before leaping forward with his gun blazing. People screamed and shouted. The gun held eight bullets and, despite the strenuous efforts of the powerfully built Karl Uecker, the hotel's assistant maître d', who wrestled the gunman's arm to a nearby steam table, he fought like a man possessed and continued shooting until the chamber was empty.

By now, Kennedy was lying on the floor in a pool of blood. A hotel employee, the busboy Juan Romero, whose hand had been shaken by Kennedy only moments before, knelt by the senator's side, comforting him and gently cradling his head. Kennedy asked, "Is everybody all right?" Even though the pantry was packed with over seventy people, Daniel Curtin pushed through the crowd in spite of the commotion and passed rosary beads to Romero for the senator. "Come on Mr. Kennedy. You can make it," Romero said gently. Ethel, the senator's wife, was soon at his side, and he said, "Oh, Ethel, Ethel, am I all right?" Later, he asked her, "Am I going to die?"

Others had also been shot. Paul Schrade, Kennedy's friend, had been shot in the forehead; Continental News Service's Ira Goldstein had been wounded in the buttock; Irwin Stroll had caught one in his left leg; William Weisel, of the American Broadcasting Company, was shot in his abdomen; and a deflected bullet hit Elizabeth Evans, a political supporter, in the head. Kennedy had been shot three times, with a fourth bullet passing through his jacket shoulder pad. Seventeen minutes later, the injured were taken by ambulance to the

Central Receiving Hospital. Shortly after arriving at the hospital, Senator Kennedy was quickly rerouted to the Good Samaritan Hospital because he required brain surgery. He arrived there at 1:00 A.M., three-quarters of an hour after the shooting. The doctors directed him to an operating room, where they began a three-hour operation to try and save him.

Police Chief Tom Reddin was quickly informed of events, and back at the Ambassador Hotel the police officers and FBI agents had quickly descended on the place. An investigation began at once. Soon, the place was awash with officers as every available man was sent there. The gunman was quickly arrested and his questioning began immediately. He refused to cooperate with the police. He would neither give his name nor answer their questions. His appearance gave cause for concern. His eyes were peaceful and he continued to smile. He looked as though he might have been in a trance. He was elsewhere; his body may have been shooting at Senator Kennedy in the pantry at the Ambassador Hotel, but it seemed his mind was absent. At one point while being questioned, he became somewhat incoherent: he had no memory of his attack on the senator.

Those who had noticed him in various parts of the hotel said he was in the company of a couple, a man and a woman, which would suggest the shooting had been the outcome of a conspiracy. The Los Angeles Police Department (LAPD) showed its hand when it declared its investigation would be thorough *since it was determined Los Angeles would not become another Dallas*. Very much like Dallas, however, from the beginning the LAPD set its face against any assertion there had been a conspiracy, even when its investigators were tripping over clear indications that a conspiracy had taken place. If resisting such evidence was the LAPD's priority rather than hunting down whoever had shot Kennedy, it would explain a great deal. The investigation was curious to say the least.

DeWayne Wolfer, the LAPD's forensic expert, began working out the bullet trajectories. He accounted for all eight bullets from the shooter's gun and produced a "map" showing where all the bullets went. This involved examining the walls and woodwork for bullet marks and holes, and his end product earned him full marks from the police department. Individuals were interviewed through the night and, after the crowds had all gone home, the pantry was examined from stem to stern.

The shooting of Senator Kennedy became a case of murder at 1:44 on the afternoon of June 6, 1968, although hopes for his recovery had been abandoned at about 6:30 that morning. When the surgery the doctors carried out on him was over, they had not achieved what they had hoped to achieve. He was wheeled to the hospital's intensive care unit where hospital staff cared for him as well as they could. They had tried to the best of their abilities to restore the senator, but his injuries were such that even if he had survived he could no longer have been a presidential candidate much less a senator. Some might have said that he would no longer have been a man.

During the morning, and well after surgery had been abandoned on Senator Kennedy, the face of the gunman was shown on television and in newspapers. He was recognized by his two brothers, who immediately went to the police. He was identified as Sirhan Bishara Sirhan, who had been born in Jerusalem and, with his family, had survived the trauma and tragedy of having become a refugee in Israeli-held territory. The police declared it open and shut. There was only one gunman and he was now in custody. The case was wrapped up.

CHAPTER 25

The Case for Conspiracy

*Who controls the past controls the future: who controls
the present controls the past.*

—George Orwell, *Nineteen Eighty-Four*

IT DID NOT matter what was dug out of the woodwork, either actually or metaphorically. Anything shown to be in contradiction to
the official version of events was unacceptable. Where have we
heard that before? Even when it was FBI agents digging additional
bullets out of the woodwork it was unacceptable. An FBI agent told
me personally he *knows* there were more bullets fired in the Ambassador pantry than were accounted for by the DeWayne Wolfer
"map," but it did not register with the LAPD. It was switched off.

William Bailey, now retired from the FBI and a college lecturer,
told me he witnessed the existence of two bullet holes in the center
door divider. According to Bailey, many other people examined them
also, news reporters, photographers, and hotel staff among them.
They were conspicuous by their absence from Wolfer's trajectory
"map." Even the coroner Dr. Thomas Noguchi who had conducted
the autopsy on Marilyn Monroe, witnessed the existence of the two
bullet holes in the door frame and was photographed pointing to
them. Another photograph featured police officers, Robert Rozzi
and Charles Wright, bending down to examine another hole in the
door frame about eighteen inches from the floor. The caption to this
Associated Press photograph stated the two officers were examining a bullet hole.

Photographs of four holes marked "bullet holes" were taken and later released by the FBI and a different group of four holes was shown circled in chalk in a LAPD photo in which one hole had been labeled "bullet hole." The label had been ascribed by an FBI agent, though the chalk marks were apparently the work of Officer W. Tew, of the sheriff's office, whose chalked up name also appeared in the photograph. In his conversation with me, Bailey did not discount the existence of other bullet holes in the various parts of the pantry, but those he personally witnessed took the total beyond the eight-bullet capacity of Sirhan Bishera Sirhan's gun. The discovery of a ninth bullet hole should have been enough to constitute grounds for recognizing that a conspiracy had taken place, and to ignore it represented a blatant refusal on the part of the LAPD to accept the facts.

Sirhan's companions proved to be another example of the LAPD being switched off. The male companion was ignored, and the woman, who was described by several witnesses as wearing a polka-dot dress, provoked little interest. But the witness evidence of the existence of the two was unchallengeable. The LAPD, however, went to extraordinary lengths to resist the notion that Sirhan had two companions, or even one, for that matter. The three had been seen in the ballroom during the evening, though they left at some point and re-entered at about 11:30 P.M. Sandra Serrano had opened a door to a fire escape exit and had taken a seat on the stairs to get some air. While she was sitting there, Sirhan, with the attractive woman and tall man, dashed up the stairs to get in through the door Serrano had left open. The woman asked to be excused as she squeezed past Serrano.

Susan Locke witnessed the presence of the woman in the polka-dot dress in the hotel ballroom, when she took particular note the woman did not wear a badge authorizing her presence at the event. Booker Griffin saw the woman with Sirhan and described her as wearing a dress that was mainly white and maybe another color. In fact, Griffin recalled seeing the woman three times in the ballroom. The first time he saw her she was with Sirhan, the second time she was with Sirhan and the tall man, and the third time she was with the tall man but not Sirhan. He recalled they looked miserable, which was extremely noticeable amid a happy, exuberant gathering. Griffin was later interviewed for television and made no secret of what he had seen.

Sirhan and the woman in the polka-dot dress were also seen together in the bar by the witness Lonny L. Worthy, though before the shooting they drifted to the pantry area, where they drank coffee. Darnell Johnson, who entered the pantry in advance of the senator, saw five persons in a group, one of which was Sirhan, another the woman in the polka-dot dress, and the tall man, who was wearing a blue jacket. In the pandemonium immediately after the shooting of Senator Kennedy, the woman in the polka-dot dress and the man in the blue jacket ran out of the pantry as others struggled to get in to see what had happened. Griffin caught sight of them and cried out, "They're getting away." Jack J. Merritt, an employee of the Ace Guard Service, saw them dashing away, and saw another man running to get away through the rear exit of the kitchen. They were not miserable now. "They seemed to be smiling," Merritt said. The witness George Green saw the tall man and woman running away, while the photographer Evan Freed saw two men and a woman— the woman possibly wearing a polka-dot dress—running to the east end exit of the kitchen pantry. Richard Houston also saw the woman in the polka-dot dress racing out to the terrace area. "We killed him," he heard her say.

Police Sergeant Paul Sharaga was driving his car close to the Ambassador Hotel when he heard a report of the shooting. He made his way there at once and, as the first supervising officer at the hotel, he began the standard procedure of setting up a command post in the car park. He was walking toward the main entrance to the hotel when he encountered the Bernsteins, who were running out in a greatly distressed state. Asked what they were running from, they told Sharaga that when they had been on the balcony, just outside the Embassy Room, they had been passed by a man and a woman in a polka-dot dress running out crying jubilantly, "We shot him! We shot him!" Mrs. Bernstein asked, "Who did you shoot?" and the woman answered, "Kennedy. We shot him. We shot him."

Serrano, in her location on the fire exit stairs, had her second look at the woman in the polka-dot dress and the tall man in the blue jacket. She had heard the bangs inside, but did not know what had happened. As the two ran past her down the stairs, presumably just before passing the Bernsteins, the woman said to Serrano, "We shot him! We shot him!" Puzzled, Serrano asked, "Who did you shoot?" Loud and clear, the answer was, "Senator Kennedy." Sergeant Sharaga had put out an APB as soon as the Bernsteins had described the couple to him, but a little later Detective Inspector John Powers asked him to withdraw it. Sharaga refused to do this but Powers canceled it anyway. There was to have been no conspiracy in the Kennedy killing.

Sergeant Sharaga had written up an account of what the Bernsteins had told him. He did this by hand and sent it by courier to headquarters. The report disappeared. Undaunted, he later dictated a complete report to Officer J. M. Steele and filed this with his watch commander, but when he later enquired about it, he was told it had not been received. It should have been collected by officers of the Special Unit Senator team, which had been set up to conduct the investigation into the shooting of Senator Kennedy. Enquiring further, he was told it had never been picked up. Fortunately, this time Sergeant Sharaga had kept a copy for himself. It was a year later that Sharaga left the LAPD, disillusioned. He had had his efficiency ratings reduced, and it was clear he had fallen from grace for pursuing the matter of the woman in the polka-dot dress and her companion. Twenty years later, he discovered he was on record for having said he had changed his mind, and that the Bernsteins' account of the woman in the polka-dot dress was a product of their hysteria. Sharaga made it clear that he made no such statement and was never interviewed by an investigating officer. He said that the report was "not based on any interview of me by any officials in the LAPD at any time. Further, it also contains false and deliberately misleading statements." It is noted that in the book he wrote, *Special Unit Senator*, published in 1970, Chief of Detectives Robert Houghton chooses not to mention Sharaga's command post at all.

The woman in the polka-dot dress was real to everyone who saw her, but the LAPD chose to disinvent her. When it could not evade the issue any further, it identified a woman it said was the woman the witnesses had all seen. She was the only one wearing a polka-dot dress that night, it asserted. She was Valeria Schulte, a blonde who was a volunteer worker. Unfortunately, she was not wearing a white dress with black dots; instead, she wore a green dress with yellow spots. Furthermore, she could not have been dashing anywhere: one of her legs was encased in a plaster cast from top to ankle and she needed a crutch to walk. The crassness of this assertion requires no serious comment.

There is evidence of careful orchestration in the movements of the woman in the polka-dot dress, which includes indications there were more than one. If the sightings of this woman were accurate, then it would seem that part of the plan was to deploy two—or even more—women wearing the same distinctive dress in a clear plan to cause confusion. It has not been overlooked that any woman wearing a polka-dot dress is crying out to be noticed. If the Ace Guard Service employee Jack J. Merritt saw a man—apart from the woman in the polka-dot dress and the man in the blue blazer—dashing in another direction, and the photographer Evan Freed saw *two* men and a woman running to the east exit, this, if Sirhan is added, accounts for the group of five persons seen by Darnell Johnson in the pantry.

× × ×

No witness was officially credited with having seen a second gunman in the pantry area at the Ambassador Hotel when Kennedy was shot. This did not mean there were none. Such evidence from

Donald Schulman will be introduced in chapter 23, which deals with the Ace Guard Service employee Thane Eugene Cesar, but he was not alone. Two women came forward and said that they clearly saw another gun in the near vicinity to Senator Kennedy, and there may well have been more. Since it was not a question the police asked of witnesses, it is hardly surprising if it was left to a very few to come forward and tell what they had seen. Lisa Urso was one of the two women who saw what happened. She said she saw a man—not in uniform—whom she assumed was a "security guard" with a gun in his hand immediately after the shooting. She described him as blond and said he was wearing a gray suit. Urso said the man was right by Senator Kennedy. She twice offered her testimony to those seeking information about the killing. On one of the two occasions, she said they did not want to know. On the second occasion, she said they were hostile to her. Urso also saw the uniformed Ace Guard Service employee Thane Eugene Cesar remove his gun from its holster and later replace it.

The second of the two women witnesses told how she saw a man she described as a Caucasian firing a gun. She said he was something over six feet tall and had dark, wavy hair. He, too, was wearing a suit, she said, and fired only once or twice before running away.

Reminiscent of the John F. Kennedy assassination, where, according to the government enquiry, only one rifle was involved, it was later revealed that there were several weapons in the Texas School Book Depository at the time the president was killed. In the case of the Robert F. Kennedy murder, there were more guns seen in the pantry area than were ever mentioned by the investigators. One is reminded of a saying by Napoléon Bonaparte, "The art of the police consists of not seeing what there is no use seeing."

In this case, it was no use to those dedicated to establishing that no conspiracy had taken place. This certainly applied to those taking statements from witnesses in the kitchen pantry at the Ambassador

Hotel. There was much that would come into the category of it being "no use seeing." The LAPD had made up its mind what had happened, regardless of what people saw.

And those unfortunate enough to have seen the wrong things were given a bad time by those investigating this event.

CHAPTER 26

Unwelcome Evidence

It is better to choose the culprits than to seek them out.
—Marcel Pagnol

BOOKER GRIFFIN WAS subjected to the rigors of police questioning as though he were a criminal. The interrogation relating to his sightings of the woman in the polka-dot dress, after a congenial television interview, must have come as a nasty shock. Investigators demanded ultrascrupulous accuracy and, when not satisfied, completely threw out his evidence. Their treatment of Griffin made it look as though they simply did not want to know what he had to say. They said he had likely seen Judy Royer, who worked for Senator Robert F. Kennedy, talking to Sirhan Bishara Sirhan, then "mentally projected" the image of Royer to the fleeing woman in the polka-dot dress. Griffin did not know what to think, but the attempt to discredit him was followed by an assertion that made him angry. In a similar experience to that of Police Sergeant Paul Sharaga, in 1988 he read a document released by the police asserting that he stated he had lied to them about the woman in the polka-dot dress. Griffin denied that any such statement had ever been made by him and he confirmed the details of what he had seen. "I know what I saw," was his answer to the police who tried to dispose of his evidence. He recounted he had suggested that he be given a polygraph lie detector test, which the police said was unreliable.

However, it was not unreliable in the case of two other polka-dot

woman witnesses subjected to the test who were said to have "failed."
One of these was Sandra Serrano, who had been sitting on the fire
escape steps. After being taken out to dinner by Police Sergeant
Enrique Hernandez, when try as he might he could not get her to
change her story, it was after 10:00 P.M. when he took her to headquarters for a polygraph test. When Hernandez interrogated her, his
techniques were less than professional, to say the least. He started
by disposing of her evidence before she gave it. "Okay, now, we
have statements here that obviously are incorrect," he began, and
Serrano was subjected a process nearer to torture than interview.
She repeatedly described what she had seen and time after time
Hernandez doggedly refused to accept it. He had made his mind up
and would not have it. The following is a combination of extracts
from a videotape of the interview and printed extracts of what was
said, the asterisk (*) denotes points where Serrano protested in the
background:

Hernandez: I think you owe it to Senator Kennedy—the late
   Senator Kennedy—to come forward and be a woman about
   this. If he—and you don't know whether he is a witness right
   now in this room watching what we are doing in here—don't
   shame his death by keeping this thing up. I have compassion
   for you. I wanna know why, I wanna know why you did what
   you did. This is a very serious thing.

Serrano: I seen [sic] those people.

Hernandez: No, no, no, no, Sandy. Remember what I told you
   about it? You can't say that you saw something. . . .

Serrano: Well I don't feel that I am doing anything wrong. . . . I
   remember seeing the girl!

Hernandez: No. I am talking about what you have told here
   about seeing a person tell you, "We have shot Kennedy." And
   that's wrong.

Serrano: That's what she said. [*Garbled*]

Hernandez: Sandy, look:* I can, I can explain this to the [investi-
   gators] and you won't have to talk to them and they won't

come to you. I can do this. But please, in the name of Kennedy. . . .

Serrano: [Don't say in the] name of Kennedy. . . .

Hernandez: [*Garbled*]

Serrano: I remember seeing the girl.

Hernandez: [*Garbled*] . . . brushing it off with a smirk on your face, with a smile, when you know that deep inside. . . .

Serrano: I remember seeing the girl.

Hernandez: No, no. [I have in my] notebook you have told the [*garbled*] saying a person told you "[We] have shot Kennedy" and that's nonsense.

Serrano: That's what she said.

Hernandez: No it isn't, Sandy. [*Voice rises*] Please don't [*garbled*] * I love * this* man, and if you don't * change he will be [able to hear] right now and [*garbled*] he can remember it.

Serrano: Stop shouting at me.

Hernandez: Well, I'm trying not to shout. I'm sorry but this is a very emotional thing for me, too. If you love this man, the least you owe him, the least you owe him, is the courtesy of letting him rest in peace.

Serrano: I'm not gonna say nobody told me ["We shot him!"] just to satisfy anybody else.

Hernandez: This didn't happen.

Serrano: It happened.

Hernandez: No. It didn't happen. . . . Nobody told you, "We shot him!"

Serrano: Yes.

Hernandez: No.

Serrano: I'm sorry but that's true. That is true. . . .

Hernandez: [*Garbled*] . . . bad for the heart. . . . This is gonna make an old woman out of you before your time . . . something that's a deep wound that will grow with you like a disease—like a cancer.

Serrano: The results of this test [the polygraph], how far will they go?

Hernandez: Just between you and me.

Serrano: I don't want any of this stuff made public.

Hernandez: We're not dealing with publicity.

It is interesting to note how precisely Serrano described the woman in the polka-dot dress to the FBI. She said the woman was "a white female, 23 to 27 years of age, 5ft 6in tall, of medium build, 125 pounds. She had dark brown hair, ear length and wore a white voile cloth dress with black quarter-inch polka dots. The dots were about one and a half inches to two inches apart. This dress had three-quarter length sleeves, a bib collar with a small black bow, and was A-lined. [She] wore black shoes and [had] no purse.

Serrano also commented on the shape of the woman's nose, which she said was like Bob Hope's.

For between forty and fifty minutes Serrano was subjected to Hernandez's intense harassment. He suggested to her that she had picked up the description of the "girl in the polka-dot dress" from Thomas Vincent DiPierro, a college student who was working part time as a hotel employee and who had also supposedly seen the woman. When interviewing DiPierro, Hernandez suggested he had picked up the description from Serrano. Serrano finally yielded under the pressure and conceded she got the description of the woman from DiPierro, and Hernandez accepted that as victory. To return to facts and reality, however, Serrano and DiPierro did not meet at the Ambassador Hotel that night. About an hour after the senator was shot, Serrano was collared to be interviewed by Sander Vanocur on NBC television. DiPierro was also interviewed and they met for the first time after the transmission. Another vital point is that, criticized for not speaking up before this about the three who ran past her up the fire escape steps to get into the Embassy Room, it was not until Serrano saw pictures of Sirhan on that program that she recognized him as the man with the woman in the polka-dot dress and her other companion.

Lieutenant Manny Pena, who oversaw all that happened in the investigation, was asked about Hernandez's treatment of Serrano.

"That's just interrogating," he said. "I don't see anything wrong with those words to draw out compassion. It's an interrogative technique." Of Serrano, he said, "She was a young kid, and she was projected into a national limelight. . . . She was a real celebrity. . . . It was very difficult for her to say, 'Well, I'm mistaken.' " He went on to say he still thought he was correct in dropping further enquiries into "the girl in the polka-dot dress."

The tailpiece to these witness interviews reflects no credit on the LAPD investigation. Serrano gave up her job as a keypunch operator and fled back to her mother's home in Ohio to escape the attention that she could no longer bear. So much for Pena's assertions that she was enjoying the whole thing. It was all of twenty years afterward that the documents relevant to the case were released to the public, and with them was a box of videotapes that, almost certainly, was released in error. Included was the tape of Hernandez tormenting Serrano. Serrano was sought out to ask what had gone on and she said, "I was just twenty years old and I became unglued. . . . I said what they wanted me to say." As to the honesty of what was in the videotaped interview, she asserted that what she had said in her original statement was true.

Because he was an eyewitness, DiPierro was required to give evidence before a grand jury a few days after the shooting, and as a consequence Sirhan was indicted. Here, he mentioned the woman in the polka-dot dress, which drew much public attention. What bothered Hernandez was whether DiPierro would rehearse what he had said in the grand jury all over again at Sirhan's trial. He finally persuaded DiPierro that he did not see the woman in the polka-dot dress standing next to Sirhan and talking to him as he had previously stated and that he had confused this with a sighting of Valeria Schulte, the woman with the cast on her leg. DiPierro caved in to Hernandez and withdrew further reference to what he had seen of the woman.

The description of the woman in the polka-dot dress given to the grand jury by DiPierro, while masculine, was accurate and very interesting. He said it was the woman he noticed first talking to this man, who proved to be Sirhan. The reason she caught his attention was that she was "very good looking." He said, "I would never forget what she looked like because she had a very good looking figure, and the dress was kind of lousy. . . . It looked like it was a white dress and it had either black or dark-purple polka dots on it."

He then described the scoop neck of her dress and went on to say she had brown hair and also commented on her nose, which he described as "podgy."

As time went by, DiPierro became unhappy with his capitulation to Hernandez, and when he heard a radio broadcast about the Kennedy shooting on local station KHJ, he wrote his congratulations. On the subject of the woman in the polka-dot dress, he said he was "deeply interested in hearing the facts straight for a change" and offered help on the subject. When the radio reporter stopped by to see DiPierro, he found he was unable to speak to the young man. His father answered the door looking disturbed. He told him that they had been visited by someone claiming to be from the FBI and, as a consequence of this, begged his son to be left alone since his life might be in danger.

In spite of the determination of the LAPD to discredit any hint of suggestion that a conspiracy had taken place, the existence of the woman in the polka-dot dress was extremely well established. There was a ruthlessness evident in the actions of the LAPD, in the persons of CIA-connected individuals, desperately anxious to erase all records of sightings of the woman in the polka-dot dress. This was also reflected in making false statements in the records of the case, as I recounted earlier. Did the conspirators make an error in having their woman—or women—wear a conspicuous polka-dot dress? It would appear she was deliberately meant to be seen.

CHAPTER 27

Unwelcome Evidence of a Different Kind

I am a camera with its shutter open, quite passive, recording, not thinking.

—Christopher Isherwood

FIFTEEN-YEAR-OLD Scott Enyart's encounter with the police colored his understanding and belief of what went on during the investigation into Senator Robert F. Kennedy's murder for the rest of his life. His father had bought him an expensive, professional-quality Nikon "F" camera with a 50 mm lens. Anxious to put it to use, he took it to the Ambassador Hotel, where he was determined to make an extensive record of events on Kennedy's victory night for his school magazine. He snapped away inside the ballroom and did not miss a thing when it came to photographing the senator making what would be his last speech that night. As the senator withdrew from the stage and made his way to the pantry area, Enyart followed, taking more photographs. Into and through the pantry area, he was in close attendance, jumping on the tables there to get the best possible shots. Right up until the senator was shot he was taking photos from his vantage position. In the pantry alone, he said he took eighteen pictures.

An officer spoke to Enyart afterward. He told the officer that "the shots started to be fired and I took pictures and kept taking pictures." The officer asked, "While the shots were being fired?" Scott replied, "While the shots were being fired." A few minutes later, he was chased by two men as he made to leave the hotel. He did not know they were officers and was afraid. He ran out of the automatic doors as they were closing but, he said, "I was blinded by lights. [Police spotlights] I was grabbed. I was put down on my face on the red carpet. My camera was taken, my wallet was taken, my pockets were emptied. . . . I looked up and saw guns pointed at me." In an interview for television, he asserted, "They took me and tossed me into the back of a squad car which was sitting . . . right in front of the entrance." The police asked him if he had witnessed the shooting and he replied he could not tell without looking at the photographs he had taken, as they had been his preoccupation.

Enyart was driven to the rear of the hotel, where the police had a holding room. From there, he was transported to Rampart Station by jailbus. He was not interviewed until 6:00 A.M., not the best time for a fifteen year old who had been up all night to be questioned. Enyart submitted details of his movements taking pictures in a drawing he made of the area while he was being questioned by the police. The sketch, when sought some years later, had disappeared.

The LAPD promised Enyart he would have his camera and all his pictures back, but getting them back was another matter. When he went for them, he found that they were locked up. "I was not allowed to look at the film," he said. "They took a stack of prints and one of the detectives shuffled through them and separated it into two piles and, basically, he gave me the photographs from one roll of film leading up to the assassination and then after the assassination. Everything that I had taken in the pantry was gone." The astute young man then made an observation that constituted a somber indictment of the LAPD action. "If the police department was right [about what had happened in the pantry], then my photographs would only have proved that they were right, so for them to destroy it [sic] only leads me to believe that something's being covered up."

Well put and right on target. Add to this the distress caused during the interrogation of other witnesses, the experience of Sergeant Paul Sharaga, and the LAPD's refusal to do a straight count of bul-

Joe Junior, Kathleen (Kick), and John Fitzgerald Kennedy in London in 1939. (Courtesy John F. Kennedy Library)

President John F. Kennedy. (Courtesy John F. Kennedy Library)

Sam Giancana, bad boy of
the Chicago Cosa Nostra.
(Author's collection)

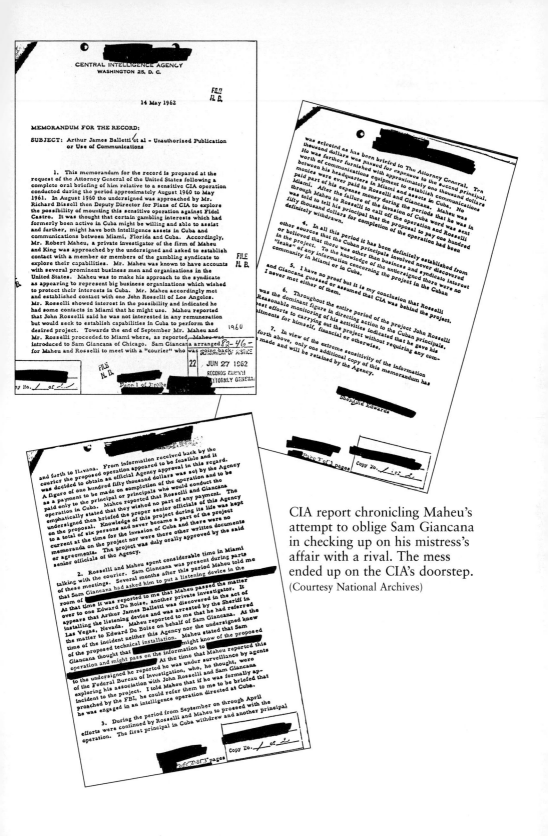

CIA report chronicling Maheu's attempt to oblige Sam Giancana in checking up on his mistress's affair with a rival. The mess ended up on the CIA's doorstep. (Courtesy National Archives)

"Happy birthday, Mr. President..." Marilyn Monroe at JFK's birthday party at Madison Square Garden. (Courtesy John F. Kennedy Library)

The front lawn of Marilyn Monroe's house shortly after her death. The stuffed animals eye the policemen warily. (AP/WideWorld)

Jack Clemmons at his interview with the author. (Author's collection)

Psychiatrist Ralph Greenson.
(Author's collection)

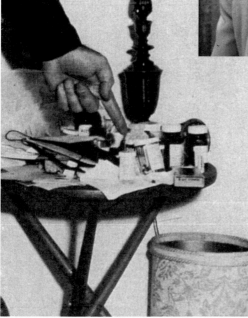

A finger points to the many empty pill bottles on Marilyn Monroe's bedside table. (AP/WideWorld)

Los Angeles Assistant Police Chief Tom Reddin. (Author's collection)

Los Angeles coroner Theodore Curphey claimed Monroe had killed herself by swallowing 47 Nembutal tablets, when Abbott Laboratories, which manufactured Nembutal, said it would have taken twice that many to kill her. The autopsy revealed no sign of the drug in her stomach.
(Author's collection)

THE WHITE HOUSE
WASHINGTON

~~TOP SECRET~~ - EYES ONLY   October 11, 1963

NATIONAL SECURITY ACTION MEMORANDUM NO. 263

TO: Secretary of State
            Secretary of Defense
            Chairman of the Joint Chiefs of Staff

SUBJECT: South Vietnam

At a meeting on October 5, 1963, the President considered the
recommendations contained in the report of Secretary McNamara
and General Taylor on their mission to South Vietnam.

The President approved the military recommendations contained
in Section I B (1-3) of the report, but directed that no formal
announcement be made of the implementation of plans to withdraw 1,000 U.S. militiary personnel by the end of 1963.

After discussion of the remaining recommendations of the report,
the President approved an instruction to Ambassador Lodge which
is set forth in State Department telegram No. 534 to Saigon.

                                    McGeorge Bundy

Copy furnished:
    Director of Central Intelligence
    Administrator, Agency for International Development

                        cc:
                            Mr. Bundy ✓
                            Mr. Forrestal
                            Mr. Johnson
            ~~TOP SECRET — EYES ONLY~~ NSC Files

            Committee Print of Pentagon Papers
            by MSS   4/13/77

Letter showing
President Kennedy's
decision to begin
withdrawing troops
from Vietnam.
(Author's collection)

A sketch showing Elm
Street and the site of the
JFK assassination
(Author's collection)

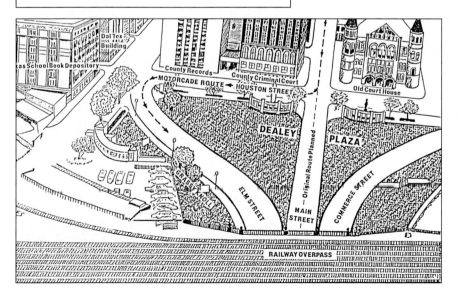

The scene at Parkland Hospital as the news of the President's death was announced. (Courtesy National Archives)

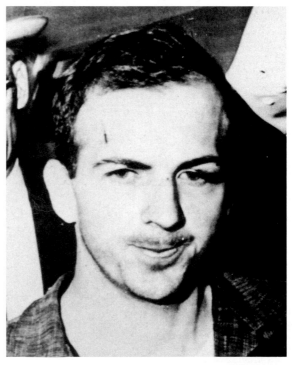

Lee Harvey Oswald.
(Courtesy National Archives)

Oswald and Marina in Minsk. (Courtesy National Archives)

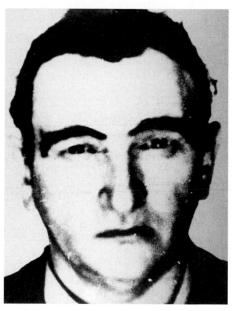

Dave Ferrie. He worked with
Bannister in New Orleans
(Courtesy National Archives)

Roscoe White. His "diary" said
he was a shooter at the JFK
assassination; he then went on to
kill Officer Tippit. The latter is
more likely. (Author's collection)

The Warren Commission. (Courtesy National Archives)

THE WARREN COMMISSION

| Richard B. RUSSELL | John Sherman COOPER | Hale BOGGS | Earl WARREN | Gerald FORD | Allen W. DULLES | John J. McCLOY |

J. Lee RANKIN

Norman REDLICH   Howard P. WILLENS   Alfred GOLDBERG
Melvin A. EISENBERG   Charles N. SHAFFER, Jr.

| I. Basic Facts of Assassination | II. Identity of Assassin | III. LHO's Background | IV. Possible Conspiratorial Relationships | V. Oswald's Death | VI. Presidential Protection |

SENIOR COUNSELS

| Francis W.H. ADAMS | Joseph BALL | Albert JENNER | William COLEMAN | Leon HUBERT | |

JUNIOR COUNSELS

| Arlen SPECTER | David BELIN | Wesley LIEBELER | W. David SLAWSON | Burt GRIFFIN | Samuel A. STERN |

LIAISONS

Jim Davis - assigned from State Dept. to consult   Thomas Kelley - Secret Service
    with WC about approaching USSR   Abram Chayes - State Department
Ted Sorensen - White House   H. Miller - Justice Department
Adam Yarmolinsky - Defense Department   R. Helms - CIA
James J. Malley - FBI

Mrs. Helen Markham (*far left*) at the spot from which she witnessed the Tippit killing. (Courtesy National Archives)

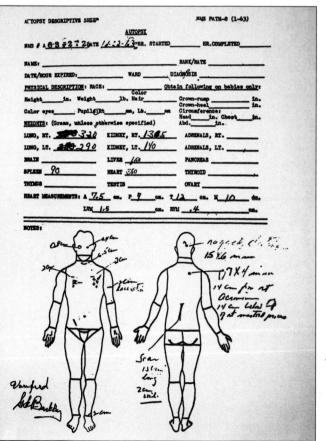

JFK autopsy
diagram.
(Courtesy National
Archives)

Robert F. Kennedy while he was still alive. (Courtesy John F. Kennedy Library)

Robert Kennedy at the Ambassador Hotel, Los Angeles. This would be his last speech. (Courtesy Scott Enyart)

Coroner Thomas Noguchi examines the bullet holes for himself. (Courtesy S.E. Massachusetts University, RFK Assassination Archives)

The pantry where the shooting took place. (Courtesy S.E. Massachusetts University, RFK Assassination Archives)

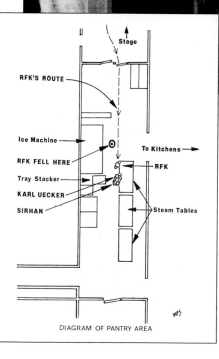

Stage

RFK'S ROUTE

Ice Machine

To Kitchens

RFK FELL HERE

RFK

Tray Stacker

KARL UECKER

SIRHAN

Steam Tables

DIAGRAM OF PANTRY AREA

The pantry area detailed. (Author's collection)

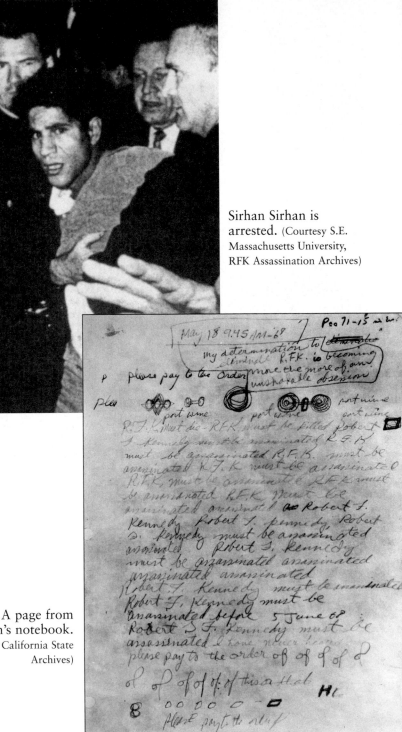

Sirhan Sirhan is arrested. (Courtesy S.E. Massachusetts University, RFK Assassination Archives)

A page from Sirhan's notebook. (Courtesy California State Archives)

Edward M. Kennedy in a rare sober moment.
(Courtesy John F. Kennedy Library)

A sketch of
Chappaquiddick Island.
(Author's collection)

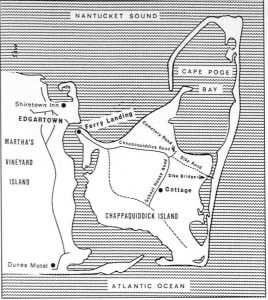

Mary Jo Kopechne. (Courtesy AP/WideWorld)

Mary Jo Kopechne. Scuba diver John Farrar pictured with the car after he
had taken the body of Mary Jo Kopechne from the backseat.
(Author's collection)

lets and bullet holes found in the pantry woodwork, and we are looking at all the ingredients of a cover-up. In 1988, when the LAPD files on the shooting of Robert Kennedy had been placed in the public domain, Enyart, then thirty-five, wrote to the chief of police at that time, Darryl Gates, asking for his photographs back. He wrote an eloquent, complimentary letter, and asked for signed pictures of Gates for his two children. A month later, Gates replied telling Enyart that everything the LAPD had was now passed over to the state of California. He enclosed the name and telephone number of Laren Metzer, who was the state archivist, thanked Enyart for his help in the Kennedy investigation, and enclosed two autographed pictures. Enyart then wrote to Metzer, who replied he could not find the pictures and suggested they were among the 2,400 photographs destroyed by the LAPD in 1968.

Enyart was unhappy that his pictures had not been among the documents and other pictures released by the LAPD. In 1989, he filed a lawsuit against the city of Los Angeles for compensation in respect of the photographs not returned. This was challenged by the city, on the grounds that the statute of limitations had run out in respect of them. The court agreed and threw out the case. An appeal was made in 1993, however, that resulted in the Court of Appeals overturning the earlier decision, in respect of the secrecy imposed by the LAPD for over twenty years.

Then, like a bolt from the blue, attorneys for the city claimed to have found both prints and negatives answering to the description of those belonging to Enyart. They had been filed under another name, they said. But when Enyart and his lawyer went to the archives in Sacramento to examine what they had found, he was faced with more questions than answers. The negatives, a set of thirty, were on 125 ASA Ilford, while he had used 400 ASA Kodak Tri-X. The sequence of the pictures was wrong, and the single roll contained some of the pictures from all three of the rolls he had used. Enyart, who was a professional photographer, recognized he was being offered a second-generation version of his pictures—in other words, a copy, but an incomplete one. The one glaring omission was that there were none of the pictures he had taken in the pantry area of the hotel. The judge, Emilie Elias, ordered the find to be brought to the courtroom where they could be used as evidence.

The courier, who had traveled by air to Los Angeles International from Sacramento, hired a car to take him the rest of the journey. He reported that his white Mazda began making a thumping noise, and, when he got out to identify the source of the noise he found his right rear tire had been slashed. Returning to the car, his briefcase had vanished with the critical photographic evidence it contained. The question must arise whether, as Enyart's lawyer hinted, "Somebody, for some reason, is making sure those photographs do not reach public view," or whether, in fact, somebody, somewhere, was making sure the pictures identified by Enyart as copies were not reaching the courtroom. "Just a petty theft," was the comment of the city's leading lawyer, Skip Miller.

It was June 1996 when the trial began. Enyart was subjected to the derogatory sniping of Skip Miller, who questioned the number of rolls of film he had used, whether he was in the pantry area at all, and whether he actually took important pictures of the shooting. He told the jury members they should make up their own minds about the theft of the photographic evidence from the courier's car, referring scornfully to the suggestion it might be part of "the Evil Empire's twenty-eight-year [old] plot," and defending the LAPD's secrecy of the documentation relating to the shooting of Kennedy. The city attorney spoke up for the handling of evidence in the Kennedy case on the part of the LAPD and said that if the jury members believed the LAPD had anything to do with the photographic evidence being stolen then they believed in the tooth fairy.

Enyart described his encounter with police officers when his camera and film were confiscated and gave a detailed account of the interview that eventually followed. In a somewhat thorny trial, one of the most curious, indeed fascinating new facts to emerge was that the log numbers given to Enyart's pictures were the same as those given at first—later changed—to the bullet fragments retrieved from Senator Kennedy's head. Enyart's attorney spoke of "a consistent and deliberate attempt [on the part of the city] to erase Scott Enyart and his photographs from the record of this case," while the city's attorney declared Enyart's claims as "fabricated with smoke and mirrors."

In spite of counsel for the prosecution, in his summation the city's defending counsel told the jury Enyart was trying to pull a fast one and did not deserve a dime, "This case is all about profit, personal gain, self-promotion, and greed." When the jury returned from deliberation, it awarded Enyart a total of $625,600 in compensation for the failure of the LAPD to return his film, which included accrued interest. "We definitely thought the city and police screwed up all the way through," commented the jury foreman. Understandably, a delighted Enyart said he would much rather have had his three rolls of film. Quite apart from the fact their worth would probably have been many times more than the total of his compensation, we might actually have got to see who actually shot Senator Kennedy.

The Scott Enyart saga did not quite finish there, however. The city of Los Angeles made an appeal against the award to him, which was upheld. Devastated, Enyart made it clear that he was prepared to go to litigation again to have this new appeal quashed and that he had no intention of handing victory to the city in what was fast becoming a game of legal ping-pong. The city then reconsidered and settled out of court in the sum of $100,000.

I give credit to Enyart that the chief inspiration for his battle with the LAPD, and his lawsuits with the city of Los Angeles, was the hope of recovering his pictures. This he did not achieve, but his actions appeared to underline, even more than we had thought before, that there was something special about the pictures in question, something the LAPD had gone to great lengths to keep secret. Since I cannot accept that Sirhan Bishara Sirhan was responsible for

Senator Kennedy's death, the question remaining for me must essentially be: Could the LAPD and city authorities have wished to protect the identity of the real killer?

Curiouser and curiouser. Then there was the Thane Eugene Cesar mystery.

CHAPTER 28

Thane Eugene Cesar

We live and learn but not the wiser grow.

—John Pomfret

THANE EUGENE CESAR was employed by the Ace Guard Service, which was contracted to provide security to the Ambassador Hotel and was in no way engaged by Robert F. Kennedy. While the senator could make decisions about the presence of those who would provide personal protection, he could not prevent the hotel providing security services. Except for Bill Barry, his personal friend, Kennedy had forbidden the presence of any others to provide security for him, whether official or unofficial. Therefore, it was somewhat ironic that when he entered the pantry area of the Ambassador, Cesar was sticking to him like glue. Karl Uecker, the hotel's assistant maître d', was also in close attendance, slightly preceding Cesar and holding the senator's wrist. When the shooting started, Uecker threw himself at Sirhan Bishara Sirhan, putting Sirhan's head under his arm in a headlock and driving Sirhan's gun hand down to the steam table, desperate to get him to give up the gun. Cesar, as he himself admitted, ducked, stumbled, and fell to the floor. His clip-on bow tie flew off and is seen in photographs of the prostrate senator.

So much for the Ace Guard Service. Cesar was asked how long he had worked for the company, and he replied, "Six months." This was not true. Further research showed that Cesar had been given his first job for Ace as recently as May 31, 1968, only weeks before.

Furthermore, he had not, as he claimed, worked several times previously at the Ambassador for Ace; this was his first engagement at the hotel. As for Cesar's involvement in events, the witness Donald Schulman said he saw him draw and fire his gun in the pantry. He said:

> I was standing behind Kennedy as he was taking his assigned route into the kitchen. A Caucasian gentleman stepped out and fired. *The security guard* [Cesar] *hit Kennedy all three times*. Kennedy slumped to the floor. The security guard fired back [at Sirhan] and I saw the man who shot Kennedy in the leg, he—before they could get to him, he shot a—it looked like he shot a woman and he shot two other men. They then proceeded to carry Kennedy into the kitchen . . . he . . . was definitely hit three times.

Jeff Brent, the reporter who had been taking Schulman's statement, wanted to make sure of one thing. He asked if he had got it correct that it was the security guard he had spoken of when he referred to the firing. "Yes," Schulman replied. The fourth bullet had missed, of course, and had merely passed through the senator's shoulder pad. The shot to the leg attributed to Sirhan was wrong, and this assertion may reflect that Schulman's vantage point was related to Cesar's position rather than Sirhan's. In a later interview when Schulman was not quite so hassled, he told the researcher Theodore Charach, "The things I did see I'm sure about. And that is about Kennedy being shot three times. And a guard definitely pulled out his gun and fired. . . . He wasn't very far from Kennedy. He was just behind Mr. Uecker and on Kennedy's right side, but there was another guard in front of Senator Kennedy and one on Kennedy's left side in the very crowded sardine-like conditions."

The question must be asked: Why was Kennedy hemmed in by three guards when he had specifically asked for no guards to be in attendance? Clearly, they were not very effective as guards.

While others were not sure how many bullets had hit the senator, Cesar was exactly right when he was asked the question. It was a radio reporter who asked:

> *Reporter:* Officer, can you confirm the fact that the Senator has been shot?
>
> *Cesar:* Yes. I was there holding his arm when they shot him.
>
> *Reporter:* What happened?
>
> *Cesar:* I dunno—gentleman by the lunch counter there and as he walked up he pulled a gun and shot at him.
>
> *Reporter:* Was it just one man?
>
> *Cesar:* No—yeah, one man.
>
> *Reporter:* And what sort of wound did the Senator receive?
>
> *Cesar:* Well, from where I could see, it looked like he was shot in the head and the chest and the shoulder, but . . .
>
> *Reporter:* How many shots did you hear?
>
> *Cesar:* Four.

This statement sequence is important for several things. First, the incredible accuracy of the number of bullets fired at Senator Kennedy, without confusion of any shots that might have come from Sirhan's gun. He never mentioned that. Second, describing Sirhan as having "shot at" the senator was exactly accurate. He did not claim Sirhan had shot Senator Kennedy. The question put to him, "Was it just one man?" draws the somewhat uncertain, eerie answer, "No—yeah, one man."

On this evidence alone, Cesar merited the highest level of interrogation on the part of the LAPD. This was not to be so. Test bullets were never fired from Cesar's gun and he was promptly cleared of suspicion. The gun Cesar carried was a .38 caliber, and it would not, in the normal way, have been difficult to differentiate the bullets it used from those used in the .22 caliber gun used by Sirhan. The one bullet retrieved from Senator Kennedy's body, however, was so distorted the LAPD could not say with certainty it was a .22, or that it had come from Sirhan's gun.

Arguably, in a professional killing such as this, it would have been unthinkable for a gun to be used that did not match the caliber of Sirhan's gun. But then who was to say that Cesar had not been carrying a .22 as well as his service issue? Or for that matter, a .38 that had been modified to shoot .22 caliber bullets. Cesar had, in fact, possessed a .22 caliber gun similar to that used by Sirhan. He said he had sold it before the time of the shooting at the Ambassador, but there is evidence that this was another lie. LAPD Sergeant Phil Sartuche said he checked it out with the person to whom Cesar had sold the gun and declared this was all in order. However, Charach carried out the same check and found himself looking at a receipt for the .22 made out some three months *after* Senator Kennedy was murdered. Jim Yoder, who bought the gun from Cesar, told how it was later stolen and he had never seen it again. It was a long time after this (in 1974) that Cesar conceded he was not sure whether he had sold his .22 caliber gun before or after the shooting of Senator Kennedy. If it was afterward, this leaves an even greater glaring hole in the investigation and reflects an even poorer enquiry than already observed.

Cesar said he was instructed by his superiors to walk beside Senator Kennedy as he made his way through the pantry area, but this was not so. The Ambassador Hotel's security chief, William Gardner, talking to the FBI, said he had no guard assigned to escort the senator, since he had specifically forbidden uniformed security guards or anyone carrying weapons in his proximity. In view of Gardner's respect for the wishes of the senator, it was not only strange that Cesar was so close to him, it was stranger still that when Cesar ducked and fell, he was helped up by *another* security man, "I think it was Murphy," he said. In fact, there were three Ace guards in close proximity to Kennedy when he was killed. Gardner had engaged only eight men in total for the evening, and a statement was obtained by the FBI that ran, "the Senator did not want any uniformed security guards in his presence nor did he want any armed individuals as guards. Mr. Gardner said this is one of the reasons why he did not have any guard assigned to escort the Senator through the hotel during the visit."

Did this not merit investigation?

× × ×

At this point, it is worth recounting that we have seen incredibly clear evidence of complicity by others, even if Sirhan had killed Senator Kennedy. But this is challenged by the many who have claimed to recognize strong indications that Sirhan was under the influence of hypnotism—which will be examined in the next chapter—and that he was a patsy set up to cause distraction while someone else killed Senator Kennedy. There is also ample evidence that it was the intention of the woman—or women—in the polka-dot dress to create further diversion immediately after the shooting. Apart from the striking design of the dress, calculated to be remembered, the involvement of the woman was clearly advertised—"We shot Senator Kennedy"—over and over again, but the woman in the polka-dot dress, the man in the blue jacket, and another man who made up the group successfully melted away, never to be seen again. The possible role of Cesar has never been fully investigated and we cannot rule him out of the equation simply because he says he was not involved. This was a cleverly devised murder, and the only participant brought to justice still languishes in jail.

Sergeant Paul Sharaga might have been said to have caught a mental glimpse of the alliance between the CIA renegades and those from the Establishment who sought to destroy the Kennedys when, many years after the senator's death, in a television program, he commented, "I think we have a structure in this country and I refer to them [sic] as a corporate war machine, or you can refer to them as anything you want. I believe they did and will do anything that they need to—or that they want to—to preserve their status quo."

Not, perhaps, completely on target, but near enough to an awareness of forces offstage and out of sight pulling the strings and watching their intentions carried out, even if that involved murder.

But what Sharaga was not aware of, in common with most of those directly involved, was that there were many strange activities engaged in by officers of the LAPD after the shooting of Senator Kennedy and well into the investigation that ensued. And the same might apply to the run up of Sirhan's trial and then during the time of his trial.

CHAPTER 29

Mind Games

Art thou but a dagger of the mind, a false creation,
proceeding from the heat-oppressed brain?
—Shakespeare, *Macbeth*

SIRHAN BISHARA SIRHAN acted in a very peculiar way when he shot at Senator Robert F. Kennedy. He was tranquil and smiling and the look in his eyes betrayed his mind was far away. This was well noted at the time and, as far as I am aware, has never been challenged. No one present in the pantry area who saw Sirhan has ever said this was not the case, and a man who smiles throughout a bloody attack on another human being cannot be said to be acting rationally. It is a sign of derangement, and it has to be asked why this young man, who acted rationally beforehand and returned to rationality soon afterward, should address himself to firing off every round in his gun with such vehemence between these times, while wearing this unnatural smile.

Perhaps, the most obvious explanation proposed was that Sirhan was hypnotized. I must confess that for many years I could not accept this. To me it seemed as though this explanation was a huge gloss: something to explain a situation that was otherwise difficult to explain. But when I came to researching what was going on at this time—and for some time before this—in the CIA under the heading of mind control, I had to think again.

During World War II, the CIA was interested in the techniques developed by the Nazis in mind control by way of hypnotism and the use of drugs. During the Korean War, the CIA acquired a heightened awareness that the Komitet Gosudarstvennoĭ Bezopasnosti (KGB; State Security Committee) was pushing ahead with research into aspects of mind control. Early in the 1950s, the CIA was examining the consequences of administering the drug LSD and 1953 was the year that Richard Helms proposed to the CIA director that a study of the "covert use of biological and chemical materials" should be undertaken. It was about 1954 when a project named the "Artichoke" program was adopted by the CIA. In this the subject, under hypnotism, was to respond to a "trigger" to carry out the murder of a designated person. The "trigger" could be a word, an action, the appearance of an object—almost anything. The CIA denied ever using it, but from this time forward the notions of Richard Condon in his gripping novel *The Manchurian Candidate* were no longer the reserve of those with inventive minds who wished to fascinate and entertain us with the impossible. The impossible was now in the process of becoming reality.

It was the agency's ambition to use drugs for the purpose of obtaining data on behavioral change, memory disturbance, discrediting by aberrant behavior, altering sex patterns, acquiring information, suggestibility, and creating dependency. Once in possession of such data, the application of it was subhuman, the stuff of which nightmares are made. Terms such as "depatterning" and "differential amnesia" now entered the parlance of a new breed of CIA agent.

The CIA's dedication to learning about mind and behavioral control having been established, a top-secret program known as "Mkultra" was introduced in which Dr. Sidney Gottlieb violated all ethical boundaries in the experimentation linked to this new study. One of Dr. Gottlieb's techniques involved surreptitiously administrating LSD to members of agency staff so that he could observe behavioral changes. Data obtained from veteran CIA agents, combined with the content of documents obtained under the Freedom of Information Act, revealed details of the unthinkable consequences to one of Dr. Gottlieb's experimental dopings. It involved an Army Chemical Corps scientist, Dr. Frank Olson, who attended a conference at a secret venue along with other colleagues. Dr. Gottlieb "spiked" Dr. Olson's after dinner drink with LSD, and probably did the same to the drinks of other participants, because the conference offerings deteriorated to such a level it was abandoned. A depressed Dr. Olson confided to his wife that he had made a fool of himself, and he offered his resignation to his senior officer. The senior officer, who had also attended the conference, was puzzled and persuaded Dr. Olson to change his mind, since he knew the doctor's behavior at the meeting had been above reproach. Dr. Olson, however, sank into a state of deep depression and began to suffer from paranoia. He believed the CIA "was out to get him."

Dr. Gottlieb responded by sending him to a doctor in New York who was funded by the CIA. Suffering from delusions, Dr. Olson wandered the streets believing he was acting on orders, tore up his money, and, after some time, was found sitting in his hotel lobby. The New York doctor could not help Dr. Olson and, after a second unsuccessful attempt, recommended he should be admitted to a hospital. With a CIA agent to accompany him, Dr. Olson booked into a hotel where, in the early hours of the morning, the agent was awakened by the doctor plunging through the closed window against which the blind had been drawn. He fell to his death, after which the whole affair was carefully covered up by the agency.

In another example, Dr. Gottlieb secretly administered LSD to an agent in Washington who went missing. He was eventually found cowering near a bridge across the Potomac in a state of shock. Shaking with fear, he was terrified when cars approached him. He perceived them as grotesque monsters. Against a background such as this, a program of mind control calculated to produce the actions of Sirhan Bishara Sirhan becomes a distinct possibility. It is interesting to assemble the accounts of Sirhan's appearance and behavior as given by a variety of people at different times.

Yosio Niwa was a cook at the Ambassador Hotel, and he saw Sirhan shooting at Senator Kennedy. "I'll never forget that guy's face," he said. "I'll never forget. I was so upset. I told him, 'You got mother or father?' He was smiling, too. . . . He was looking at me. I was so excited, upset. He was smiling. . . . I don't know why." Another witness, the writer George Plimpton, spoke of Sirhan having a "trance-like appearance," mumbling rapidly in a weak voice, incoherent and reticent, and taking breaths in deep draughts. His eyes, said Plimpton, were "dark brown and enormously peaceful."

The waiter Martin Patruski witnessed the shooting and observed, "The guy looked like he was smiling." Mary Grohs was a Western Union teletype machine operator, and Sirhan came over to where she was at about 10:30 P.M. Questioned by the author Robert Kaiser, she told him, "Well, he came over to my machine and started staring at it. Just staring. I'll never forget his eyes. I asked him what he wanted. He didn't answer. He just kept staring. I asked him again. No answer. I said that if he wanted to check the latest figures on Senator Kennedy, he'd have to check the other machine. He still didn't answer. He just kept staring."

Another witness, Joseph Lahaiv, spoke of Sirhan as being "very tranquil" during the struggle to stop him shooting. The strongest memory of the waiter Thomas Vincent DiPierro was of his smile, "That stupid smile. . . . That very sickly looking smile."

At the time Sirhan was arrested, he did not speak to the police. He remained silent during his first interrogation. Officer Arthur Placencia flashed a torch into his eyes and noted the response, the details of which had to be elicited from him by counsel. He was not helpful in establishing that the behavior of Sirhan's eyes indicated that he was under the influence of alcohol, drugs, or, for that matter, hypnotism, the latter of which was unlikely to occur to the officer. Sergeant William Jordan was also with Sirhan during the first few hours after his arrest, and he said that by the third attempt to interrogate him he was quite talkative and that "he would talk about various things." This was entirely compatible with the effects of hypnotism wearing off, but that was not the only change noted by the sergeant. Whether Placencia had told him about Sirhan's eyes or not, Sergeant Jordan went on record as observing they had cleared by the time he was arraigned. There is here a clear assumption on the part of two officers that his eyes were previously abnormal. When he finally decided to talk, Sirhan did not talk about the shooting of Senator Kennedy. It appeared he had no memory of the event.

It was interesting to learn that the last person to talk to Sirhan before he made his way to the Ambassador Hotel was Gamoard Mistri. Mistri was a fellow student of Sirhan. He said that Sirhan showed him the bullet that he had in his pocket when he was later arrested. The presence of a metal object is regarded as highly significant in relation to hypnotism.

CHAPTER 30

The Trial

Trial by jury itself, instead of being a security to persons who are accused, will be a delusion, a mockery, and a snare.

—Lord Denman

"[SIRHAN BISHARA SIRHAN] was a member of numerous Communist institutions, including the Rosicrucians," declared Mayor Sam Yorty.

"The Rosicrucians aren't a Communist organization," said a reporter.

"Well," continued Yorty, "it appears that Sirhan Sirhan was a sort of loner who harbored Communist inclinations, favored Communists of all types. He said the U.S. must fall. Indicated that RFK must be assassinated before June 5, 1968. It was a May 18 notation in a ringed notebook."

In another pronouncement, bringing his fist down on the ringed notebook, he declared that an "evil Communist organization has played a part in inflaming the assassination of President Kennedy." Of course, he did not mean *President* Kennedy, he meant Senator Kennedy, but this was one of his lesser blunders that day. It was said that Mayor Yorty "shot from the lip," and this well described his elephantine bumbling into the news on the day Robert F. Kennedy died. The listening reporters soon found out that Sirhan had no connection with communist groups, but Mayor Yorty was always good for copy, always good for a quote. It was to be hoped that the readers of what was written by the reporters knew Yorty as well as the reporters did. The ringed notebook mentioned by Yorty would prove important, however, which was exactly why Yorty should not have been mentioning it at all. It had been obtained from Sirhan's home without a warrant. Whether it was really Sirhan's and whether he had made the inflammatory entries had not been ascertained. And the mayor's blundering was doing its best to ensure the notebook would not be accepted as evidence by the court that would try him.

Robert Houghton, the LAPD's chief of detectives, was assigned the investigation into Kennedy's murder and brought the operation "Special Unit Senator" into being exclusively to investigate the assassination of the second Kennedy to die by the bullet. As I have already indicated, his position was that another Dallas had not occurred in Los Angeles and would not be perceived as having occurred in that city. Once Sirhan had been indicted for the murder of Senator Kennedy, the blinkered LAPD investigation proceded in a straight line toward the trial and conviction of the accused, without deviating to the left or right to consider options that independent parties clearly saw required looking into.

With the exception of one single FBI agent, who was quoted as supporting the LAPD investigation, there was a marked rift between the police and the federal agents. Roger J. LaJeunesse, the senior FBI agent, received instructions directly from President Lyndon B. Johnson that he was to take charge of the case, but from the first meeting attended by LaJeunesse at LAPD Headquarters, it was plain that the FBI was not welcome. Houghton, having been placed in charge of Special Unit Senator, had been assured by the local FBI chief that the bureau would not become involved in the investigation, but this was prior to the instructions from the president. As the LAPD arrangements unfolded, LaJeunesse noted an unusual degree of possessiveness on Houghton's part. "They elbowed us out of it right away," he said.

Houghton had placed Chief of Homicide Detectives Hugh Brown in overall control of what became known as Special Unit Senator, and gave him freedom to choose his team, though with the proviso that Lieutenant Manny Pena was placed in day-to-day control of the investigation. Pena's decisions were not to be questioned, so, in the long run, where this left Brown is quite baffling. Sergeant Enrique Hernandez was appointed to the Background Conspiracy Team, designated to examine Sirhan's background and, as the title implied, to search out and identify any possible conspiracy behind the murder of Senator Kennedy. Thus, Pena and Hernandez were effectively running the show. LAPD officers were subject to them, and the FBI had been shunted off. This is important to understand because it emphasizes that what proceeded from the investigation into the trial proceedings was, to all intents and purposes, filtered through the CIA.

Pena, according to Houghton, in his book *Special Unit Senator*, was an officer of immense experience. He "spoke French and Spanish, and had connections with various intelligence agencies in several countries." However, he did not tell us about the well-established relationships both Pena and Hernandez had with the CIA. At one time, Pena had retired from the police department to take up a post with the State Department's Agency for National Development Office. The Office of Public Safety of the Agency for International Development has been exposed as a cover for the CIA. It specialized in teaching intelligence agents of foreign countries how to carry out assassinations. To those who understood its function, it was thought of as the Department of Dirty Tricks. Enrique Hernandez had also served in the ultrasecret Office of Public Safety. Both of these agents had opted to return to the LAPD. And here they were, effectively controlling the investigation of Senator Kennedy's murder.

Technically, the trial began the following January, where witnesses were flanked by only a handful of the general public and about thirty men and women from the more prestigious news outlets. About seventy other reporters watched the proceedings on closed-circuit television in another courtroom, several floors beneath, which became their "home" for the three months of the trial. However, the required deliberations relating to the selection of a jury and other matters resulted in the actual trial proceedings not beginning until February 13, 1969. One of the other matters related to criminal proceedings that were hanging over the chief defense advocate, Grant Cooper, and the proceedings against Sirhan Bishara Sirhan could not begin until they had been satisfactorily "tidied up."

The prosecution conducted a strong case against Sirhan, with his defense counsel less than effective in representing the interests of their client. The defense team, led by Cooper, had hammered out a plea bargain with the prosecution that Judge Herbert V. Walker would not accept. The defense had obtained agreement from Sirhan that he would plead guilty either to murder in the second degree, which did not carry the death penalty, or to murder in the first degree, provided that he was guaranteed life imprisonment as opposed to being sentenced to death. In spite of any such arrangement being unacceptable to Judge Walker Cooper followed a strategy of making life as easy as possible for the prosecution and seeking to raise challenges to prosecution assertions as seldom as possible. It has to be said that his team did not agree with him on this. Cooper believed that, regardless of the judge's position, what he proposed to do would still obtain a result in which the prosecution would not demand the death penalty. The consequences were that the trial was distinctly lop-sided in favor of the prosecution. The defense team ignored opportunities to oppose assertions made and declined even to cross-examine witnesses where that would have been a normal procedure.

There was no doubt that Cooper believed that Sirhan was under the effects of something that changed his behavior at the time of the shooting. He asserted that Sirhan was sick but, frankly, the young man baffled not only Cooper but the entire defense team. In the long run, the various psychiatrists engaged by the defense did little to help. By arrangement, one defense psychiatrist worked in cooperation with a prosecution psychiatrist, which was not calculated to produce much help for the accused.

Much was made by the prosecution of the notebook found at Sirhan's home that featured incriminating entries. Over and over again in an entry dated May 18, the statement was repeated, "RFK must be assassinated, RFK must be assassinated, RFK must be assassinated . . . before 5 June 68." At first glance, it supported the case against Sirhan without doubt, but various anomalies in the writings were observed. There were a number of entries written in the third person, "Sirhan must begin work on . . ." and "Sirhan heard the order of . . . ," while others were in the first person, "I advocate . . ." and "I firmly support . . ." Others, again, were straightforward statements. When, confronted with his May 1 writings in court which occupied but two pages of his notebook, Sirhan had no recollection of them. Cooper questioned him thus:

Cooper: Well, now, let me ask you this. You still don't remember writing this?

Sirhan: I don't remember it. I don't remember writing it.

Cooper: Do you remember writing this: "Please pay to the order of of of of of . . . this or that"?

Sirhan: No, sir, I don't remember that.

Cooper: What significance does this have for you?

Sirhan: Nothing to me. I don't have a bank account. I don't understand it.

Cooper: Well, can you understand why you put the name of a racehorse in there, "Port Wine"?

Sirhan: No, I don't.

Cooper: But you don't deny writing it.

Sirhan: No, I don't deny it. It is my writing.

The defense psychiatrist Dr. Bernard Diamond had questioned Sirhan on this subject under hypnosis in jail. Sirhan wrote his answers:

Diamond: Is this crazy writing?

Sirhan: Yes, yes, yes, yes, yes, yes, yes, yes.

Diamond: Are you crazy?

Sirhan: No, no, no, no.

Diamond: Why are you writing crazy?

Sirhan: Practice, practice, practice, practice, practice.

Diamond: Practice for what?

Sirhan: Mind control, mind control, mind control, mind control.

Diamond: Who wrote your notebooks?

Sirhan: I, I, I, I, I.

Diamond: Were you hypnotized when you wrote the notebook?

Sirhan: Yes, yes, yes.

Diamond: Who hypnotized you when you wrote the notebook?

Sirhan: Mirror, mirror, my mirror, my mirror, my mirror, my mirror, my mirror.

When he was brought out of the trance, Sirhan was shown what he had written. "This is not Sirhan," he said.

There was a great deal about the "mechanical, repetitive" writing in the notebook to suggest quite strongly that these certain entries had been written while Sirhan was under hypnotism. From the very beginning, when first the witnesses of the shooting at the Ambassador Hotel had seen Sirhan, there had been a deep suspicion he had been under hypnotic control. Therefore, in some way this otherwise devastating evidence of the notebook could arguably have supported that Sirhan was a victim just as much as Kennedy.

Cooper was devastated that, when push came to shove, Sirhan asked for the death sentence. Cooper's strategy had been totally wrong. Sirhan was, indeed, sentenced to death, and, in the final analysis, it was the rejection of the death sentence by the state of California that intervened and allowed a commutation of Sirhan's sentence to one of life imprisonment. Small wonder Sirhan's mother complained he had not had a fair trial.

The defense team had not engaged a ballistics expert. William W. Harper, a noted criminologist and ballistics expert, had, earlier in the proceedings, telephoned Cooper to pass on some advice he thought Cooper should have. It was to the effect that DeWayne Wolfer was not to be trusted. He warned that the LAPD criminologist was too happy to oblige the police department. Harper, who had been a consultant in hundreds of homicide trials over a lifetime's work, knew Wolfer and his work, which, he said, was not scientific. "He's not competent," he declared. In what appeared to be his blissful ignorance, Cooper thanked Harper but told him he was not concerned. It is thought that Harper may have tactfully been offering his services to Cooper but his gesture went unnoticed or was ignored.

Wolfer gave evidence to the effect that test bullets had been fired from the .22 caliber Iver Johnson Cadet handgun with the serial number H18602 and that the bullets that struck the victims were fired "by this gun and no other." This is curious in view of the fact the gun bearing that serial number had been logged in the case of a robbery suspect, Jake Williams, and had been in the possession of the LAPD for more than a year before the Kennedy killing. "This gun and no other"? This defies belief.

Wolfer did not state that the gun Sirhan had used, also an Iver Johnson Cadet, bore the serial number H53725. Therefore, the incompetent defense team did not recognize that the prosecution had submitted ballistics evidence that came from another gun, not Sirhan's. This came to light in a probe carried out by Harper after the trial was over. Frankly, in this case it did not require an expert to note that the serial number quoted was incorrect.

The prosecuting counsel David Fitts asserted that Sirhan had put his gun "to the very vicinity of the Senator's head and at point-blank range in rapid succession fired eight shots." Not only was this patently inaccurate because of various other people in the pantry area being shot, it was inaccurate because the various witnesses could not place Sirhan close enough to get a near-touching shot at Kennedy, and certainly not in the back of his head. The general opinion rendered was that he did not get closer than three feet in front of him. Unbelievably, there was no challenge from the defense team.

Under questioning, Wolfer declared that he fired three test shots that he used for comparison, and the markings indicated that the bullets fired in the pantry came from that gun (H18602) and no other. His prosecution questioner then asked if the markings were "analogous to fingerprints," to which Wolfer replied, "That is correct," which, showing his ignorance, was not correct. There is a near likeness to the uniqueness of fingerprints, but these markings are not as reliable as fingerprints. Wolfer also asserted he had tested all the bullets recovered from the victims and compared them with test shots fired from Sirhan's gun. "I am able to say they were fired from that gun," but, quite remarkably, Wolfer offered no corroborating documentation whatever. He made a bald declaration and the defense team, once again, failed to challenge it. Had they been listening, they would have realized that Wolfer had, effectively, cleared their client of having any part in the killing of Kennedy by clearly specifying the gun H18602 to be the murder weapon.

When it came to the question of the bullet said to have been recovered from Kennedy's head, the prosecution was unable to match this bullet to Sirhan's gun, the gun entered in error, or any other gun, for that matter. Again, quite remarkably, the defense said nothing; this was another lost opportunity in Sirhan's defense that any ballistics expert—and particularly Harper—would have picked up immediately. The bullet recovered from Kennedy's neck had been marked by the autopsist Dr. Thomas Noguchi with his initials TN and the number 31, the last two digits of the coroner's case. This became known as People's Exhibit 47. The bullet brought into the trial as People's Exhibit 47 had DW TN engraved into it, however, and was clearly not the bullet it was purported to be. The prosecution again escaped being taken to task by the defense.

In summary, the trial proceedings in relation to the ballistics evidence were a shambles. Since the LAPD's ten-volume *Special Unit Investigative Report* was sealed for twenty years after Kennedy's murder, this tended to spike the guns of those who might have challenged its findings. In fact, an improper meeting took place not long after the trial finished in which Houghton, Judge Walker, Fitts, and two clerks met to discuss how to prevent investigators obtaining the investigative data logged by the LAPD. This was strictly in defiance of the proper availability of such. It is to be noted that no member of the defense team had been asked to participate in this meeting, and in the account of the meeting recorded, Fitts declared that the defense team had been given all the documentation they had asked for and nothing more. Fitts stated, "They asked for interviews and interviews they got," but he admitted he had not handed over those documents that contained police conclusions. When it came to the records of arrests made, he said, "As far as I am concerned we are not going to release any of that." He gave as his reasons the confidentiality of the criminal record of those arrested. Since this was not a case in which multiple arrests were made, one wonders what it was all about, other than preserving secrecy. Undaunted, and regardless of the absence of help from official sources, Harper made a detailed study of the ballistics evidence, with no support from the defense team, when the trial was over.

Wolfer was said to have fired four bullets from gun H53725 (Sirhan's gun) on June 5, 1968, and on June 7 four bullets were entered into evidence with the grand jury hearing. According to Wolfer, his initials were engraved on the test bullets, and in a statement elsewhere, Wolfer said he also crimped the noses of his test bullets. When the four test bullets were examined, there were no identifying initials from Wolfer. No identifications were placed on the bullets until 1975, and there was no crimping. It was claimed that "unknown parties" had substituted the four bullets, but no hard evidence ever emerged to support this. Three bullets marked with Wolfer's initials were entered into evidence at Sirhan's trial as People's Exhibit 55, and the noses were crimped. Strangely, they were also marked A, B, and C, where the four bullets submitted by Wolfer to the grand jury had been marked, in 1975, as D, E, F, and G.

In 1975, Judge Robert A. Wenke ordered that test bullets be fired, but the California State Archives received neither the bullets nor the casings of the bullets that had been fired. It seems they vanished. With bullet substitutions, evidence envelope substitutions, and missing evidence, it is impossible for the state of California to prove that Sirhan fired the fatal shots. I have no doubt Sirhan did not fire them. Much of the data quoted earlier was obtained by the researcher Rose Lynn Mangan, a trusted friend of Sirhan, who worked tirelessly on his behalf. She told me, "the State has no proper chain of custody, nor can one be created. This appalling record is found in the Court Order #2 Evidence Inventory which Deputy Attorney General Karlin has . . . tried to disown and discredit. The fact is, the State has tampered with the ballistics evidence, and the State cannot prove that Sirhan Sirhan shot Senator Kennedy."

When questioned in 1975 about the Iver Johnson Cadet .22 caliber revolver he had wrongly quoted as Sirhan's—H18602—Wolfer said it was available for comparisons to be made, though police records showed it had been destroyed in July 1968, long before the Sirhan trial. In fact, in 1971 it was discovered the gun had not been destroyed until July 1969.

A year after Sirhan's trial Harper, a brilliant criminologist and an established expert in the study of ballistics, made a study of the evidence put forward at the Sirhan trial. Following his investigation, and in a signed affidavit dated December 28, 1970, Harper, having considered other extremely pertinent details, concluded his report with the following:

> The physical evidence shows that the gun that fired the three test bullets was gun No. H18602, not the Sirhan gun. Thus, the only gun placed at the scene by scientific evidence is gun No. H18602. Sirhan's gun was taken from him by citizens at the scene. I have no information regarding the background history of gun No. H18602 nor how the police came into possession of it.
>
> No test bullets recovered from the Sirhan gun are in evidence. This gun was never identified scientifically as having fired any of the bullets removed from any of the victims. Other than the apparent self-evident fact that gun No. H53725 was forcibly removed from Sirhan at the scene, it has not been connected by microscopic examinations or other scientific testing to the actual shooting.
>
> The only reasonable conclusion from the evidence developed by the police, in spite of their protestations to the contrary, is that two guns were being fired in the kitchen pantry of the Ambassador Hotel at the time of the shooting of Senator Kennedy.
>
> From the general circumstances of the shooting the only reason-

able assumption is that the bullet removed from victim Weisel was in fact fired by the Sirhan gun. This bullet is in near perfect condition. I have, therefore, chosen it as a "test" bullet from the Sirhan gun and compared it with the bullet removed from the Senator's neck. The bullet removed from the Senator's neck, Exhibit 47, was one of those fired from *Firing Position B* [from behind], while the bullet removed from Weisel, Exhibit 54, was one of those fired from *Firing Position A*, the position of Sirhan. My examinations disclosed no individual characteristics establishing that Exhibit 47 and Exhibit 54 had been fired by the same gun. In fact, my examinations disclosed that bullet Exhibit 47 has a rifling angle approximately 23 minutes (14%) greater than the rifling angle of bullet Exhibit 54. It is, therefore, my opinion that bullets 47 and 54 could not have been fired from the same gun.

The above finding stands as independent proof that two guns were being fired concurrently in the kitchen pantry of the Ambassador Hotel at the time of the shooting.

The conclusions I have arrived at based upon my findings are as follows:

1. Two .22 caliber guns were involved in the assassination.
2. Senator Kennedy was killed by one of the shots fired from *Firing Position B,* fired by a second gunman.
3. The five surviving victims were wounded by Sirhan shooting from *Firing Position A*.
4. It is extremely unlikely that any of the bullets fired from the Sirhan gun ever struck the body of Senator Kennedy.
5. It is also unlikely that the shooting of the Senator could have accidentally resulted from an attempt to shoot Sirhan.

Dated December 28, 1970

William W. Harper
State of California
County of Los Angeles

CHAPTER 31

Thrown to the Wolves?

Sir, I have found you an argument; but I am not obliged to find you an understanding.

—Samuel Johnson

AT THE TIME Robert F. Kennedy was murdered, Jon Kimche was the Middle Eastern correspondent for the *London Evening Standard*. Kimche had connections in the Middle East: the best being his brother, David, who was listed as a senior officer in the Israeli Foreign Office and was a well-known Israeli secret service agent. This connection, among many others, gave Kimche a special insight into what was happening in his area of interest.

Within days of the Kennedy tragedy, he was researching Sirhan Bishara Sirhan's background, but this was a different background than that reported in the United States. His first article appeared on June 13, and ran as follows:

> Startling new evidence about the identity of the man charged with killing Robert Kennedy has been produced by an Arab government. The government has been making an intensive investigation into the background of Sirhan Bishara.
>
> The new information, which is being communicated to the United States authorities, may open up an entirely new line of inquiry into the motivation and organisation of the attack on Kennedy. It also indicates considerable variation in the accounts so far given of Sirhan's past and movements.

His full name is given as Sirhan Bishara Sirhan Abu Khatar. He was first brought to the United States as a four-year-old child in 1948—not in 1957. He returned to Jordan in 1957 and the records show that he was married in the Orthodox Church at Es Salt, 15 miles west of Amman on June 27, 1957, when he was only 13, to Leila Yussef Mikhael from Es Salt. Later that year Sirhan returned to the United States and three months later his wife was brought to him. The records of his journey are not very precise and probably not very important, as both husband and wife were little more than children.

Rather more interest centres on three later journeys which Sirhan made, especially on the last two which, according to this investigation, were made in 1964 and 1966. In 1964 Sirhan, according to these records, returned to the Middle East for seven months, four of which he spent in Damascus. Where he was for the rest of the time is not stated.

In 1966 he is said to have spent an even longer period in the Middle East, including a stretch of five months in Cairo. He returned to the United States, according to this report, at the beginning of 1967. The Arab government is convinced that its records are accurate but they are being sent to the United States so that they can be checked with the information assembled by the FBI.

Last week Sirhan's father cursed his son. Yesterday he was denouncing Kennedy and preparing to go to Los Angeles to stand by his son.

Kimche was in a privileged position in regard to obtaining data of this sort because of David's appointment within the Knesset. It is unlikely, however, that he would feature in his reports what he had not checked elsewhere. His reputation as a journalist and author would have been compromised and buried overnight if it were thought he was merely acting as a conduit for Israeli disinformation. Sufficient to say that David Kimche's alliances were not secret, and it would be extremely unlikely that the editors at the *London Evening Standard* were less than fully cognizant of this family relationship. The fact that the *Evening Standard* published three reports in this series from Jon Kimche would serve to underline that its editors were satisfied with Kimche's sources' bona fides.

The second of Kimche's reports was published on June 17 along-side a report by New York–based Leo Armati, who wrote about Sirhan creating a rumpus in the Max Raffery victory party. Kimche's report said:

> The Federal Bureau of Investigation at home and United States offi-cials abroad have been active over the weekend in seeking to pene-trate the sickening smoke screen which is settling on the Robert Kennedy assassination—especially over Sirhan Bishara Sirhan's im-mediate past.
>
> They have been probing new information covering at least four foreign countries concerning Sirhan's movements. In doing so they are satisfied that Sirhan's constitutional rights for a fair trial will not be jeopardised. On the contrary, it is thought that timely action and revelation may protect his life more effectively than formalistic si-lence—especially if Sirhan shows any inclination to talk freely.
>
> New information which has reached the U.S. Government claims to give details of Sirhan's journey to Syria in 1964, the time he went, where he went, how he went, and what he did.

This development was getting more interesting because of the in-formation that was reaching the U.S. government. It appears there was nothing being raised that would be featured in Sirhan's trial. Whatever was reaching the government was going no further. In his third article, Kimche combined news emanating from Los Angeles with his developed data relating to Sirhan from his Middle Eastern contacts. In the article dated July 18, a month after the last one, he stated:

> Curious moves have taken place before the trial of Robert Kennedy's alleged assassin starts in Los Angeles tomorrow. Extracts from Sirhan Bishara Sirhan's diaries have been circulated to interested and important politicians and others. Apparently the aim is to show that the young man was mentally unbalanced and not responsible for his action.
>
> This is indicated, it is claimed, by names of other prominent

American statesmen who were listed in the diary for assassination after Kennedy. A closer inspection, however, shows that these were all men directly involved in Middle East politics and accused by the Arab spokesmen of being pro-Israel.

But more important has been the attempt to blanket the information about Sirhan's own earlier movements. Though these are now known and recorded by at least three Arab governments—and presumably must be known by the FBI—there appears to be a desire not to bring this part of the case into court. Earlier details of Sirhan's journeys to the Middle East have now been fully investigated by the Arab governments concerned and they have filled in the missing details in the earlier report.

These show that: Sirhan left the United States at the end of January 1964, and travelled via Canada. From February 5 to February 21 he lived in the al Hamra suburb of Beirut with a Christian Arab family called Alquas al Mouishi. He then went to Damascus and from February 23 to March 5, 1964, he lodged with Halim al Halibi in Ghouta. From there he went to the training camp at Qataneh, outside Damascus. With him at the camp were 10 other Palestinian and some Iraqis and others. The two officers in charge of the camp at the time were Lieut. Colonel Aziz al Marouf and an Algerian Major known as Ahmed Belcasim.

There are no further details of the way he returned to the U.S. But the record shows that Sirhan left again in April 1966. This time he signed on as a member of the crew of a ship going to Alexandria. He is reported as arriving in Alexandria on May 22, 1966, and living for a week in Cairo at a small hotel. After that he moved to the house of a Lebanese family known as the Karam family. He stayed with them until he was taken to a training camp in the Ma'adi district of Cairo.

On August 3 he was again moved to a camp in Gaza. There he stayed until the end of September before returning to the United States—again there are no details about the return journey.

Kimche confided to me that his three Arab sources comparing notes were Egypt, Syria, and Lebanon. Sirhan's clandestine movements looked very much like those of a spy, but if so, for whom would he be spying? Certainly, it would not be for any of the three countries passing information to the U.S. government. It is also unlikely Sirhan was spying for any other Arab state, either, since it would be unlikely a devotee to an Arab cause, official or unofficial, would have had evidence provided against him. It would not be they who would throw him to the wolves. They would merely have remained silent. It would be different, however, if they knew he was working for the CIA. The statements made at this time in relation to the activities of Sirhan in the Middle East may have been a sharp reminder to the United States not to place the blame for the assassination of Senator Kennedy on to an innocent Arab country.

In examining the details of Sirhan's whereabouts, according to the data given by the Middle Eastern countries, there are two points where they differ from the records in the United States. One relates to the period August 3 to the end of September 1966, where the Middle Eastern sources said he was in Gaza and the records in the United States said he was working at Granja Vista Del Rio Farms in Corona, California. He was said to have had an accident there in September, and worked there until December. The second discrepancy concerns April 1966, where U.S. records place Sirhan opening a bank account on April 5 (remember that during his trial Sirhan categorically denied having a bank account) and Middle Eastern sources place him being a crew member on a ship that arrived in Alexandria, Egypt, in May. It can be said that it would not have been the first time the CIA placed doubles in a desired place. These records may relate to Sirhan's supposed whereabouts in the United States as much as to his supposed whereabouts in the Middle East.

If Sirhan worked for the CIA, then it would come as no surprise. Nor would it be surprising if he was left remembering nothing of this affiliation. The advancements in the development of hypnotic techniques at this time made it possible to erase from the subject's mind all memories of certain aspects of background, as well as all memories of who was causing this to happen. Therefore, it would not be significant if Sirhan recalled nothing of a bygone employ-ment with the CIA. Neither would it be significant if he remem-bered nothing of his work for it in the Middle East. As it is today, if such memories "leaked" into his mind, and this is extremely un-likely, it would be understandable if Sirhan was prepared to quietly forget them in favor of winning the parole so elusive to him over all these years.

I sent copies of the three Kimche articles to Sirhan's lawyer, Lawrence Teeter, in advance of the publication of this book. He dis-missed them out of hand, giving me the impression he thought they were Israeli disinformation. What the Israelis would gain from such disinformation I am not at all sure, but the attribution of the data to three named Arab countries hardly supports this thesis. Further-more, the publication of the three articles in the *London Evening Standard* not only supports their authenticity but it also draws at-tention that the reports were likely read by all the London-based diplomats for the various Arab states, and copies of the articles were almost certainly transmitted back to their countries. I am not aware of a single contradiction or complaint arising from the publi-cation of Kimche's reports. However, it is strange that they never reached the U.S. press. There would seem to be no doubt whatever that full details were in the hands of the FBI, and if that were the case, it would be exceedingly unlikely that the CIA was not also in full possession of the claims.

It had not passed notice that Sirhan had bought a car, a 1956 De Soto, a few days before his attack on Kennedy and that he had in his pocket $400, a princely sum in 1968. He certainly was not lack-ing in money. Neither was he lacking in incriminating evidence. Two extra .22 caliber bullets and a used cartridge case were also in his pockets, as though to make it as easy as possible to link the shooting to him. To this should be added a key belonging to a car owned by Robert Grindrod, an Ambassador Hotel employee. Grin-drod was not involved in Kennedy's killing, but he was "listed" by the Secret Service—someone it was "interested in"—which likely was a red herring thrown in to add to the discomfort of Sirhan.

It also added to his discomfort that he appeared to know so little about the gun he used. Did he have it when he went to the Ambassador, or was he passed it by the tall man or the woman in the polka-dot dress? It has been pointed out that, under hypnosis, it is easier to program a person to go through the motions of shooting a gun than to program a person to kill someone. This is exactly what appears to have happened: he engaged in the motions of shooting while Kennedy was killed during the mayhem he created. On analysis, it was his entries in his notebook that left a great deal open for investigation. For instance, while his "anti-Kennedy" rantings occurred in only two pages of his notebook, there were few references to anything concerning Arabs, and anti-Israeli references were totally absent.

To put it at its simplest in his trial, Sirhan did not have a leg to stand on. Instead of producing every scrap of evidence to account for his actions or to somehow attempt to justify them, he simply asked to die. The absence of any memory of his actions combined with the damning "automatic" writing in his so-called notebook made it difficult for any defense team to protect him. But then the fact that his defense team appeared worse than useless did nothing to improve his position. Accusations of communist affiliations were raised because of entries in his notebook in which he writes over and over, "pay to the order of," and says:

I have often wondered what or how it feels to be rich, rich, rich, rich, rich. . . . I advocate the overthrow of the current president . . . of the United States of America. I have no absolute plans yet—but soon will compose some. . . . I firmly support the communist cause and its people—wether [sic] Russian Chinese Albanian Hungarians—workers of the world unite you have nothing to lose but your chains.

This was quite mysterious and another reason for questioning how the entries came to be made in the notebook, since his communist friend Walter Crowe told how he had tried to interest Sirhan in the politics of the far left without success. Sirhan simply was not interested.

There was, as many have pointed out, something extremely odd about the whole affair. The indications of Sirhan's spying activities were real and needed addressing. However, they never were addressed because they were never introduced into the trial proceedings, in spite of Kimche's assurances that all the data he collected was in the hands of the FBI.

There is little doubt that Lee Harvey Oswald was a CIA agent and that he was set up to take the blame for the killing of President John F. Kennedy in 1963. The CIA agents who were the survivors of the Bay of Pigs debacle, with their Establishment allies, were dedicated to ridding the White House of Kennedys, and in their conspiracy to kill Kennedy they thought nothing of mercilessly sacrificing a fellow agent, Oswald, in their quest to change the rule of government to get what they wanted. In the case of Robert F. Kennedy, he appeared to be in no danger until he became a front-runner in his bid for the presidency. Here was another Kennedy knocking on the door of the White House, and neither the conspirators' intense hatred of him had abated, nor had their ruthless determination to keep him from power. After killing a president, the conspirators were unlikely to balk at killing a senator, and having achieved the more difficult task of the assassination of John Kennedy, they were not going to stand back and allow another Kennedy to assume the presidency. It was all part of the scenario described to Wayne January by the CIA pilot the day before John Kennedy was murdered.

Many writers and researchers have already underlined that the so-called investigation into the killing of Robert Kennedy was almost exclusively in the hands of CIA operatives. The FBI was shouldered out of the picture and the officers of the LAPD were made subordinate to the CIA men. There were too many instances of the investigation being conducted strictly in blinkers for it to pass without question. Sirhan's trial was something of a mockery, where his defense was almost totally ineffective in deference to the prosecution, a situation that would be difficult to match in legal history.

It is hard to contemplate a young man so pathetically without help and prepared to accept what was coming to him. But then those capable of programming a "Manchurian candidate" were also capable of programming him to self-destruct. It would be easy to see in all of this another Lee Harvey Oswald, another CIA man being thrown to the wolves by those determined to dictate the presidency of the United States. Bizarrely, therefore, Sirhan was entirely prepared to accept the responsibility for the murder of Senator Kennedy, even if he did not do it. There surely had to be something very, very odd about that.

CHAPTER 32

Unexplained, Mislaid, and Other Anomalies

Half the truth is often a whole lie.

—Proverb

THE WOMAN IN the polka-dot dress is a classic example of the unexplained left to dangle, without explanation by those investigating the murder of Robert F. Kennedy. Clearly, she was a key figure in what occurred at the Ambassador Hotel the night Kennedy was killed. The so-called investigation that resulted in a woman on crutches, patently not the woman in question, being put forward in all seriousness by LAPD defies belief. The trouble was that the evidence put forward by those present at the time was, necessarily, discarded by those dedicated to the idea that there was one shooter, one killer, and that they had him in detention.

That Police Sergeant Paul Sharaga's accounting of the reports he had received on the presence of the woman in the polka-dot dress went "missing" is a prime example of the ruthlessness and determination of Lieutenant Manny Pena and Sergeant Enrique Hernandez to "direct" the investigation. To all intents and purposes, they "airbrushed" the woman completely out of the picture. To have followed that line of enquiry would have taken them into the realms of conspiracy, against which they were totally dedicated.

When the first batch of LAPD files—the Summary Report—was finally released, it added little to what was already known about the case. It was thought that further waiting would be rewarded in 1988 with the release of the full details of the entire file. However, when it happened the file was found to be missing some of the physical evidence, such as the .22 caliber bullet that had been found in Sirhan Bishara Sirhan's pocket and over 2,400 photographs of the crime scene, bullets, and ballistics. This made mockery of the media reports following the release of the Summary Report. They had then reported that the conclusion reached by the LAPD was that most people making conspiracy charges were "lying for one reason or another."

× × ×

There was a great deal of explaining to do in regard to the remarkable attack made on the integrity of the coroner, Dr. Thomas Noguchi. It was stated in the *Los Angeles Herald Examiner* that having said that the bullets that killed Kennedy were fired from behind and at very close range, Dr. Noguchi was asked by a member of the district attorney's staff to change the "one to three inches" statement he had made after his examination to "one to three feet." He refused, but by now he wondered what it was all about. He decided he would take the matter further and have a neutron activation analysis carried out on the bullets that had been removed from Senator Kennedy. He was promptly prevented from carrying out these tests, both by the LAPD and the Office of the District Attorney. They simply made it impossible for him to have access to the bullets. This was not the end of the affair, however. As time went by, he was accused of incompetence in his handling of the Kennedy autopsy. After being accused of taking drugs, he was suspended; put simply, he had been fired.

Dr. Noguchi was not the man to take this lying down. He vigorously fought back in a public hearing of his case. When his lawyer proposed a detailed review of the Kennedy autopsy, Warten Weekes, the defense counsel for the county, suddenly became ill at ease, insisting the details of the Kennedy assassination should not be represented in public for fear of "international" reactions. Weekes conceded that Dr. Noguchi's autopsy had been "superior" and drew matters to a close. Of course, the aforementioned expected explanations were not forthcoming. In the long run, they were not necessary.

The authorities had displayed to the world their motives in trying to get rid of Dr. Noguchi, and the implications in respect of the enquiry into Kennedy's death were glaringly obvious to see.

Dr. Noguchi was reinstated in 2003 and continued to be the coroner of Los Angeles until he retired. I spoke to Dr. Noguchi, in the company of his lawyer, Godfrey Isaac, who acted for him in his retaliatory action against the city of Los Angeles. Dr. Noguchi was both accomplished and honest, and we have him to thank for knowing the truth about the proximity of the weapon and the location of the shots that killed Kennedy, which the authorities appeared to be desperate to have hushed up.

× × ×

It is unbelievable that Dr. Noguchi did not give his vital evidence at Sirhan's trial. He appeared and was fully prepared to give the results of the autopsy when he was stopped. Questioning the coroner, the district attorney was engaged in developing a "fencing match" designed to keep key questions from being answered by Dr. Noguchi, when—of all people—a member of the *defense* team intruded to say that the coroner's evidence was not desirable, explaining that he should not recite the gory details of the nature and location of the wounds inflicted on Senator Kennedy. Hence, his explosive evidence was never heard in court, courtesy Sirhan's lawyers. An interesting question is: When was critical evidence from a coroner describing the wounds of a murdered man in a trial of the man accused of the killing prevented from being given? And since the description the coroner had to give would have clearly favored the accused, another interesting question might be: How often does defense counsel publicly shoot itself and its client in the foot with one bullet?

× × ×

If the previous problems in the investigation are regarded as inexplicable, there are other instances even more obvious and begging explanation. Little has been said about the hairy experience of

William W. Harper, the renowned criminologist who investigated the ballistics evidence relating to the Sirhan trial after it drew to a close. Harper was on his way to pick up his wife when he observed that he was being followed. He pulled ahead and could not shake off his pursuer. It developed into a regular car chase through the streets of Pasadena, California, when he suddenly drove over the crest of a hill and dropped sharply on the other side. At that moment, he heard what he knew was a bullet hitting his car. A later examination confirmed this, and the location of it indicated that had he not dropped over the hill at that moment, he would have been shot in the back of the head. The culprits were never found, and their motives never obtained.

× × ×

Should there be any doubt that the LAPD was deceitful and dishonest in regard to the investigation of the Senator Kennedy assassination, there is an example that will serve amply to illustrate stealth and deception. It was the response of Assistant Police Chief Daryl F. Gates to reports on activities of the outspoken Allard Lowenstein, who had been a congressman representing New York and who made no bones of saying he believed Sirhan innocent. Lowenstein held a press conference in the New York Statler Hilton jointly with Paul Schrade, one of those shot in the Ambassador pantry at the time of the Kennedy slaying. Its purpose was to exert pressure on the authorities to have the secret police files on the Kennedy murder made available to the public. This movement had begun not long after Sirhan's trial had ended, but it was not until 1988 that the files were opened. Here in 1974, the press conference resulted in a seventy-six-page memo being submitted to Gates. The fly sheet on the memo said, "This separate addenda [sic] contains confidential information relative to the questions submitted by Allard Lowenstein. The information has not been revealed prior to this report and may conflict with previous statements made by the Chief of Police and other officials. Serious consideration should be given to the release of this information."

Perhaps the last line should have said that "Serious consideration should be given to *withholding* this information."

Gates knew what it meant. The data was not released.

× × ×

The unhappy tailpiece to this chapter relates to Lowenstein, who was shot dead by Dennis Sweeney. A former member of the civil rights movement, Sweeney was known to fifty-one-year-old Lowenstein and was said to be deranged. Whether the murder was a consequence of Lowenstein's high profile in the Kennedy aftermath was not ascertained. A close friend made the comment that "Dennis Sweeney was a nut. The only question is whether he was a handled nut."

CHAPTER 33

A Law unto Themselves

Who to himself is law, no law doth need.

—George Chapman

FROM THE VERY beginning of the investigation into the death of Senator Robert F. Kennedy, the LAPD exercised its own law. It might have been expected that in a shooting situation where the number of bullets fired were critical to determining in which direction the investigation should proceed there would be no argument when the counting was done. The gun Sirhan Bishara Sirhan fired in the pantry area of the Ambassador Hotel held a total of eight bullets. His gun was empty after his shooting spree. The enquiry team involved itself in accounting for the eight bullets fired and, to its own satisfaction, did so. Unhappily for the LAPD, there were others accounting for bullets fired that night, and they did not stop at eight. When a ninth bullet was identified, and even a tenth, it would have been expected that the investigating officers would have acknowledged that at least two guns were fired in the area and that the two guns fired would have identified that a conspiracy had taken place. Not so for the LAPD investigators, who doggedly stuck to their predetermined no conspiracy line.

In another direction, they showed themselves quite resolute in denying there was ever a woman with Sirhan, the woman in the polka-dot dress. She was obviously a figment of the multiple imaginations of all those who saw her, but then, an accomplice would have indicated that a conspiracy had taken place. When it finally became necessary to answer the torrent of eyewitness statements, they "identified" the woman as a Kennedy volunteer, Valeria Schulte, a blonde, who wore a green dress with yellow polka dots, showing total disregard to the consistency of the descriptions of the witnesses who said she had brown hair and that she was wearing a white dress with black dots on it. Furthermore, Schulte had one leg in a cast, from top to toe, requiring her to use a crutch. Her description could not have been further from the woman the witnesses had described.

In their anxiety to expunge all references in their records to the woman in the polka-dot dress, the interrogator Sergeant Enrique Hernandez virtually made liars of two young people, who knew what they saw. Sandra Serrano and Thomas Vincent DiPierro were hounded until they said what Hernandez wanted them to say. CIA linked as Hernandez was, Lieutenant Manny Pena went on record as saying he had no criticism of Hernandez's interrogation "technique." Booker Griffin and Sergeant Paul Sharaga were both misrepresented in false statements found, twenty years later, in the LAPD files. They had both asserted knowledge of the woman in the polka-dot dress, and that was not to be allowed in the official record.

Scott Enyart, desperate to make a complete record of events with his camera that night at the Ambassador, did a superb job of covering Kennedy's movements. Since the press representatives had all gone to telephones to phone in their stories to meet their deadlines when the senator finished his speech in the ballroom, Enyart was alone in making a continuous record of Kennedy's progress through the pantry area. He was extremely excited in carrying out his task, but this gave way to devastation when his hero was shot down. It was not long before the press photographers were back in the throng, but he had got the vital sequence they had missed. He told the police what he had been doing and was terrified when he was chased by plainclothes officers, who held him at gunpoint to take from him his treasured film. The story of his efforts to recover his pictures and the subsequent court cases, in which he, too, was branded a liar, are to be found elsewhere. It would seem that the pictures taken by Enyart were not to be seen by the public.

Hidden away in the mass of data relating to the court cases in which Enyart invested $250,000 to achieve an award of $100,000 were references that merit the closest attention. This might just be a clue to the kind of things to be seen in Enyart's pictures, if we had ever been allowed to see them. Two of Enyart's pictures had been given the log numbers 24 and 25. These numbers coincided with the numbers logged for People's Exhibit 48, a bullet and bullet fragment retrieved from Kennedy's neck. Had the Enyart pictures been given identical numbers because they corresponded with the shots fired at the senator? The numbers on the exhibits were crudely altered from 24 and 25 to 26 and 27. This raises the possibility that they were renumbered so as to avoid them being linked to Enyart's pictures.

I have spoken to Enyart on a number of occasions. While it cannot be said that he is in any way happy with the treatment he received at the hands of the LAPD and the city of Los Angeles, I detected no bitterness. He said he felt vindicated in spite of receiving a derisory award from the court. "We proved that the LAPD is crooked," he said, "and we beat Skip Miller." Louis "Skip" Miller, a top lawyer, defended the city and attracted little merit for his performance in view of the questionable tactics he used. In the first trial, the jury foreman was excused to return to his work, whereupon Miller went to see him to discuss what had transpired in the jury room. He was seeking hints of improprieties that might give him grounds for seeking a mistrial. Quoting the former jury foreman, Miller sought a mistrial and had Enyart's petition thrown out by the judge. The law had been changed some four years earlier prohibiting such consultations between counsel and jury members. Miller was reported to the state bar and consequently found himself a defendant in a case in which he was accused of willfully violating the code of professional conduct. He claimed he was unaware of the change in the law, a remarkable admission from a lawyer who demanded $225 an hour for his services. Translated into today's values that amounts to quite a fortune in fees.

The catastrophe of the ballistics evidence is quite unbelievable. The catalog of errors is bewildering. Bullets handed in as evidence were always marked so that the person handing it in could be properly identified at a later time. In an amazing number of instances, such bullets were found to have different markings when examined later, making it impossible to identify which was which. A bullet removed from Senator Kennedy's neck was confused with a bullet removed from the buttock of Ira Goldstein, who had also been injured in the shooting; faulty microscope optics were blamed. This was investigated and no fault was found in the optics of the microscope in question. The confusion between the two guns in the courtroom defies belief. There is, of course, an unthinkable aspect to this confusion. If the Iver Johnson Cadet gun with the serial number 18602, which had been in the possession of the LAPD for over a year, having been taken from Jake Williams, a robbery suspect, really was the gun that had killed Kennedy, as DeWayne Wolfer asserted (see chapter 30), where did this leave the LAPD? And why was Sirhan not discharged immediately?

It is known that 2,410 photographs relating to Kennedy's killing were destroyed by the LAPD. They were incinerated at a local hospital on August 21, 1968, while the investigation was still in progress and months before Sirhan's trial began. The LAPD also destroyed a doorpost containing evidence—bullet holes—on the grounds that it could not be accommodated in a filing cabinet. Altogether, the LAPD showed an unbelievable disregard for evidence.

Add to this the attempt to discredit the coroner Dr. Thomas Noguchi and his vital evidence, and the picture assumes proportions in which distortion becomes the norm. Were it not such a serious matter, it would qualify as an example of "Through the Looking Glass" justice.

CHAPTER 34

Consequences

*They spend their time mostly looking forward to
the past.*

—John Osborne

TO HIS MANY followers, Robert F. Kennedy was a shining light. For some, he was the means of rekindling the promise of the new beginning in politics that had been glimpsed in John F. Kennedy. To others, regardless of family connection, here was a man of compassion, a man to be trusted with affairs of state and with the development of a caring government. When Kennedy died, there was an enormous political vacuum. To many, there was only the consolation of looking to Edward M. Kennedy to take up where his brothers had left off. This might well be said to have been looking forward to the past.

The wise ones in the Democratic Party had already looked, considered, and decided, correctly, that Edward Kennedy was too young and inexperienced to take up where Robert had left off, though it is thought to have been proposed by some. In any case, he would never have crassly jumped into his brother's shoes. That would have been unthinkable to him. When he was asked to add his name to the ticket as a candidate for the vice presidency, he declined. He said:

Over the last few weeks, many prominent Democrats have raised the possibility of my running for Vice-President on the Democratic ticket

223

this fall. I deeply appreciate their confidence. Under normal circumstances such a possibility would be a high honor and a challenge to
further public service. But for me, this year, it is impossible. . . . I
know that [you] will understand these reasons without further elab-
oration.

Politically, it was a tragedy to add to tragedy, for the Democrats
had reached that magic moment when there was a roller coaster of
popular opinion ready to sweep their soon-to-be-adopted candidate
into the White House. Magic moments of that kind do not turn up
very often, and it was thought by no means to be out of the question for any candidate they nominated to be swept into the presidency on the coattails of Edward Kennedy running for the vice
presidency. But it was not to be, and Richard Nixon had a walkover
victory when the day came.

All that sparkling enthusiasm, hard earned by Robert Kennedy,
the new-bred confidence, the wonderful surge of popular support, the
new-era-around-the-corner feeling was going to be wasted. It was
simply going to dissipate, disappear, die, for there was nobody else
to stand in who could possibly deliver what Kennedy had promised.
Perhaps in 1972 it would be Edward Kennedy. Perhaps this was the
way forward. It needed time.

Kennedy was buried the Saturday following his murder. In New
York, the crowds had gathered to pay their last respects to the
fallen senator. A select few of Kennedy's friends stood as honor
guard by the coffin throughout the night, and the morning had
brought a packed requiem Mass at Saint Patrick's for him. Edward
Kennedy eulogized, but there were few who needed to be reminded
of the great loss they had suffered. The rousing "Battle Hymn of the
Republic" provided an outlet for the pent up feelings of those who
found it difficult to let their hero go, and then it was on to Washington
for the burial.

It was dark when the pallbearers carried the coffin into Arlington
Cemetery, and the darkness provided a fitting shroud for those who
were present, but who resented having to bear witness to the rever-

ent concealing in the earth of a man they had known as so full of political promise, so dynamic, so full of compassion, so forward looking, so full of vigor, so full of hope: too full of life to be quenched by the uncaring bullet, too bright a light to be extinguished by the hatred of the assassin.

× × ×

So now it was to the task of facing the future without Robert Kennedy. Edward Kennedy was in the forefront of many people's minds. This would be the last chance to embrace a shining Camelot, the last chance for a whole generation to rise above the dictates of those who sought to impose government by the gun.

John F. Kennedy had said, "Just as I went into politics because Joe died, if anything happened to me tomorrow, my brother Bobby would run for my seat in the Senate. And if Bobby died, Teddy would take over for him."

This was a code of honor. Robert may not have taken Jack's seat in the Senate, but he fought for and took a seat. Then he campaigned to take his brother's place in the White House and failed through no fault of his own. Now the Democrats looked to Edward. Before he had left the hospital in which Robert died, Allard Lowenstein bellowed at Edward, "You've got to take the leadership! Now that Bobby's gone you're all we've got!" Sadly to be reflected on, Lowenstein, a campaigner against the Vietnam War, would be shot down and killed himself (see chapter 32).

Even though he was advised to quit politics and practice law, Edward could not turn his back on politics. Robert had realized there was somebody out there who wanted to kill him, and it did not stop him, and Edward felt exactly the same way about it. He said, "I know I'm going to get my ass shot off just like Bobby," and he took sensible precautions, for what they were worth. In his first speech after Robert's death, he said, "There is no safety in hiding. Not for me; not for any of us here today; not for our children, who will inherit the world we make for them. . . . Like my brothers before me, I pick up a fallen standard."

The sentiment was not echoed in his immediate actions, however. In 1969, Edward Kennedy ran for majority whip in the U.S. Senate. This was very much a fetching and carrying appointment, a mundane move clearly in the opposite direction from running for president. It came as a great surprise to many, and no doubt a disappointment, too. The logic could not be deduced. It may have been a compromise of sorts between Edward and his family in return for him staying in politics, but otherwise it was difficult to understand.

There was little doubt that the mood of the Democrats in marking Edward as their future presidential candidate had not escaped notice of the conspirators, who were standing by their dire threat: they would kill John Kennedy, Robert Kennedy, and any other Kennedy who went in the direction of the White House. But there was no doubt that the conspirators had problems. To kill two Kennedys five years apart was something that might escape close investigation, but to kill another Kennedy would be inviting exposure. There must be another way of keeping the third Kennedy out of the White House.

Senator Edward M. Kennedy

CHAPTER 35

Reorientation

We must travel in the direction of our fear.
                                                —John Berryman

WHEN THE INAUGURATION of John F. Kennedy as president took place, the grateful Kennedy gave to each of his chief workers an engraved cigarette case. On Robert's it said, "To Robert F. Kennedy. After I am through, how about you?" The inscription on Edward's ran, "And the last shall be first." Both, of course, were very meaningful.

Edward M. Kennedy had had reason to be grateful that he was a member of his illustrious family. At Harvard, he thoroughly disgraced himself by getting another student to sit an examination in Spanish for him. Dismissed in ignominy, it was the drubbing his father gave him that drove home that Kennedys did not cheat. He first sought to expiate himself by enlisting in the armed forces, but he was bound to return to the scene of his failure and put matters right. It was likely family influence that secured a second chance for him, and he would not let the family down this time. He plied himself, graduated, and went on to earn a law degree.

But there was no suggestion he was taking up a career in law when he was appointed assistant to the district attorney of Suffolk County, Massachusetts. He contributed little to the job: he rarely took a case and was not that brilliant when he did. It would appear he was sitting it out in preparation for his next stepping-stone. It was certainly observed that he had ability when he cared to show it, which was not often. He was learning about politics. Honest enough to refuse payment for his appointment—he accepted one dollar a year—there were those who quipped he was overpaid. The writer Jack Olsen said, "He was as bad on his last day as he was on his first . . . and when he left, a colleague recounted, 'No one was unhappy to see him go.' "

But of his political aspirations, Olsen spoke of people calling him "the best politician in the family." John Kennedy certainly endorsed this. Olsen said, "Of all the Kennedys he had the heartiest laugh, the most spontaneous smile, the most refreshing Irish humor, the gladdest hand." In 1962, Edward Kennedy campaigned for the September primary although thoroughly unready for it. But he was well schooled, and with his family staunchly behind him he made a remarkably strong candidate. With the election campaign all but won, he recklessly agreed to a television debate with his opponent, Eddie McCormack. In the debate, McCormack wiped the floor with him. His leaning on family connections, his lack of experience, and his seeking for "qualifications" by visiting foreign countries all came under a torrent of fire from the explosive McCormack. McCormack had the edge over Kennedy in every direction. He exploited every weakness he perceived in his opponent. Had the contest been scored by an umpire on points, there was not the slightest doubt that the hesitant, monosyllabic Kennedy would have been buried without a trace. As it was, the viewers to the debate reached a totally different conclusion. Whether it was because the viewers were far more discerning than given credit for, or whether the medium was far more ephemeral than ever believed, the decision went hands down to Kennedy. He had demonstrated restraint, a well-balanced attitude, gentlemanliness, and all the features that recommend a candidate to the voters. His election win was 559,303 to 257,403, a whopping 69 percent of the vote. Here it was, another Kennedy for Massachusetts: unsurprising, but in remarkable circumstances. His course was set: another bright Kennedy light was twinkling.

When Edward was approaching election to the U.S. Senate, his brother, the president, had just delighted the nation by seeing off the peril of a war with Cuba and the Soviet Union. His success in the Cuban missile crisis brought him enormous political kudos, and this rubbed off onto Edward. Edward's formidable opponent, George Lodge, would, at any other time, have given him huge problems, but now the way was paved for him. He took the seat with 1,162,611 votes against 877,669, a tidy majority.

This did not alter the fact that Edward lacked Jack's charisma and Robert's resolution and tenacity. But Edward was establishing himself as his own man, and he had his own talents and assets. He could tackle the tedious and the humdrum without complaint, and at the same time stand up as a bright star when his moment arose. He had enormous ability to bring to his tasks in the Senate, and he was thus making his way when the crisis of his brother's murder took place in Dallas in 1963. Robert and Edward were probably more greatly valued after this tragedy and looked to for resistance to the violence that had savaged the presidency. When it came to Robert's death in 1968, however, there were many who would not have blamed the survivor if he had chosen to hide himself away and work in obscurity.

This would not be his way, however. When, at the age of thirty, he had been sworn in as the junior member of the U.S. Senate for Massachusetts, he had ceased to become the baby of the Kennedy family. He felt he had overcome the weakness he displayed in the Spanish examination episode and could preen himself that he had brought home honor and distinction to rank with his brothers. And his endeavors were acknowledged. Soon after Edward's swearing in, addressing an audience at Harrisburg, Pennsylvania, President Kennedy smilingly began, "I should introduce myself. I am Teddy Kennedy's brother."

That it had suddenly become a new ballgame with the death of Robert might well influence the thinking and the attitudes of the last brother, but it would not prevent him, as he had already said, from picking up the fallen standard.

CHAPTER 36

Sailing and Celebrations

You can only predict things after they have happened.
—Eugene Ionesco

THE YEAR AFTER Robert F. Kennedy died, Edward M. Kennedy made his usual plans to take part in the famous summer regatta off the coast of Martha's Vineyard at Edgartown, Massachusetts. The Edgartown Regatta attracted the rich and famous, and competing in the event had become a tradition for the Kennedys. This year, Edward would have as his sailing companion his nephew, Joseph P. Kennedy III.

The regatta was not the only attraction to Martha's Vineyard that year, however. Edward had rented the Lawrence cottage on the tiny island of Chappaquiddick, just off the coast of Martha's Vineyard, in which to entertain some of his staff and friends. This was a "thank you" for the likes of Mary Jo Kopechne, who had been a "boiler room girl"—one who boiled down the news so that it could be quickly assimilated—for Robert Kennedy and who had now joined his team. There were six women and six men in the party, if Kennedy's sixty-year-old driver was included. The venue offered peace and quiet, sandy beaches, exclusive bathing, hopefully sunshine, and countryside.

Though the island would be used for holiday pursuits and the cottage for parties, barbecues, and other celebrational activities, the party guests had been booked in to hotels in Edgartown. The six women invited were sisters Maryellen and Nance Lyons, Susan

Tannenbaum, Esther Newberg, Rosemary Keough, and Mary Jo Kopechne. The men in the party were Joseph P. Gargan, Edward's cousin, Charles C. Tretter, Raymond S. LaRosa, and Paul Markham a close friend of Edward's. These four, with Edward himself and Jack Crimmins, his driver, made up the six men. There had been other such gatherings at other venues, but Chappaquiddick offered the privacy that Edward liked for his partying. And if the comments of the neighbors, such few as there were, were anything to go by, the laughter emanating from the cottage marked it out as a great success.

The Friday night activity was a barbecue, with Gargan as chief cook. As it grew late, the senator asked Crimmins for his car keys because he had decided to make it an early night. As early nights go, it was not that early. Crimmins said it was about 11:15 P.M., but others made it much later. Crimmins would stay the night at the cottage, which had some, but not much, sleeping capacity, and it was reported that the senator left with Kopechne. They assumed that he was giving her a lift.

Early the next morning, two anglers made a shocking discovery at Chappaquiddick. They were at the Dike Bridge searching for a suitable place to start fishing when, looking into the dark waters, they saw the shape of a large car lying upside down in about eight feet of water. They lost no time in contacting the police, and Edgartown's police chief, Jim Arena, was soon in charge of the operation to try to save the life or lives of anyone who might still be in the vehicle. He borrowed a pair of trunks from one of the residents and swam to the car to get a better look. The vicious currents in what was called Poucha Pond were so strong he could see nothing, so he called the fire department and asked it to quickly send a scuba diver. The investigation took a nasty turn when the diver saw the body of a woman in the back of the car. The scuba diver, John Farrar, ascertained that the body was in an advanced state of rigor mortis. He saw how she had desperately orientated her head and mouth to assume a position in which she could take advantage of the last remaining air in the car. With the car being upside down, she had moved toward the floor of the car above her, but she had had little chance of survival. She was brought to the surface with her arms stiffly fixed in an outstretched position from clutching at the upholstery of a seat in front of her.

By that time, there was a doctor in attendance, and he confirmed that she had died by drowning. He further described to a reporter that "the body was rigid as a statue, the teeth were gritted, there was froth around the nose, and the hands were in a claw-like position." The license plate and the description of the vehicle, when it was raised, identified it as belonging to Senator Kennedy, and a handbag found in the car indicated the woman was Rosemary Keough. Reports said that Senator Kennedy had arrived at Chappaquiddick via the ferry earlier in the morning and had spent some time making a telephone call from the payphone at the ferryhouse. He returned to Edgartown before getting in touch with the police to give an accident report. Kennedy corrected the police chief's assumption that the dead woman was Rosemary Keough. "It's not Cricket Keough," he said, using the name by which she was called. "It's Mary Jo Kopechne, and I have already notified her family."

Somewhat curiously, after discussions with Markham, who was a lawyer, the senator opted to make his statement in writing, which he prepared with Markham at police headquarters. The statement handed to Police Chief Arena, which was unsigned, read as follows:

On July 18, 1969, at approximately 11:15 P.M., on Chappaquiddick Island, Martha's Vineyard, I was driving my car on Main Street on my way to get the ferry back to Edgartown. I was unfamiliar with the road and turned on to Dike Road instead of bearing left on Main Street. After proceeding for approximately a half mile on Dike Road I descended a hill and came upon a narrow bridge. The car went off the side of the bridge. There was one passenger in the car with me, Miss ——, a former secretary of my brother Robert Kennedy. The car turned over and sank into the water and landed with the roof resting on the bottom.

I attempted to open the door and window of the car but have no recollection of how I got out of the car. I came to the surface and then repeatedly dove down to the car in an attempt to see if the passenger was still in the car. I was unsuccessful in the attempt.

I was exhausted and in a state of shock. I recall walking back to where my friends were eating. There was a car parked in front of the cottage and I climbed into the back seat. I then asked for someone to bring me back to Edgartown. I remember walking around for a period of time and then going back to my hotel room. When I fully realized what happened this morning, I immediately contacted the police.

This was the signal for sixteen of those around the Kennedy family who might offer friendly and expert advice on Edward's predicament to gather at Hyannis Port, Massachusetts, "taking every spare bed," as *Time* magazine expressed it. The list of the distinguished gathering read like a Who's Who of all the Kennedy big guns, and included Robert McNamara, Richard Goodwin, Arthur M. Schlesinger Jr., John Kenneth Galbraith, Robert J. Clark, Stephen Smith, Burke Marshall, and Theodore Sorensen, as well as Joseph P. Gargan and Paul Markham, who were both guests at the Lawrence cottage on Chappaquiddick, on July 19.

Kennedy's brief, pointed explanation of events satisfied the judge that he had committed no more than the offense of failing to report an accident. He left out Kopechne's name because he did not know how to spell her surname. The judge gave him a minimal two-month suspended sentence, but the public at large was more curious than the judge and far more demanding by way of seeking an explanation. Kennedy appeared on television to give more details of what had happened. He began:

My fellow citizens:

I have requested this opportunity to talk to the people of Massachusetts about the tragedy which happened last Friday evening. This morning I entered a plea of guilty to the charge of leaving the scene of an accident. Prior to my appearance in court it would have been improper of me to comment on these matters. But tonight I am free to tell you what happened and to say what it means to me.

On the weekend of July 18 I was on Martha's Vineyard Island participating with my nephew Joe Kennedy—as for thirty years my family has participated—in the annual Edgartown sailing regatta. Only reasons of health prevented my wife from accompanying me.

On Chappaquiddick Island, off Martha's Vineyard, I attended on Friday evening, July 18, a cookout I had encouraged and helped sponsor for a devoted group of Kennedy campaign secretaries. When I left the party, around 11:15 P.M., I was accompanied by one of these girls, Miss Mary Jo Kopechne. Mary Jo was one of the most devoted members of the staff of Senator Robert Kennedy. She worked for him for four years and was broken up over his death. For this reason, and because she was such a gentle, kind, and idealistic person, all of us tried to help her feel that she still had a home with the Kennedy family.

There is no truth, no truth whatever, to the widely circulated suspicions of immoral conduct that have been leveled at my behavior and hers regarding that evening. There has never been a private relationship between us of any kind. I know of nothing in Mary Jo's conduct on that or any other occasion—the same is true of the other girls at that party—that would lend any substance to such ugly speculation about their character. Nor was I driving under the influence of liquor.

Little over one mile away, the car that I was driving on an unlit road went off a narrow bridge which had no guardrails and was built on a left angle to the road. The car overturned in a deep pond and immediately filled with water. I remember thinking as the cold water rushed in around my head that I was for certain drowning. Then water entered my lungs and I actually felt the sensation of drowning. But somehow I struggled to the surface alive. I made immediate and repeated efforts to save Mary Jo by diving into the strong and murky current but succeeded only in increasing my state of utter exhaustion and alarm.

My conduct and conversations during the next several hours to the extent that I can remember them make no sense to me at all. Although my doctors informed me that I suffered a cerebral concussion as well as shock, I do not seek to escape responsibility for my actions by placing the blame either on the physical, emotional trauma brought on by the accident or on anyone else. I regard as indefensible the fact that I did not report the accident to the police immediately.

Instead of looking for a telephone after lying exhausted in the grass for an undetermined time, I walked back to the cottage where the party was being held and requested the help of two friends, my cousin Joseph Gargan and Paul Markham, and directed them to return immediately to the scene with me—this was sometime after midnight—in order to undertake a new effort to dive down and locate Miss Kopechne. Their strenuous efforts, undertaken at some risks to their own lives, also proved futile.

All kinds of scrambled thoughts—all of them confused, some of them irrational, many of them which I cannot recall, and some of which I would not have seriously entertained under normal circumstances—went through my mind at this period. They were reflected in the various inexplicable, inconsistent, and inconclusive things I said and did, including such questions as whether the girl might still be alive somewhere out of that immediate area, whether some awful curse did actually hang over all the Kennedys, whether there was some justifiable reason for me to doubt what had happened and to delay my report, whether somehow the awful weight of this incredible accident might in some way pass from my shoulders. I was overcome, I'm frank to say, by a jumble of emotions—grief, fear, doubt, exhaustion, panic, confusion, and shock.

Instructing Gargan and Markham not to alarm Mary Jo's friends that night, I had them take me to the ferry crossing. The ferry having shut down for the night, I suddenly jumped into the water and impulsively swam across, nearly drowning once again in the effort, and returning to my hotel about 2:00 A.M. and collapsed in my room. I remember going out at one point and saying something to the room clerk.

In the morning, with my mind somewhat more lucid, I made an effort to call a family legal adviser, Burke Marshall, from a public telephone on the Chappaquiddick side of the ferry and belatedly reported the accident to the Martha's Vineyard police.

Today, as I have mentioned, I felt morally obliged to plead guily to the charge of leaving the scene of an accident. No words on my part can possibly express the pain and suffering I feel over this tragic incident. This last week has been an agonizing one for me and the members of my family, and the grief we feel over the loss of a wonderful friend will remain with us the rest of our lives.

These events, the publicity, the inuendo and whispers which have surrounded them, and my admission of guilt this morning raise the question in my mind of whether my standing among the people of my state has been so impaired that I should resign my seat in the United States Senate. If at any time the citizens of Massachusetts should lack confidence in their senator's character or ability, with or without justification, he could not in my opinion adequately perform his duty and should not continue in office.

The people of this state, the state which sent John Quincy Adams and Daniel Webster and Charles Sumner and Henry Cabot Lodge and John Kennedy to the United States Senate, are entitled to representation in that body of men who inspire their utmost confidence. For this reason, I would understand full well why some might think it right for me to resign. For me this will be a difficult decision to make.

It has been seven years since my first election to the Senate. You and I share many memories—some of them have been glorious, some have been very sad. The opportunity to work with you and serve Massachusetts has made my life worthwhile.

And so I ask you tonight, people of Massachusetts, to think this through with me. In facing this decision, I seek your advice and opinion. In making it, I seek your prayers. For this is a decision that I will have finally to make on my own.

It has been written a man does what he must in spite of personal consequences, in spite of obstacles and dangers and pressures, and that is the basis of all human morality. Whatever the sacrifices he faces, if he follows his conscience—the loss of his friends, his fortune, his contentment, even the esteem of his fellow men—each man must decide for himself the course he will follow. The stories of past courage cannot supply courage itself. For this, each man must look into his own soul.

I pray that I can have the courage to make the right decision. Whatever is decided and whatever the future holds for me, I hope that I shall be able to put this most recent tragedy behind me and make some further contribution to our state and mankind, whether it be in public or private life.

Thank you and good night.

Thirty thousand telegrams and thousands of letters brought the reactions of people who watched Kennedy that night. They comforted him in generating hope that his political future could be salvaged. Reactions from the press were not as generous, however. Some reports expressed a degree of satisfaction and some merely expressed satisfaction and distinctly no more. At the other end of the spectrum, those who received it with hostility called it a "cold, heartless, political maneuver." Doubt was begetting doubt in the minds of many Americans; questions there at the beginning remained unanswered, and, as further evidence came tumbling out and a blanket of secrecy shrouded the aftermath of events, greater doubt came to beget even greater doubt.

CHAPTER 37

Bones of Contention

Swindon: *What will history say?*
Burgoyne: *History, sir, will tell lies as usual.*
—George Bernard Shaw, *The Devil's Disciple*

PEOPLE OUTSIDE THE state of Massachusetts did not reflect the same feelings in the volume of mail—or in the absence of volume of mail—sent to Senator Edward M. Kennedy. Investigations by journalists were set in motion and those who carried them out were not impressed by the way the few people who could shed light on events had closed ranks. The formal inquest on Mary Jo Kopechne was not open to the public; it was "top secret" in accordance with Kennedy's request to the Massachusetts Supreme Court. Documents relating to the proceedings were available only to witnesses and their counsel for the purpose of checking accuracy, and an application for an autopsy to be carried out was turned down. In fact, it was a neat package: but if there was no mystery remaining, if we had heard the truth in what the senator said, why the secrecy? Surely if everything had been as was stated the inquest would have supported this at all points, dispelling the circulating rumors. Featuring among the anomalies was Kennedy's strange behavior. He came out of it as having acted selfishly and this was not part of his character. Neither was cowardice, the accusations of which began to mount.

In the statement made on television, Kennedy offered no explanation for being on the Dike Bridge at Poucha Pond. In his brief statement to the police, he would have us believe he took the wrong road. To begin with, this is highly questionable. Earlier in the week, he had driven backward and forward to the ferry. From the Lawrence cottage, this involved turning left at the only junction— where a reflecting arrow pointed toward the ferry—and traveling on the only available road at that point, via Main Street. The only alternative was to turn right instead of left at the junction and drive on the rough and bumpy road in the opposite direction from the ferry. In relation to his statement, it is curious to say the least that on the night in question he turned right instead of left. He also said that he was unfamiliar with the road. This assumes that both he and Kopechne were unfamiliar with it and that they both failed to see the arrow. In neither case does it make any sense. On the day the tragedy happened, the senator had been driven on the Chappaquiddick road three times and Kopechne five times. On that same day, the senator had been driven on Dike Road and across the Dike Bridge twice, as had Kopechne.

Sheriff Huck Look put the proverbial cat among the pigeons when he made a witness statement to the effect he saw the senator's Oldsmobile as he drove home after 12:30 that morning. The big black car approached him from the opposite direction he was taking down School Road. With his headlights, he saw the driver and a woman sitting beside him. Look drew his Pontiac to a halt when he saw the Oldsmobile turn off into what he knew was the entrance to the local cemetery. But the car had stopped at once and Look thought the driver might be seeking directions. He got out of his car and walked back to help, but he never spoke to the driver. The big black car quickly backed out of the cemetery and sped down the road toward the road that led to the Dike Bridge and Poucha Pond. Sheriff Look was an able man who could recognize the various makes of cars. He could not see clearly in the dark, but he read off some of the numbers of the license plate, which he later found corresponded to the numbers on the senator's car. Look said he could not be certain what he saw in the backseat of the car. He said it could have been another passenger or a coat hanging up. In view of the fact that Kopechne's body was recovered from the backseat of the car, it seems likely he saw her there. This would beg the question of who it was traveling next to the senator.

But it was the *time* Sheriff Look saw the car that scrambled Kennedy's explanation of things. At half past midnight, how could he have been heading for the ferry to take himself and Kopechne back to Edgartown? The ferry closed down at midnight. This suggests the senator had other ideas when he left the cottage and that he had no notion of taking the ferry back to Edgartown. The mystery of who sat next to the senator might be explained by the presence of a handbag found in the car when it was lifted out of the water. This handbag, which was found on the underside of the car's roof, belonged to Rosemary Keough. Since Kopechne's mother said her daughter never went anywhere without her purse, it would seem that when she stepped into the Oldsmobile, she was planning on returning to the cottage, rather than going to the hotel. These circumstances present a scenario in which Kennedy was romancing Keough that night, while Kopechne was merely there to afterward take the two to the ferry landing, where they would find their prearranged means of reaching Edgartown. Kopechne would then drive the car back to the cottage. This scenario makes sense.

The handbag evidence became even more significant when it was revealed that two hotel room keys, one belonging to Keough and the other to Kopechne, were found inside it. They were sharing a room. If Kopechne had been returning to her hotel room when she left with Kennedy, how did she expect to get into her room? Why did she not sort out the keys with Keough, and more mysterious still, why did she not take her own handbag with her? This all supported the theory that it was Keough who was out with Kennedy that night, and it was most curious that Charles C. Tretter made a point in providing an alibi for Keough for the particular time in question. It should be noted that no one provided alibis for the Lyons sisters, Susan Tannenbaum, and Esther Newberg. Tretter told how he took Keogh out for a walk at 12:25 A.M.

What an odd time to be taking anyone out for a walk, especially by a married man. If it was questionable for Kennedy to be taking women off privately, why was it not also questionable for Tretter? While they were out walking, he claimed he saw the Valient, a car hired for the general use of any of the partygoers, driving toward the ferry crossing, which raised more questions than it answered since the ferry closed at midnight. Wondering what had happened, Tretter said they walked back to the cottage to find only Jack Crimmins in bed and asleep. There was no explanation of where the others were. Joseph P. Gargan and Paul Markham might be accounted for if they were searching for Kopechne, but what about Raymond S. LaRosa and the other women?

In relation to Kennedy's account of returning to the cottage and having raised the alarm, the timing of the nocturnal walk raises a great many questions and makes it difficult for us to know where, in fact, the partygoers were. Incredibly, Tretter went on to tell how, finding only Crimmins there, he and Keogh went out walking again. They did not return to the cottage, he said, until 2:20 A.M. This would appear to account for Keough's whereabouts during the entire time of the crisis. It is noted, however, that Tretter did not mention anyone who might corroborate his alibi. In fact, a sleeping Crimmins was the only one mentioned. On consideration, however, it would seem far more likely that Keough returned to Edgartown with Kennedy, as planned.

At this point, one pertinent and worrying question arises: If I can detect and identify so many questions and anomalies after all these years, why was it the police could not—or did not—raise them at the time? I can find no record that they did. The investigation, or anything approaching an investigation, into the events at the Dike Bridge was extremely Kennedy-friendly and left a great deal to be desired. A morsel released by Police Chief Jim Arena, however, provided another disturbing reason to call into doubt Keough's whereabouts. At about ten o'clock on the morning in question, when Chief Arena rang into his office from Chappaquiddick, where he was supervising matters, he was told that Kennedy was there. Arena asked to speak to the senator and a fragment of their conversation surfaced (this is understood to be as reported by Arena):

Arena: Do you know whether there were any other passengers in
the car?
Kennedy: Yes, there were.
Arena: Well, do you think they might still be in the water?
Kennedy: Well, no. Say, can I see you?

Chief Arena obligingly returned to his office at Kennedy's request. At this time, the dead woman was being identified as Rosemary Keough, and it was Kennedy who corrected Chief Arena and
informed him the victim was Mary Jo Kopechne. One is left to
wonder who Kennedy had in mind when he said, "Yes, there were,"
to the question, "Do you know whether there were any other passengers in the car?" He did not answer, "Yes, there was," meaning
himself, which would have fit his story. "Yes, there were" implies
there was a third person. This offers support to the theory that the
other one in the car that night had been Keogh, the owner of the
handbag, and that Kennedy had not, at this point, quite worked out
how he could explain Keough's absence and the presence of her bag
without disclosing his relationship with her.

Kennedy said that after he had reached the cottage following the
accident, he sat in the backseat of the Valient and asked to be taken
to the ferry landing. Since the ferry had closed down at midnight,
this was an odd thing for him to request, and an even odder thing
for those around him to accede to. "I believe that I looked at the
Valient's clock and believe that it was 12:20 A.M.," Kennedy said
later. He could not have done this because there was no clock in the
Valient, though he tried to wriggle out of it by saying he obtained
the time from Paul Markham. The time quoted by the senator was
probably greatly in error, which made the proposal to drive to the
ferry landing even more curious. It may have been as much as an
hour after that time, if not more. Finding there was no ferry,
Kennedy said he dived into the water and impulsively swam back to
Edgartown. According to locals who know the waters in those
parts, this was most unlikely. Some tried it and commented that the
currents and the dark would have made it a perilous proposition at

night. Hardly the thing a man injured and traumatized from the harrowing experience he described would even contemplate taking on.

A clue as to what really happened may be found in what Gargan and Markham later told Maryellen Lyons. They said they had been looking for a boat at the ferry slip, while yet another huge clue involved Kennedy's sailing partner and nephew, Joseph P. Kennedy III. Joe was reported as being seen, soaked to the skin—apparently straight off a boat—in Edgartown shortly before 3:00 A.M. Someone driving at that time of night, who knew him, spotted him and offered to give him a ride back to his hotel. He was staying at the same hotel as his uncle, the Shiretown Inn. Joe was reluctant to accept a ride, but then, perhaps because totally refusing it might have created more unwanted questions than accepting it, he agreed and was taken to his hotel. Joe was reported as not being very communicative on that ride. On the face of it, considering what we know about that night—especially the timing of the movements of the principals—it would appear a far more likely scenario that he—in a launch—had been the means by which Kennedy had returned to Edgartown.

But it is not entirely guesswork: Remington Ballou, an Edgartown resident, and his family witnessed a fifteen- to seventeen-foot motorboat making for the direction of a small sailboat that was moored in the harbor. The lights were extinguished promptly, but not before Ballou had counted three persons aboard the launch. The time was just about 2:00 A.M. The third person on the boat may have been Keough or one of the other women—or for that matter, one of the men.

An extremely likely sequence of events appears to be that after spending time with Keough, he was to escort her back to the car to retrieve her handbag and hotel key. They would then be driven to the ferryslip and taken back to Edgartown in the launch with Joe, while Kopechne took the car back to the cottage. This would account for the keys in Keough's bag and the absence of Kopechne's purse. But when Keough and Kennedy returned to the car, it was not there.

Kennedy probably searched and could not find it anywhere. When he had exhausted all possibilities, he walked Keough back to the cottage, which would account for his rejection of the idea of stopping at a house on the way and seeking help. When he reached the cottage, he obtained the services of Gargan and Markham, who extended the area of search for Kopechne and the missing car. It would have been unlikely that any one of them would have considered that the car might be in the water. In any case, they would not have been able to see it. The mystery could not be immediately resolved, but it was important to establish the whereabouts of Keough and Kennedy. Tretter provided for the one, and a clever device assisted in providing for the other.

Allowing for Joe to have spent some time mooring the launch in which he had brought Kennedy and Keough back to Edgartown, it would seem to fit, time-wise, that the senator reached his hotel before his nephew, but well after 2:00 A.M., and that he appeared from his room, fully dressed and dry, to speak to the room clerk at the Shiretown. Russell E. Peachey said the senator had probably been disturbed by the noise in the next room to his, and, saying he could not find his watch, had asked the time. It was then 2:25 A.M. said Peachey. On the one hand, this evidenced that Kennedy had not returned to the hotel with his nephew, which would have been extremely undesirable, and, on the other hand, in the best tradition of detective fiction, this established he was in his room at the time stated. Realistically, this smacked of someone involved in a deep problem the cause and nature of which he was ignorant, but against which he felt he needed protection. But there was also a hint that had he not encountered Peachey, Kennedy may have put into operation a preferred plan, to sneak off and make his way by a specially arranged plane to Hyannis Port, far away from Chappaquiddick and Martha's Vineyard.

CHAPTER 38

Murkier and Murkier

They make haste to shed innocent blood.

—Isaiah 59:7

Two SEPARATE AND distinct mysteries could be identified as relating to the hours following the tragedy. One involved Edward M. Kennedy's actions and attitudes that morning. Between 8:00 and 8:30 he stood outside his hotel visiting with friends whereafter—at about 8:30—he walked into the foyer of the Shiretown looking for newspapers. The day clerk, Mrs. Stewart, occupied herself in providing for his needs. He wanted Boston and Washington papers that, she told him, she could get for him a little later. He then found he did not have a dime with which to make a telephone call. She obliged, and he went off to a pay phone to make a call; and this was a call that gave rise to a fair degree of speculation. The question was whom could he have been calling from Edgartown with a dime? Not the Lawrence cottage on Chappaquiddick, because the only phone there was reserved for the use of the owner and was locked up. The best answer put forward was that he made a collect long-distance call to obtain a number on which he could reach his brother-in-law, Steve Smith, who was vacationing in Spain.

On the contrary, a collect call hardly explained Stewart hearing him shouting, "No, no, no! It's M, M, M!" as she later recounted, which suggested he had not got through to his party. One way or another, he returned the borrowed dime to Stewart very quickly, so either he did not use it or he was very speedy in going up to his room for his money and back again. Though there is considerable uncertainty about it, it was claimed he had already made seventeen telephone calls from his hotel room that morning, but if this was so, it raised the question of why this one had to be made from a pay phone. Joseph P. Gargan, who was now seen dripping wet, and Paul Markham joined Kennedy at about 8:30 A.M., and they disappeared to his room until they made their way to the Chappaquiddick ferry landing

Kennedy had been noted to be quite relaxed and pleasant, elegantly dressed in light blue pants and a white polo shirt, and sporting canvas deck shoes. His preoccupation was the relatively normal one of seeking the particular newspapers he wanted. He was not tearing about asking questions or, for that matter, making excuses for himself. In short, he did not act at all like a man who knew his car had crashed into Poucha Pond with a woman inside. What would he talk to Gargan and Markham about? More than likely, they told him about the fishermen having spotted a car in Poucha Pond. Gargan's wet state suggested he identified it as the senator's and had dashed across by the next ferry to bring the news. He was surly, it appears, and he probably said they were still looking for Mary Jo Kopechne.

The answer to the dime telephone call might possibly be connected to the second mystery of the morning. At about nine o'clock, Kennedy, Gargan, and Markham crossed by the ferry to Chappaquiddick. Since the senator did not show concern about Kopechne, his car, which by then was being raised from the waters, or the questions the locals were asking, there had to be another compelling reason for him to be there. This was doubly underlined by the fact that he returned to Edgartown as soon as the one task he undertook was fulfilled. Having obtained his wallet from his bedroom before leaving, that one task was to make use of his credit card to make telephone calls from the ferryhouse or else to accept calls there. And it was at this time that the ferryman Dick Hewitt shouted a question in the senator's direction. "Senator Kennedy, are you aware of the accident?" One of Kennedy's aides shouted back a very revealing answer, "Yes," he said. "We just heard about it."

Just heard about it? What a strange reply in respect of Kennedy's later story of having escaped from the car, of failing to rescue Kopechne, and of eventually swimming back to Edgartown. The aide's reply strongly supports that Kennedy's real shock came when he was approached by Tony Bettencourt, a permanent resident on the tiny island, who arrived in his car. He called out, "Senator, do you know there's been a girl found dead in your car?" Kennedy appeared to be totally nonplussed. Clearly, the news of his car being found submerged in water had provided him with news that did not faze him. What had happened to the car was not important to him. But the news of the dead woman shattered him. Totally at a loss, he remained silent until asked by Bettencourt if he wanted a ride to the scene of the tragedy, when he declined, saying he would return to Edgartown.

He had made—or received—telephone calls that were, apparently, so private he could not make them—or receive them—in his hotel room, indicating there was something special about them. But after Bettencourt's bombshell, he ponderously made his way, without delay, back to Martha's Vineyard in a different mood.

Kennedy's mood change by the ferryhouse on Chappaquiddick seemed to indicate that everything had clicked into place. The news about Kopechne in some way seemed to link with the telephone calls at the ferryhouse. The timing of the calls appeared significant, too. It is my belief that he was told to expect to hear impending news of a tragedy from whomever it was he spoke to in one of his mysterious telephone calls. This would fit. It would also fit if the person at the other end of the line was responsible for what had happened and if Kennedy had been told to accept this as a warning of what would befall him if he pursued his ambition to reach the presidency.

× × ×

Consideration of the known details about the tragedy itself throws great doubt on the story told by Senator Kennedy for anyone looking for the reality of the situation. When, for instance, he said that the Dike Bridge was unlit, this was true. That car headlights would have provided more than ample illumination, however, would also be true, and the senator's attempt to provide an excuse for the car plunging over the side of the unrailed bridge was not realistic. He explained he had approached the bridge by driving down a hill, and it came as a shock to him when the car leveled and his headlights picked up the bridge, then it was all too late. There is a "bump" but no hill on the approach to the bridge, and car headlights show the bridge from a distance of about a hundred yards away. Besides all this, Kennedy was quite familiar with the bridge and where it led to, as witnessed by many previous visits with his brother, Jack.

The unrailed bridge, however, was not exactly what it at first sounded to be. The edge of the bridge on both sides was lined with substantial timber placements, reminiscent of railway sleepers almost a foot high, end to end along the full extent. This would surely have alerted any driver driving too close to the edge. The bridge was also stated to be narrow. It was actually twelve feet wide, and its width provided no hazard to a driver. If this was an accident, it was the first time in the twenty years of the bridge's existence that any car had suffered such a fate. Furthermore, it has to be asked how easily a car might have rolled over the edge. The timber sleeper linings would likely have created a problem. If the front wheel or wheels of the car had gone over the edge, there was a good possibility that the car would have become wedged or "perched" on the substantial ledge. And the same would apply even if it had gone backward over the edge.

Before delving further, the evidence of Sylvia Malm should be considered. Malm and her daughter lived in a house located less than 200 yards from the Dike Bridge. They heard a car racing toward the bridge about half an hour or more *before* Sheriff Huck Look saw Kennedy's car. The car was "going faster than usual," Malm said. If the car was racing to catch the ferry, it was going in the wrong direction. It would seem its only destination could have been the bridge. Could it have been that someone shadowing him, with the knowledge of where it was the senator was heading to that night, raced ahead to lie in wait for him?

Police Chief Jim Arena made some interesting comments relating to the tire marks found on the wooden bridge. He said they "weren't really what you could call skid marks. They were more like scuff marks that probably were brought about by tires going sideways, sliding more than skidding across something." In other words, they were consistent with the car having been pushed over the edge of the bridge by those dedicated to compromising the senator, but hard to explain otherwise.

The damage to the car also gave rise to questions. It was expected the roof of the car would be found damaged, but what accounted for the excessive damage to the right side of the car? Inside the car, there was broken glass everywhere. All the windows were smashed except for the driver's window, which was rolled down, and the window to the left rear. Could this damage have been sustained when the car was rolled on its side en route for the waters of Poucha Pond? By that time, Kopechne was probably unconscious, and if she came to, she did not do so until the water revived her. But whether the water was actually responsible for her death is another question.

To add to the mystery surrounding Kopechne's death, the Massachusetts Department of Public Safety ran a check on her clothing, and the results were sinister. Blood was found on the left sleeve and on the back of her blouse. Melvin Topjian, the analytic chemist responsible for the submission, was asked at the inquest if anything other than blood could have caused the reaction to his test. "In my opinion, no sir," was his answer. This discovery raised the possibility of Kopechne having been attacked before the car plunged into the water. Dr. John J. McHugh, of the Massachusetts Department of Public Safety, who had supervised the benzidine tests carried out by Topjian, testified as to what a benzidine test was and went on to explain that "gross examination of this item [the blouse] under visible and ultra-violet light disclosed the presence of reddish brown and brown washed-out stains principally on the back and left and left sleeve surfaces. Most of these stains gave positive benzidine reaction indicating the presence of residual traces of blood."

The tests were not run immediately after Kopechne had been discovered, but her blouse was so deeply penetrated by blood that when the tests were eventually carried out, there was, according to Dr. McHugh, still an "unusually strong" response to the benzidine.

A blood sample taken from Kopechne showed a high content of ethyl alcohol. Translated into a volume of 80 to 90 percent proof spirit, this would suggest she had had some five or six drinks during the hour before she died, or even more over a longer period. This came as a great surprise to those who knew her. She drank very little indeed, and such drinking would have been out of character for her. Esther Newberg testified to this:

> *Newberg:* Five or six drinks would have been completely out of order with the way she lived. And if a girl who didn't drink had that much to drink you would certainly be able to tell if she was more jovial than normal, and she was not.
> *Court:* I am only telling you what a chemical analysis shows and the chemical analysis is practically irrefutable.
> *Newberg:* Then I am the wrong person to be asked, because as far as I was concerned she was completely sober.
> *Court:* And you saw her the time she left?
> *Newberg:* Exactly the time she left.

One theory that had been suggested was that Kennedy and Kopechne got so drunk the car could not be controlled and the fatal accident ensued. However, this raised far more questions than it answered, leaving the senator guilty of more than one criminal offense. It would not explain his behavior afterward and would involve his guests in various offenses as well, since the men in the party were all conversant with the requirements of law in these circumstances. It would also make nonsense of his behavior the following morning. The difficulty of a car rolling off the bridge would also have to be considered, hacking at the roots of such a scenario, while the excessive damage to the car would not support this, either. Also, such a theory would leave a riddle surrounding the presence in the car of the handbag belonging to Rosemary Keough, the unexplained presence of both hotel keys in the bag, and Joseph P. Kennedy III's middle of the night soaking and reluctance to talk about it. Looking at it from every angle, the theory is a nonstarter.

But if Kopechne did not embark on a heavy drinking spree after she left the cottage with the senator, how did the alcohol, in such quantity, get into her bloodstream? Logically, it would appear there was no other explanation possible other than that indicated by the blood deposit found on her blouse sleeve. If she did not drink the alcohol, then she had to be injected with it. This would correspond with a situation in which she was attacked and killed, or was knocked out by the injection and left to recover in the water, then drown. It would also be consistent with the intentions of those who carried out the attack: to discredit Kennedy and make him unelectable. And it would also explain why Markham and Gargan arrived back at the cottage at about 2:15 A.M., having searched the island for the car without success.

According to the story Kennedy told, Markham and Gargan had supposedly been diving into Poucha Pond to try and rescue Kopechne, but one of the women at the cottage described them both as dry and looking "normal" when they appeared. Unable to sleep, Gargan was up and around early that next morning. According to the *New York Times*, it was at this point he was reported as saying, "We can't find Mary Jo." There was no talk about her being in the car in Poucha Pond; no talk about him and Markham having dived in repeatedly to try and save her; and no devastating, "She must be drowned by now." Gargan said simply, "We can't find Mary Jo." That would appear to support conclusively that the senator's story was fiction and that at that time he had no more idea about where Kopechne was than Gargan or Markham had.

The trouble for Kennedy was that he was caught between a rock and a hard place. Assuming that he had been told by the conspirators, in the mysterious telephone call made or received at the ferryhouse, that they were responsible for Kopechne's death, he could have reported all he knew to the police. It would also be assumed that he had been warned against doing this, and told that if he gave trouble he would be eliminated just as his brothers had been. I am not at all sure Kennedy would have succumbed to such threats, but if this was the rock, the hard place represented what would have had to be made public if he took the problem to the police. The hard place involved telling the world about his womanizing, his rendezvous with Rosemary Keough, and the appearance he had *two* women with him that night. Since his wife, who had had two miscarriages, was at that time pregnant again and staying only a few miles away at Squaw Island, admitting this would have devastated his political career.

He decided on the alternative that left him with a slim chance of surviving in politics. He survived, more by good luck than good management, but he knew what the consequences would be of offering himself for the presidency. Regardless, he eventually did so, but the conspirators' reckoning was superior to his. In each instance, the public was reminded about the affair at Chappaquiddick, and the senator's bid for the presidency was sunk without a trace.

The inquest into Kopechne's death proved to be extremely Kennedy friendly. For instance, Judge James Boyle heard the account given by Sheriff Huck Look of recognizing the senator's car on the night in question and proceeded to demolish it:

Court: And what did you observe about the car at that time, if anything?

Look: That it was a dark car and that it was a Massachusetts registration.

Court: What did you notice, if anything, about the registration?

Look: That it began with an L and it had a 7 at the beginning and one at the end.

Court: May I have the photograph of the car that is in exhibit?

The judge was handed a photograph of Kennedy's black Oldsmobile bearing the license plate number L 78207, and Look was asked a couple more questions. He had, in fact, said it all. Unless the court could be shown that big dark cars bearing Massachusetts license plates abounded on Chappaquiddick, Look had settled the matter. Even if evidence could have been produced that at least one other car of the size and description and bearing Massachusetts plates had been seen on the island, the outcome might possibly have been justified. But Judge Boyle's additional questions were along the lines of requiring Sheriff Look to be 100 percent positive about the car he saw, a requirement rarely pursued in court in such circumstances.

Court: Well, you are unable to positively identify the car taken out of the water as the identical same car you saw the previous night?
Look: In my opinion.
Court: No, I'm talking about the positive identification.
Look: No, I can't.

And so the sheriff's significant evidence was disposed of. On the contrary, Judge Boyle was not so demanding when the evidence of Dr. Donald Mills, the local doctor, was given to the court. He asked only for an "opinion" and "reasonable certainty" when the critical subject of the blood found present on Kopechne's blouse was raised:

Court: Expert evidence already introduced has indicated that the white blouse was subjected to chemical analysis and shows evidence of blood. . . . Are you able to express a medical opinion with reasonable certainty whether the presence of that blood is consistent with your diagnosis of death by drowning?
Mills: Yes.
Court: And what is that opinion, that it is consistent or that it is not consistent?
Mills: That it is consistent.

Court: With your diagnosis?

Mills: With my diagnosis of death by drowning.

Court: Could you explain to the court the reasons why you formed that opinion?

Mills: In a drowning case when a person drowns there is what we call an exacerbation of blood or a putting out of blood from the lungs in the violent attempts to gain air and blood may and I believe usually perhaps more often than not, may be evidenced in the mouth and the nose of the decedent. The blood might, in the efforts, the physical evidence to avoid drowning, might spread I suppose almost anywhere to the person's clothing.

Court: Are you able, Doctor, to render an opinion as to how much blood normally is released from this kind of death? . . . Off the record. [A discussion took place in the court that was not recorded.] Can you render an opinion?

Mills: A very small amount. I mean, less than half a cupful for example.

Court: I am satisfied, Doctor. I have no other questions.

All the way through this sequence of questioning, Judge Boyle was seeking only "opinions" and "reasonable certainties," which were not sought when Sheriff Look gave evidence. Look had infinitely more going for him on the basis of "opinion" and "reasonable certainties" than Dr. Mills, who, it appears, had completely disposed of any notions that Kopechne had been attacked before her death. If this was assumed to be the case, it was assumed wrongly, however. The results of the Department of Public Safety's benzidine tests were not that easily dispensed with. In any case, it seemed a reasonable challenge to Dr. Mills's theory about how the blood stained the blouse to argue that such blood would have drifted away from the body, especially if the person was thrashing around in the water. It would also have been odd if it had attached to only two limited areas of the blouse, especially if one area was on the back of the garment she was wearing.

Sheriff Look was stoic in defending his position, however. A barely possible explanation for what Look saw on that night was put forward, and if accepted, this would have had the effect of neutralizing the sheriff's evidence. It was asserted he may have seen Kennedy, Gargan, and Markham in the white Valient tearing down to the Dike Bridge to dive on the submerged car. This made little impression on Look, who replied, "I can tell black from white." Then there was the license plate detail he had written down. Look learned that there were those who were poking around trying to discredit him and his evidence. They were not successful, however, and Look came back with, "I can't help what I saw. Investigators for Kennedy are knocking on doors all over Edgartown asking old ladies if I get drunk or run around with women. Well, everybody knows that I don't, but even if I did, it wouldn't change what I saw." But at the inquest, Kennedy was supported to the hilt: his story went unchallenged.

Then, quite remarkedly, when it was all over, Judge Boyle revealed that he had misgivings, unfortunately surfacing when it was all too late for them to do anything except create further doubts. In his findings, he referred to the very basics of the events at Chappaquiddick, "I infer a reasonable and probable explanation of the totality of the facts is that Kennedy and Kopechne did *not* intend to return to Edgartown at that time; that Kennedy did *not* intend to drive to the ferry slip and his turn on Dyke [*sic*] Road was intentional."

In this declaration, Judge Boyle effectively pulled the rug from under the senator's feet in regard to his basic account of the episode. In so many words, he was calling Kennedy a liar. Judge Boyle went on to say that if Kennedy was aware how dangerous the bridge at Poucha Pond was, the driving of his car "constituted criminal conduct." It was a great pity the judge was not able to set out these premises at the beginning when a totally different result to the inquest might have been obtained. It is also a pity the judge did not advise Kopechne's parents—who opted against an autopsy— that an autopsy might reveal aspects of her death and provide answers to questions that otherwise would continue forever to be a source of mystery. Judge Boyle never again officiated in his capacity as judge after the inquest into Kopechne's death. Meanwhile, the Kopechne family had only the dubious comfort that Mary Jo had died for no reason or fault of her own. She had become involved in the dreaded politics of the 1960s, in which the people she worked for had become targets.

CHAPTER 39

Lies and Damned Lies

He who does not bellow the truth when he knows the truth makes himself the accomplice of liars.

—Charles Péguy

THE INQUEST INTO Mary Jo Kopechne's death was intended to bring all the questions surrounding the events at Dike Bridge to an end. This did not happen, however. Judge James Boyle saw to that. More than one argument had surfaced. These were not different sides of the same problem, they were quite separate though inter-related. John Farrar, the scuba diver who had brought up Ko-pechne's body from Poucha Pond, said on television twenty years afterward that if the fire department had been notified within approximately half an hour to one hour of the time the accident happened, it would have saved her life. Farrar was convinced Ko-pechne had survived, conscious, for quite some time after the car went over the edge.

On the contrary, Eugene Frieh, the undertaker who prepared Kopechne's body for the flight home to Plymouth, Pennsylvania, and who was the only one, apart from Dr. Donald Mills, to come into close contact with her body, had some interesting comments concerning the cause of her death. Having observed that "very little moisture" was produced from the body, he suggested she had died from "suffocation rather than drowning." The description of the body when it was recovered would tend to support this. The "small amount of moisture" contradicted a claim by Dr. Mills that "this girl was completely filled with water." While he would not speak to reporters on the subject, Frieh also cast doubt on Dr. Mills's report of blood emanating from Kopechne's mouth. Speaking confidentially to one of Kennedy's lawyers, he said he saw no blood from the mouth, only a pinkish exudate from her nostrils.

Of course, all these matters and the questions they raised would have been resolved if an autopsy had been conducted, but apart from the parents' views on an autopsy, an argument on this issue raged between those officials who were involved in the case. Dr. Mills, who examined the body, deferred to a district attorney's investigator on the subject, from whom the advice came that as long as foul play was not suspected there was no necessity for an autopsy.

Meanwhile, Edmund Dinis, the district attorney, almost came to blows with Dr. Mills on the matter of an autopsy, "I can't accept this man's findings at all. I can't accept anything he says. He has tried unfairly and untruthfully from the first day to shift the blame for not conducting an autopsy to this office." Dr. Mills was not taking this lying down, however. He quoted that Dinis had said, "I'm gonna keep my office out of it. I don't want another Lee Harvey Oswald affair, and if I get it it's gonna stir up a big Roman holiday in Edgartown."

The basis of the trouble was that the single, apparently superficial, examination of Kopechne's body carried out by Dr. Mills on the shore of Poucha Pond proved insufficient to settle the doubts raised by the event. Theories emerged about what had happened, and these varied; and the degree of evidence obtained tended to cast doubt on the official version. When Dr. Mills readily declared it to be a case of "death by drowning. Not a question about it," he rendered a crisp and matter-of-fact cause of death. In doing so, he effectively closed the door on the possibility of other causes of death or of other causes having contributed to her death. During the afternoon of that day, Dr. Mills was paid a visit by Dun Gifford, a legislative assistant to Senator Edward M. Kennedy. He presented the doctor with a death certificate for him to sign that was already filled in.

Notwithstanding this quick and convenient medical opinion, when the presence of alcohol at such a level was found in the bloodstream of a woman known to do little drinking, this should have set off alarm bells. When the presence of blood was confirmed on the sleeve and the back of her blouse, the district attorney should have ordered an investigation into the matter at once. Dinis eventually became aware of certain anomalies in Kennedy's story, whereupon he called in Detective Lieutenant George Killen, who approached Dr. Mills and told him Dinis wanted an autopsy. Killen reported back to Dinis at 10:00 A.M. on July 20 that it was too late; the body had already been flown out. In fact, the body had not been flown out until two hours after that time, but this explains what appeared to be the uncharacteristic lack of action by Dinis. One wonders if Dinis knew that Kopechne's body had been delivered to Gifford, who took it back to Plymouth in a Kennedy-chartered plane.

In view of all the dithering that appeared to go on, it is still fair to wonder why the glaring need for a probe passed without challenge from some quarter or other. This might simply be another instance of the inquest proving to be Kennedy friendly, or it might be just as likely the disinclination of a local official to open up a can of worms, as had been indicated by Dr. Mills. Or yet again, it might be that the district attorney was simply not fast enough in making up his mind about the necessity—or desirability—of an autopsy. Dinis did, in fact, request the Pennsylvania authorities to raise an exhumation order, so that an autopsy could finally be carried out. This caused a great deal of interstate activity, but when Dr. Robert W. Nevin, the Dukes County medical examiner, withdrew his support for the request, Dinis was left stranded and no autopsy was conducted. It is not at all clear whether Dinis was concerned about letting the matter drop, but he had at least gone through the motions. It was said that the Kopechnes' attitude toward disinterment eventually changed and that they came around to favoring an autopsy. At this point, however, the waters muddy. There was talk of the intervention of Cardinal Richard Cushing after he had spoken to the senator and of a visit by two priests to the Kopechnes. Shortly thereafter, the Kopechnes were adamant there should be *no* autopsy carried out on their daughter's body. There was also the question of a payment from Kennedy to the Kopechnes of about $100,000. It was said the payment covered a shortfall in the expected insurance payment to the Kopechnes.

An interesting, though not highly publicized, fact was that Kennedy appeared to have two things on his mind throughout the proceedings. One was that he did not want the condition of his car carefully scrutinized. The other was that he was adamant there should be no autopsy performed on Kopechne's body. He even had one of his staff stay with the body to make sure no one got too interested in it. And quite remarkably, in either case, nobody appeared to ask why.

The whole episode bore the hallmarks of strict control on the part of those who could have made an enormous difference to the investigation of the Chappaquiddick affair. Equally, open-handed Kennedy subservience was advertised, and I am not sure who benefitted by either the strict control which pervaded the investigation, on the one hand, or for that matter the blatant Kennedy subservience, on the other hand. In the long run, none of this helped Senator Kennedy; none of it contributed anything to the comforting of the Kopechne family, and certainly the cause of justice did not benefit.

A grand jury was convened in 1970 to carry out a belated investigation into matters relating to the events at the Dike Bridge. Leslie Leland, the jury foreman, made it known, "I just feel we have certain duties and responsibilities as jury members to fulfill. A great deal of time has passed since the girl died and it is time the public found out what happened."

How true, but they were not going to find out what happened. The jury members were lectured for an hour and a half about the *limitations* of their responsibilities by Judge Wilfred Paquet, and they were hedged in by so many restrictions the enquiry never got off the ground. A transcript of the inquest proceedings, which included the barbed comments of Judge James Boyle, was unavailable to the jury members, and would not be available until weeks after the enquiry had folded. It requires no comment that Judge Paquet was known to be a Democrat and a supporter of Senator Kennedy. Not only did he refuse the grand jury access to the inquest records, he forbade it to summon any of the witnesses who had given evidence to the secret inquest. What was secret would remain secret. Leland's grand jury was well and truly scuttled by Judge Paquet. The *Chicago Tribune* spoke of "this [being] the kind of thing that has hampered any effective investigation of the case from the beginning."

Meanwhile, Leland had been receiving intimidating phone calls. "Lay off, or else," threatened the caller. The caller did not have to be concerned, because the enquiry soon died from the limitation of data available to it. There is little doubt, however, that Leland and his frustrated colleagues knew by then, with greater conviction than ever before, that there was a tremendous need for an investigation into what had transpired at Chappaquiddick. An unnamed juror made a statement to a reporter, "The district attorney offered us no help at all in our investigation. In fact Dinis did everything he could to discourage our probe into the case. . . . The district attorney had all the facts and evidence before him. . . . He could have acted, but instead he played politics with the whole situation." Another juror told the press that Dinis had fought their efforts behind closed doors. "He did not want us to look into the case. He was adamant against prosecution. Without his assistance we were helpless."

It is interesting to note that Leland appeared on the same television program as the scuba diver John Farrar. Leland went on record saying that had the grand jury known there was an air pocket in the overturned car, "an indictment of manslaughter would have been brought in." If only . . . if only.

District Attorney Dinis, who it was said came to be on a first-name basis with Kennedy, had the last word on the subject when, after the failed grand jury investigation, he announced, "The case is closed. . . . This is the end of the investigation into the death of Mary Jo Kopechne."

Among the whispers, the rumors, and the frustrations of being told nothing by those who could have provided some enlightenment about what happened, it was not surprising that many viewed the events as constituting a very strange situation. Mary Jo Kopechne, a person of high moral character, was not a heavy consumer of alcohol. However, she was found apparently drowned, with her bloodstream full of alcohol, blood on her sleeve and on her back, and in the backseat of a car resting on the bottom of a lagoon. In spite of the words spoken by Kennedy, by his friends, and by those who did his bidding, no sense was ever made of what happened. Conflicting suggestions, and unlikely explanations laced with striking points of evidence, all served to muddy the waters. None of it contributed to finding out what really happened. We have never been told the truth about the events at Chappaquiddick.

To add to the mystery, it seems clear that Kennedy was completely unaware that his car was in Poucha Pond. His guests at the Lawrence cottage did not know what had happened, either. It appears nobody knew until the car was found submerged in Poucha Pond the next morning, with Kopechne's body inside.

A form of summary of the supposed features of the tragedy might be thus: Senator Kennedy made up a story to provide an explanation for what happened on that night. But the stories of people diving to try and rescue Kopechne are hollow, and the sight of any of those supposedly involved in such activity in dripping wet clothes has never been recorded. On the face of it, it is unlikely Kennedy was in the car when it went into the water. It is very unlikely he made a miraculous escape, his large frame alone is enough to dismiss such an idea. And it is extremely unlikely he swam back to Edgartown in the black of night, especially when a motorboat was seen mooring at 2:00 A.M., a very wet nephew was spotted making his way to his base, and the senator took pronounced steps to establish his whereabouts—and the time of his whereabouts—at his hotel. It must be added that it is also unlikely he was "keeping company" with Kopechne that evening. Taking everything together, it was quite a story, but not one element of it rang true.

While there were several cracks in Kennedy's version of events as they occurred at Chappaquiddick from the beginning, it was not long before the cracks were prised open even wider by the nonbelievers. The columnist Jack Anderson did not believe what he had heard and suggested that Kennedy had wanted Joseph P. Gargan to say he had been driving the car and to take the blame for the entire tragedy. Interviewed by the author Leo Damore, some years afterward, Gargan confessed that "it was made up, all of it, including thoughts and emotions."

There is a sad comparison to be made in all this with Marilyn Monroe's death. Just as I believe that Monroe was murdered by those who wished to involve Senator Robert F. Kennedy, and through him, President John F. Kennedy, in a murder investigation—which would have ruined the careers of both—I believe that Senator Edward Kennedy was "put on the spot" by the same people. The time scale? There was only eight years between Monroe's murder and Kopechne's murder. During the intervening years, not having been enmeshed in the plan to involve them in Monroe's death, both John Kennedy and Robert Kennedy were murdered.

It is important to note that in all four of the deaths, in what might be called a "serial" conspiracy, the truth was competently covered up. Police Chief William Parker, perhaps with the best of intentions, set in motion a cover-up of Monroe's death, which was only unpicked with the greatest difficulty over thirty years later, the remarkable thing being that there were so many people party to what he did. Any one of them could have exposed the fraud of Monroe's supposed suicide, but for the sake of the Kennedys lips were sealed.

The murder of President Kennedy was covered up, in part, by an extraordinary number of deaths of people connected with the case, the implication of which was never taken aboard by the Dallas authorities. This was "muscle" controlling those who were there to protect the people from such blatant interference with their liberty. Those with the know-how and expertise to detect such bloody assertion of power were, it seems, asleep or looking elsewhere. Were they really so divorced from reality they could not see what was happening to those who had evidence to bring about the death of their president? This is not to excuse the U.S. government, in the form of the Warren investigation, from preventing the truth to be known. And it is not to explain why the Senate investigation in the 1970s brushed aside its assessment of the combination of deaths related to the assassination, including those that were going on even as it deliberated.

The LAPD has a lot of explaining to do in respect to the handling of the Robert Kennedy murder investigation. Once again, it appeared from the first that the truth would simply not be revealed. From the closed eyes of those who were reluctant to see the woman in the polka-dot dress, to the harassment of witnesses, the heavy-handed police authority asserted its control on the investigation in an arrogant way, refusing to see the obvious in so many instances. The services of the FBI were dispensed with at the outset: it appeared the LAPD would have no other law enforcement agency interfering. Yet, curiously, it placed officers with direct connections to the CIA in key positions. The CIA's brief gave it no rights to intrude in such internal affairs, but it seems it assumed control through officers with strong links to the agency. This, by itself, may explain a great deal.

In the case of the Chappaquiddick affair, it was an out and out Kennedy-dominated sequence of events. It was so Kennedy friendly it was unbelievable. The one thing we can be assured of is that we did not hear the truth in relation to the death of Mary Jo Kopechne. It was a community-inspired whitewash, designed to protect the well-being of Edward Kennedy at the expense of truth. I have already said I believe Kennedy to be innocent of any wrongdoing over the death of this innocent woman, but I cannot expunge the fecklessness of his womanizing, which was the cause of the whole affair, and which, in the long run, deprived us of a dedicated

Kennedy president. The question may be asked: if Kennedy was such a "hot number" for the American presidency before the Chappaquiddick problem, why was he not killed like his brothers?

Since Senator Robert Kennedy had been killed a bare twelve months before the Chappaquiddick affair, it probably seemed prudent to the conspirators to find another way of keeping Senator Edward Kennedy out of the White House. Having declined the nomination in 1968, immediately after his brother's death, there was a good chance that he would be nominated for the 1972 election. He would have had enormous, perhaps unprecedented, popular support, but then the conspirators knew this. Their plan succeeded and Chappaquiddick killed his chances of being elected president.

If Edward Kennedy had had no skeletons in his closet, if he had not been placed in a situation where he could not tell what really had happened, he would have walked away from Chappaquiddick the strongest candidate for the presidency of all the brothers. In a somewhat remarkable way, the conspirators may have had more to fear from Edward Kennedy as president than either of his brothers. But then the conspirators knew what they were about; they well knew his weaknesses and through his weaknesses he played straight into their hands. The parallels between Monroe and Kopechne are easy to recognize. At the end of the day, the ignominy of suicide was allowed to tarnish Monroe's memory in favor of protecting Robert and John Kennedy. In the case of Kopechne, the priority of saving Edward Kennedy's political skin was placed before that of finding who killed an innocent woman.

When he returned to the Senate chamber after the Chappaquiddick episode, Edward Kennedy was led in by Senator Mike Mansfield, who loudly proclaimed, "Come in, Ted! You're right back where you belong." Mansfield accompanied Kennedy on what was to him, no doubt, a marathon walk from the back of the chamber to the very front row, where others shook his hand and made welcoming noises. But he looked uncomfortable and unwell. His loss of weight was noticeable, and thoughts were voiced that all was not well with the survivor. "This isn't Senator Ted Kennedy," said one. "This is Ted Kennedy of Chappaquiddick." A Democrat was heard saying, "Kennedy's finished. We haven't got a candidate for 1972." And in *Newsweek*, another Democratic senator had written, "All the king's horses and all the king's men cannot bring him to the White House now. I think we have finally come to the end of Camelot."

Sadly, this appears to have been the case.

CHAPTER 40

The Destruction of Camelot

And tell sad stories of the death of kings:
How some have been deposed, some slain in war, . . .
All murdered.

—Shakespeare, *Richard II*

THE DEVASTATING PATTERN of death ran in a straight line through Marilyn Monroe, President John F. Kennedy, Senator Robert F. Kennedy, and finally Mary Jo Kopechne, whose death ended the political ambitions of all the Kennedys, in respect to their White House hopes. It is a clearly marked pattern, explained and fulfilled in the words of the CIA pilot: "Tomorrow they are going to kill your President. . . . They want Robert Kennedy badly," he said, and went on to say that the Bay of Pigs CIA survivors' campaign of hatred would be extended to any of the Kennedy family that went in the direction of the White House.

Looking carefully at the pattern as it emerged, one can deduce the CIA renegades joined forces with others, money rich and power hungry, who were as determined to remove the Kennedy family from control of the presidency as the renegades themselves. This was the politics of America in the 1960s. The power to decide the future of the country fell into the hands of knaves and murderers; those determined, at any cost, to wrest power from the people and impose their own will on the country. Their dreadful acts changed the course of history, affecting not only the United States but also the rest of the world.

Looking back to the start of it all, the problems appeared to emerge from the massive power acquired by the dark forces of the country's secret agency. This might be argued to have been the consequence of presidential weakness, augmented and compounded by the legacy of war, in which clandestine activities had taken on a certain respectability. The lying, cheating, and murder that lay in obscurity behind the cloak of war had surfaced in peacetime, without the justification, no matter how dubious, of wartime necessity.

Let me be clear: There have been spies immemorial; their history goes back to the time of the Caesars and well before their day, but not on the scale encountered since World War II. And whereas agents of past eras dutifully served their masters, their new, intensified, high-tech descendants found there were opportunities to influence, and even *control,* their masters. When the world became divided by an "iron curtain," that separated the East from the West, all of the principal nations were plunged into their own covert activities to combat the covert activities of the nations they feared. The Soviet Union was the chief bogey, and it was most adept at "fielding" undercover agents, as other nations learned. But then as covert operations begot covert operations, clandestine activities were extended to finding out what was happening in friendly nations. Unhappily, it became the accepted thing that most if not all nations spied on each other. During the 1950s, as in many other countries, the United States looked to its secret services, primarily in the shape of the CIA, to establish a defense against "outside influences"—mainly communism. It was expected to perform as a kind of covert army, to know what the opposition was thinking, and to keep at least one step ahead of the enemy. And no one pretended it was any kind of game. It was for real, for deadly real.

In the case of the United States, however, the new secret "defense" system was born into a force already too extreme and powerful. During the 1950s, the CIA became an uncontrollable monster. And this was the state of things when John F. Kennedy came to power. Kennedy's most basic policy was one of finding peaceful solutions to the problems of the United States and, indeed, the world.

The problem was that here was the most powerful of all nations with an unparalleled war machine that was not allowed to flex its military muscles, while a highly developed intelligence agency stood on the touchline, suffering from the frustration of having to take orders from anyone.

The plan for Cuban rebels to oust Fidel Castro in the Bay of Pigs operation was a huge embarrassment to President Kennedy. He gave it the barest of endorsements and watched the outcome like a hawk. His difficulty related to the timing of the plan. It might be said to have been—literally—lying on his desk when he first entered the Oval Office, and cancellation of the invasion would have created many problems. Besides, everyone else concerned, including the top military, had cleared it.

However, by the early 1960s the CIA had virtually assumed making the decisions the president should have been making. The agency had become a covert form of decision-making government, and it was foreign to its thinking that the president should overrule it in such matters as those it considered necessary for the defense of the nation. Besides, the Bay of Pigs operation had the endorsement of Dwight D. Eisenhower, right? We know that the answer to this was no, it really had not; it just appeared so, and the best that might be assumed by the CIA was the cooperation of Richard Nixon, who was Eisenhower's liaison. And President Kennedy was a completely different proposition.

The CIA was prepared to flout as many of the new president's orders as it saw fit. Kennedy forbade CIA agents any practical participation in the insurgency, but this was ignored. So was the order that they should not even be present during the invasion. In fact, it is known that agents had spread the word that if the order came to rescind the operation it was to proceed in defiance of the president. The dire problems encountered in landing the rebel forces were found to be insurmountable. It was not until the plans had gone awry that the innate, deep problems between the agency and the president surfaced. The CIA had *expected* the president, regardless of his expressed policy of the nonintervention of U.S. forces, to bow to its wishes. It had expected to be able to manipulate him to satisfy its demands, and when it found it could not do so it branded the president's lack of cooperation as little short of treason.

So began the tragedy that overtook the United States during the 1960s. This was a formula of intense hatred to which the adding of the power of ruthless men, who saw the opportunity to harness the hatred of the Bay of Pigs survivors to their own ends, was overpowering. There is little doubt that those who joined with the CIA renegades saw themselves as a crusading body striving to achieve what they claimed was in the best interests of the country. It is likely they sat around a large table, in boardroom fashion, debating the pros and cons of what was to be, in reality, the theft of the nation and the frustration of its role in world politics designated by its lawful leaders.

Kennedy was a compassionate man. His feelings for people were tangible. He was not seeking to promote anything other than the development of commonsense government. He brought with him a breath of fresh air, for he was not, unlike many others who had been in his position, beholden to those who wanted to control him. He saw many who needed him, and he listened. And after he listened he acted, decisively. His vision was that of world peace and prosperity, and he wanted that peace and prosperity to pertain first to the United States. Perhaps remarkably, for a young man without the experience of poverty at any level, his feelings for the poor, the elderly, the disabled, and the unemployed were instinctive.

Robert Kennedy was quite a different proposition as a person and a politician. He earned the reputation for bullishness, a ruthless determination, and a rigorousness that made him a hard man with which to deal. That, at least, is what was evident in Robert Kennedy, the U.S. attorney general. Perhaps, they were the qualities he saw as essential to carry out his work in that office, for they were not the qualities that followed him, as time progressed, into the challenge he made for the presidency. By the time he became a presidential candidate, other vital qualities had emerged and came to dominate. It was at this time he finally stepped out of his brother's shadow and was recognized as his own man. He dedicated himself to the poor and needy, the downtrodden of all colors, faiths, and, for that matter, politics. His brief was the defense and the promotion of the underdog. It is hard to believe this was a transformation: it was the Robert Kennedy who had never stepped out before. The positive stance he took against the hostilities in Vietnam marked him as a leader rather than a follower. The 16,000 troops in Vietnam when his brother was president had, by 1967, become 400,000 and the clamor was for more. He cried "enough!" What, he asked, did the torment of war bring to the ordinary people of Vietnam? He said imagine "the vacant moment of amazed fear as a mother and child watch death by fire . . . sent by a country they barely comprehend." "Righteousness cannot obscure the agony and pain those acts bring to a single child . . . the night of death destroying yesterday's promise of family and land and home." And he wanted to know how we could ignore "the unending crescendo of violence, hatred, and savage fury." Here was another man of compassion, and what the United States—and indeed the world—needed most of all was men of compassion. He became a shining star in the political firmament before he reached Los Angeles, where the murderer who would end it all was waiting for him.

Edward Kennedy, who had supported Lyndon B. Johnson's Vietnam policy, had heard his brother's pleas and responded accordingly. His position on Vietnam was duly revised, and he fell solidly in behind Robert. Not only did he speak out against the horrors of war and the need for a "negotiated solution" to end the hostilities but he also reminded those at home what the incessant hemorrhaging of the vast sums involved in promoting the Vietnam policy was costing in policies the government was unable to implement. "We have not moved on poverty, nor have we truly met the challenges of prejudice. Our elderly and their welfare, our children and their education . . . are problems yet facing us, and these problems will not wait patiently."

We never really saw Edward Kennedy in the role of presidential candidate. His bids were overshadowed and frustrated by the events at Chappaquiddick. But he, too, became his own man, quietly making his mark in the area of foreign affairs. As a president, he may not have revealed the same visionary qualities as Jack, or the priority to place above all things the need to integrate the poor and disadvantaged into American society, which was Robert's preoccupation, in the context of a ruthless determination to make such policies work. This is not to say he lacked sympathy with, or understanding of the cause Robert had espoused. Edward was both patient and talented. He had his own insights into the needs of the country, and his growing understanding of the problems of the people of other lands would, no doubt, have formed an essential bedrock in regard to the development of his administration. He was a more than able administrator, a huge bonus for any president, because he had both an eye for detail and that "special Kennedy amalgam" as William Honan, writing in the *New York Times Magazine*, put it, "of liberalism and sophistication, steadiness and attack, which were both bred and drummed into his sinews."

The world has been deprived of the greatly needed talents, dedication, and sensitiveness of a family of gifted men who would have greatly enhanced the Office of the President of the United States. They were denied serving their country by the treasonous activities of a small group of brutal men who imposed their will on the people by bludgeon and bullet. Perhaps an even greater tragedy is that they were never identified and brought to justice.

The Warren Report has revealed a deeply flawed presidential investigation that showed clear evidence of the lack of will to identify the true culprits. This is not to mention its shortcomings in other respects. The House Assassinations Committee of the 1970s was simply inadequate. Having taken an inordinately long time to set itself up, and, of necessity, leaving the required period of time at the end for writing up its findings, the time for genuine investigation, in the middle, was about six months, which was simply not long enough. And most of its efforts seemed to be directed toward shoring up the discredited Warren Report, though credit must be given for it pointing one finger in the direction of the buildings behind the motorcade in which the president died, and another in the direction of the grassy knoll. In doing this, it indicated that a conspiracy to kill the president had existed. But had the committee listened to the early researchers, it would have known this to begin with.

Promises of further investigations have not materialized, and it would appear the resolution to account to the nation and to the world for the crimes of those who seized power in the 1960s has been abandoned. We caught a brief glimpse of what might have been in the Thousand Days of the Kennedy administration. It is small wonder the people of the nation—and many across the world—still grieve.

Bibliography

Bishop, Jim. *The Day Kennedy Was Shot*. Funk and Wagnalls, New York, 1968.

Blair, Joan, and Clay Blair Jr. *The Search for JFK*. Berkley, New York, 1976.

Blumenthal, Sid, ed. *Government by Gunplay*. Signet, New York, 1976.

Brennan, Howard L., with J. Edward Cherryholmes. *Eyewitness to History*. Texian Press, Waco, TX, 1987.

Brown, Peter Harry, and Patte B. Barham. *Marilyn: The Last Take*. Dutton, New York, 1992.

Buchanan, Thomas G. *Who Killed Kennedy?* Secker and Warburg, London, 1964.

Burke, Richard E., with William Hoffer and Marilyn Hoffer. *The Senator*. Saint Martin's Press, New York, 1992.

Capell, Frank A. *The Strange Death of Marilyn Monroe*. Herald of Freedom, Indianapolis, 1964.

Crenshaw, Charles A. *JFK Conspiracy of Silence*. Penguin, New York, 1992.

Damore, Leo. *Senatorial Privlege*. Regnery Gateway, Washington, DC, 1988.

DiEugenio, James. *Destiny Betrayed*. Sheridan Square Press, New York, 1992.

Epstein, Edward Jay. *Legend: The Secret World of Lee Harvey Oswald.* Hutchinson, London, 1978.

Fox, Sylvan. *The Unanswered Questions about President Kennedy's Assassination.* Award, New York, 1965.

Freeman, Lucy. *Why Norma Jean Killed Marilyn Monroe.* Global Right, Chicago, 1992.

Galanor, Stewart. *Cover-Up.* Kestrel, New York, 1998.

Garrison, Jim. *On the Trail of the Assassins.* Sheridan Square Press, New York, 1988.

Gatti, Arthur. *The Kennedy Curse.* Regnery, Chicago, 1976.

Giancana, Sam, and Chuck Giancana. *Double Cross: The Explosive, Inside Story of the Mobster Who Controlled America.* Warner, New York, 1992.

Gibson, Donald. *Battling Wall Street.* Sheridan Square Press, New York, 1994.

———. *The Kennedy Assassination Cover-Up.* Nova Science, New York, 2000.

Gregory, Adela, and Milo Speriglio. *Crypt 33: The Saga of Marilyn Monroe: The Final Word.* Birch Lane Press, New York, 1993.

Groden, Robert J. *The Killing of a President.* Viking Penguin, New York, 1993.

Groden, Robert J., and Harrison E. Livingstone. *High Treason.* Conservatory Press, Baltimore, MD, 1989.

Guiles, Fred Lawrence. *Norma Jean: The Life and Death of Marilyn Monroe.* Grafton, London, 1986.

Hoffman, Ed, and Ron Friedrich. *Eye Witness.* JFK Lancer, Grand Prairie, TX, 1997.

Hosty, James P., Jr. *Assignment: Oswald.* Arcade, New York, 1996.

Houghton, Robert A., with Theodore Taylor. *Special Unit Senator.* Random House, New York, 1970.

Hepburn, James. *Farewell America*. Frontiers, Vaduz, Liechtenstein, 1968.

Jordan, Ted. *Norma Jean: My Secret Life with Marilyn Monroe*. William Morrow, New York, 1989.

Kearns, Doris. *Lyndon Johnson and the American Dream*. Harper and Row, 1976.

Keith, Jim, ed. *The Gemstone File*. IllumiNet Press, Atlanta, GA, 1992.

Klaber, William, and Philip H. Melanson. *Shadow Play*. Saint Martin's Press, New York, 1997.

La Fontaine, Ray, and Mary La Fontaine. *Oswald Talked*. Pelican, Gretna, LA, 1996.

Lane, Mark. *Plausible Denial*. Thunder's Mouth Press, New York, 1991.

———. *Rush to Judgment*. Thunder's Mouth Press, New York, 1966, 1992.

Lasky, Victor. *J.F.K.: The Man and the Myth*. Macmillan, New York, 1963.

Lifton, David S. *Best Evidence*. Macmillan, New York, 1980.

Lorenz, Marita, with Ted Schwarz. *Marita*. Thunder's Mouth Press, New York, 1993.

Manchester, William. *Death of a President*. Michael Joseph, London, 1967.

———. *One Brief Shining Moment*. Little, Brown, New York, 1983.

Marks, John. *The Search for the "Manchurian Candidate."* Allen Lane, London, 1979.

Marrs, Jim. *Crossfire*. Carroll and Graf, New York, 1989.

———. *Rule by Secrecy*. HarperCollins, New York, 2000.

Marvin, Richard. *The Kennedy Curse*. Belmont, New York, n.d.

McClellan, Barr. *Blood, Money, and Power*. Hannover House, New York, 2003.

McGinniss, Joe. *The Last Brother*. Simon and Schuster, New York, 1993.

Meagher, Sylvia. *Accessories After the Fact*. Bobbs-Merrill, New York, 1967.

Melanson, Philip H. *The Robert F. Kennedy Assassination*. Shapolsky, New York, 1991.

Moldea, Dan E. *The Killing of Robert F. Kennedy*. Norton, New York, 1995.

Morrow, Robert D. *First Hand Knowledge: How I Participated in the CIA-Mafia Murder of President Kennedy*. SPI Books, New York, 1992.

————. *The Senator Must Die*. Roundtable, Santa Monica, CA, 1988.

Murray, Eunice, with Rose Shade. *The Last Months*. Pyramid, New York, 1975.

Newman, John. *Oswald and the CIA*. Carroll and Graf, New York, 1995.

Noguchi, Thomas T., with Joseph Dimona. *Coroner at Large*. Simon and Schuster, New York, 1985.

North, Mark. *Act of Treason*. Carroll and Graf, New York, 1991.

Olsen, Jack. *The Bridge at Chappaquiddick*. Ace, New York, 1970.

Otash, Fred. *Investigation Hollywood*. Regnery, Chicago, 1976.

Prouty, L. Fletcher. *The Secret Team*. Institute for Historical Review, Costa Mesa, CA, 1973, 1992.

Russell, Dick. *The Man Who Knew Too Much*. Carroll and Graf, New York, 1992.

Rust, Zad. *Teddy Bare: The Last of the Kennedy Clan*. Western Islands, Boston, 1971.

Scheim, David E. *Contract on America: The Mafia Murder of President John F. Kennedy*. Shapolsky, New York, 1988. Published in Britain as *The Mafia Killed President Kennedy*. Allen, London, 1988.

Schlesinger, Arthur M., Jr. *Robert Kennedy and His Times*. Andre Deutsch, London, 1978.

Shaw, J. Gary, with Larry Ray Harris. *Cover-Up*. Thomas, Austin, TX, 1976, 1992.

Slatzer, Robert F. *The Life and Curious Death of Marilyn Monroe.* Pinnacle, Los Angeles, 1975.

———. *The Marilyn Files.* Spi, New York, 1992.

Sorenson, Theodore C. *Kennedy.* Harper and Row, New York, 1965.

Spada, James. *Peter Lawford: The Man Who Kept Secrets.* Bantam, New York, 1992.

Speriglio, Milo. *Marilyn Monroe: Murder Cover-Up.* Seville, New York, 1982.

———, with Steven Chain. *The Marilyn Conspiracy.* Corgi, London, 1986.

Spindel, Bernard B. *The Ominous Ear.* Award, New York, 1968.

Spoto, Donald. *Marilyn Monroe: The Biography.* Arrow, London, 1994.

Steinem, Gloria, and George Barris. *Marilyn.* Victor Gollancz, London, 1987.

Strasberg, Susan. *Marilyn and Me.* Transworld, London, 1992.

Summers, Anthony. *Goddess: The Secret Lives of Marilyn Monroe.* Victor Gollancz, London, 1985.

———. *The Kennedy Conspiracy.* McGraw-Hill, New York, 1980; rev. ed., Warner, New York, 1992.

Thompson, Josiah. *Six Seconds in Dallas.* Berkley Medallion, New York, 1967.

Turner, William, and Christian Jonn. *The Assassination of Robert Kennedy.* Thunder's Mouth Press, New York, 1978, 1993.

Twyman, Noel. *Bloody Treason.* Laurel, Rancho Santa Fe, CA, 1997.

Weatherby, William J. *Conversations with Marilyn.* Paragon House, New York, 1992.

Weberman, Alan J., and Michael Canfield. *Coup d'etat in America.* Quick American Archives, San Francisco, 1975.

Wecht, Cyril, with Mark Currider and Benjamin Wecht. *Cause of Death*. Dutton, New York, 1993.

Weisberg, Harold. *Post Mortem*. Harold Weisberg, Frederick, MD, 1969.

Zirbel, Craig I. *The Texas Connection: The Assassination of John F. Kennedy*. TCC Publishers, Scottsdale, AZ, 1991.

Index